Received On:
D0016677

THE RETURN OF THE MOGULS

ALSO BY DAN KENNEDY

Little People: Learning to See the World Through My Daughter's Eyes

The Wired City: Reimagining Journalism and Civic Life in the Post-Newspaper Age

DAN KENNEDY

THE RETURN OF THE MOGULS

How Jeff Bezos and John Henry Are Remaking Newspapers for the Twenty-First Century

ForeEdge

ForeEdge
An imprint of University Press of New England
www.upne.com

Manufactured in the United States of America
Designed by Mindy Basinger Hill
Typeset in Arno Pro

Library of Congress Cataloging-in-Publication Data
available on request

Hardcover ISBN: 978-1-61168-594-7
Ebook ISBN: 978-1-5126-0178-7

5 4 3 2 1

FOR TIM AND BECKY

CONTENTS

THE RETURN OF THE MOGULS

INTRODUCTION

THE RISE AND FALL OF NEWSPAPERS IN A TIME OF TURMOIL

IN EARLY 2017, the *Washington Post* unveiled a new slogan, "Democracy Dies in Darkness." The ominous-sounding phrase, displayed prominently beneath the paper's nameplate, was a favorite saying of the *Post*'s legendary reporter Bob Woodward in describing what happens to self-government in the absence of reliable, independent journalism. Though the message seemed aimed at President Donald Trump, who had declared the news media to be "the enemy of the American People," the *Post* reported that it had been in the works for many months.[1] It was a stark slogan for stark times. "All the News That's Fit to Print," the cheerful greeting that the *New York Times* debuted before the turn of the twentieth century, had given way to something much more dystopian.

Around the same time, the *Boston Globe* published an unusual manifesto headlined "Our Mission," which began: "The truth matters. At the end of the day it may be the only thing that matters. Finding it is our job, and our pledge to anyone who takes the time to read or watch or listen to what we've found out."[2] The *Globe* also distributed bumper stickers featuring the paper's logo and the Twitter hashtag #FactsMatter in white type on a black background.

For nearly a generation the newspaper business has been in steep decline. Beset by technological advancements that hollowed out the advertising revenue that had traditionally been its main source of revenue, as well as by cultural changes and big bets on failed ideas such as free online content, newspapers had been in danger of shrinking into irrelevance. Yet the 2016 presidential campaign and the early months of the Trump presidency served to remind the public of journalism's importance — and newspapers have long served as the primary engines of the public-service journalism we need to govern ourselves.

It was precisely because of newspapers' vital role in our democracy that the business had attracted wealthy, civic-minded new owners in recent years. Over the course of one weekend in August 2013, John Henry, a financier best known as the principal owner of the Boston Red Sox, announced he would acquire the *Boston Globe*, and Jeff Bezos, the founder, chairman, and chief executive officer of the retail giant Amazon, reached an agreement to buy the *Washington Post*. At the same time, a wealthy young entrepreneur named Aaron Kushner was expanding the *Orange County Register* in Southern California, transforming the shell of a once-bankrupt newspaper he and his investors had purchased the year before into an expanded, vibrant community resource.[3] After years of pessimism and declining fortunes, the prospect of a new generation of media moguls injecting money and energy into their newspapers inspired hope.

By 2017, Kushner was long gone, the victim of his overly ambitious expansion plans. But the *Post* was thriving under Bezos, and the *Globe*, despite some setbacks and continued shrinkage of the reporting staff, was doing reasonably well under Henry. Meanwhile, the journalistic landscape had changed considerably. In a society long marred by political polarization, there was plenty of evidence that the presidential campaign and its aftermath had made things worse.

The term "fake news" degenerated in just a few months from a useful label for a certain type of for-profit scheme aimed at gaming Facebook's and Google's algorithms into an all-purpose smear directed at any news story that Trump and his supporters didn't like.[4] Slogans like "Democracy Dies in Darkness" and #FactsMatter were aimed at countering the notion that facts *didn't* matter and could always be neutralized with "alternative facts," as the presidential counselor Kellyanne Conway memorably put it.[5] Strictly as a business proposition, Trump and Trumpism were good for journalism, as many newspapers reported a sharp increase in digital subscribers.[6] But the signs were less promising with respect to the health of American democracy. Blue America clustered around mainstream news outlets such as the three major networks, NPR, and newspapers. Red America watched the Fox News Channel and logged onto Breitbart News.

There is little question that democratic self-government continues to depend on newspapers, whether in print, online, or both. Bezos, Henry, and Kushner are important not just because they are three wealthy individuals who came along hoping to save their papers and perhaps offer lessons for the rest of the beleaguered business. What's also important is that they arrived at a turning point in newspapers' long, painful transition from print to online. By the early 2010s, many people who study journalism were reaching the conclusion that nearly two decades of hoping that online ads would support free news had come to naught. The value of digital advertising was plummeting because of its very ubiquity. If newspapers were to survive, they had to convince their readers to pay — for the print edition, of course, but for online access as well.

The three moguls each took a different approach to addressing this new reality. Bezos quickly transformed the *Post* into a national digital newspaper, amassing an enormous online audience in the hope of persuading some percentage of that audience to pay a small monthly fee. Henry, faced with the challenge of serving a much more constricted regional audience, decided to impose relatively high fees. And Kushner put the physical newspaper front and center, charging as much for digital as he did for print — a strategy that might have had some success if he hadn't made the mistake of expanding too rapidly.

The lesson of Bezos, Henry, and Kushner is that there is no lesson; or, rather, that there are many lessons, some worth emulating, some cautionary. In seeking a path out of the morass into which the newspaper business has fallen, the real value lies in experimentation. Ultimately there may be no way out. Media fragmentation, changes in reading habits, and a digital advertising model that is enriching Facebook and Google at the expense of everyone else may mean that newspapers — whether online or in print — will fade away in ten, twenty, or fifty years. But given their unique role in democracy, it is of crucial importance that public-spirited people of financial means are trying to save them.

NEWSPAPERS MATTER. When I use the term "newspaper," I am not referring strictly to print. If and when a major daily newspaper successfully makes the transition to digital-only, it will still be no less a newspaper. Instead, my definition of a newspaper is a news organization whose main output consists of original, mostly text-based journalism that covers important events and issues; whose coverage is broad-based rather than niche-oriented and includes politics, government, breaking news, investigative reporting, business, sports, arts, and culture; and that appeals to a mass audience, either at the community level or nationally.

The *Huffington Post* is not a newspaper because, although it publishes some original journalism, much of its content consists of the aggregated work of others. *Politico* and *Vox* are not newspapers because they are narrowly focused on politics and policy analysis, respectively, even though they occasionally branch out into other areas. The *Washington Post*, the *Boston Globe*, and the *Orange County Register* are newspapers, and would be even if they stopped publishing their print editions altogether.

Original journalism, a broad mandate, and a mass audience are crucial to the soul of a newspaper. If journalism is not meeting the information needs of a community, self-governance becomes impossible. The media scholar Alex Jones has written about what he calls the "iron core" of journalism, which he defines as "the form of news whose purpose is to hold government and those with power accountable." By Jones's estimate, at least 85 percent of original, professionally reported accountability journalism is produced by newspapers.[7] Local television news provides little in the way of such journalism. Most commercial radio stations no longer broadcast any news at all. Community websites and blogs can provide an important service, but with very few exceptions they lack the resources to offer much original reporting. Even most large, well-funded public radio stations — and there are many — supplement their original reporting with rip-and-read stories from the local daily newspaper.

By some measures newspaper readership has been on the wane for nearly a century. It reached its peak in the 1920s, when the average household received 1.2 newspapers a day. By 2001, a time when the business was still reasonably healthy, barely more than half of households received a daily paper.[8]

What had changed was that multiple newspapers were published in most cities in the 1920s, whereas by 2016 nearly every city in the country was a one-daily town. Well into the 1950s, for instance, Boston was the home of five daily papers: the *Globe*, the *Herald* (which included the evening *Traveler*), and the *Post*, all broadsheets, and two tabloids, the *Daily Record* and the *American*.[9] By 2016, there were just two: the *Globe* and the *Herald*, a small tabloid that survived in part because it had a printing contract with its larger rival. After Eugene Meyer purchased the *Washington Post* in 1933, he and his son-in-law, Philip Graham, spent years overcoming competition from the *Times-Herald,* the tabloid *News,* and the mighty *Star,* which did not expire until the 1980s.[10] Today the *Post*'s only daily newspaper competitor is the *Washington Times,* founded in 1982 by the Unification Church.[11] The *Orange County Register* has had no local daily newspaper competition for many decades, though the *Los Angeles Times* looms over all of Southern California.

Then, too, the 1920s marked the beginning of an explosion in communications technology that crowded newspapers out of the central position they had once held. Radio was not just an entertainment medium; it was a vibrant source of news as well. After all, when we think of journalists and World War II, the first name that comes to mind is that of Edward R. Murrow, who broadcast from London while that city was enduring German bombing raids. Later on, television came to dominate after-work leisure hours, a development that hastened the demise of evening newspapers. Even though the internet has led to the fracturing of the news audience, the three network evening newscasts still command a mass viewership, with a combined average of 23.7 million as recently as 2014.[12] In contrast, the *New York Times,* one of the largest American newspapers and widely regarded as the best, reported a paid weekday circulation of a little more than 2.1 million (print and online) in 2015.[13]

Yet paradoxically, before the rise of the internet the closure of daily newspapers led not to a decline in the economics of the business but, rather, to an increase in profitability for those that remained. This may seem counterintuitive, but it should not be all that surprising. After all, the papers that survived the great shakeout that took place in city after city were left with a monopoly or close to it. Yes, radio and television commanded a significant share of the local advertising market. But for classified advertisements and for those pages and pages of Sunday department store ads, there was really no viable outlet other than the daily newspaper. Owning the only newspaper in town was a reliable way to make a lot of money, even if overall readership was on the wane. Owning the dominant paper in a two-paper town was almost as good. A half-century ago the legendary press critic A. J. Liebling took note of this reality, writing that — even then — only sixty-one of the 1,461 American cities and towns with daily papers enjoyed the benefits of competition. He continued:

> The industry's ideal is now absolute control in a moderate number of cities, or even one. These become one-ownership towns, and as the publisher turns monopolist, his troubles end. He is in the position of a feudal lord after the period of wars in the Middle Ages ended. He has his goods, but he need no longer fight for it. He is a *rentier.*
>
> Such properties fall into only three classes: good, better, and bestest. There are no poor ones, since the proprietor can impose his own terms; he gets all the advertising, all the circulation, and he can give, in return, exactly as much or little newspaper as his heart tells him. Newspaper proprietors are not distinguished as a class for large or talkative hearts.[14]

Liebling's skepticism notwithstanding, many monopoly (and near-monopoly) newspaper owners did, in fact, invest considerable resources in journalism. Reporting staffs grew. Major regional dailies took their place alongside national papers such as the *New York Times* and the *Washington Post.* Papers such as the *Boston Globe* sent reporters across the country and around the world, and built investigative reporting teams to uncover government malfeasance closer to home. The *Globe* did not win its first Pulitzer Prize until 1966; it then won twenty-five more through 2016.[15] According to one study, the quantity of news published in ten major metropolitan newspapers doubled between 1964–65 and 1988–89.[16]

In a 2009 interview aired on the public radio program *On the Media,* Steve Coll, a former managing editor of the *Washington Post* (and, as of 2017, dean of the Columbia School of Journalism), explained that the years of newspaper prosperity we have come to think of as normal were in fact a historical anomaly: "There's never been a model of newsgathering and career formation in journalism such as the one that grew up between 1960 and 2005."[17]

The journalist and scholar Philip Meyer has compared the position enjoyed by monopoly newspaper owners before the internet to that of the lords of Savoy, who for centuries extracted tolls from travelers who wished to pass by Lake Geneva. "Their monopoly newspapers were tollgates through which information passed between the local retailers and their customers," Meyer wrote. "For most of the twentieth century, that bottleneck was virtually absolute. Owning the newspaper was like having the power to levy a sales tax."[18]

The internet blew all that apart. Newspapers began experimenting with websites starting in the earliest days of the commercial web, in the mid-1990s. With dial-up modems and slow access speeds, though, the digital world didn't pose much of an economic threat in those early years. By 2007, in contrast, more than half of Americans had broadband access at home.[19] Fast, always-on access revolutionized the way people used the internet and marginalized newspapers by making it far easier for businesses to connect with their customers and prospective customers directly. That was also the year that Apple unveiled the iPhone,[20] ushering in the age of the mobile internet. The lords of Savoy had been rendered obsolete. No longer did businesses need to rely on newspaper advertising, which was expensive and inefficient.[21]

The disintegration of the newspaper business has been nothing short of breathtaking. Paid daily circulation in the United States fell from a post-1940 high of 62.5 million in 1968 to 53.3 million in 2005, the approximate moment that the economic crisis afflicting the business entered its acute stage. What happened over the next decade was even more calamitous, as long-term slippage turned into a rout. By 2016, daily circulation had declined to an estimated 34.7 million. The situation was similarly dire with Sunday editions, which, because of their relatively high volume of advertising compared with that of the daily paper, are especially important to newspaper publishers. Sunday circulation actually grew in fits and starts for quite a while after daily circulation had begun to slide, not reaching its peak until 1993, when it hit 62.6 million. By 2005, it had fallen to less than 55.3 million. By 2016, Sunday circulation had plunged to an estimated 37.8 million.[22]

Moreover, some twenty years into the digital news age, newspapers were still largely dependent on print for most of their readers and revenue. According to an analysis by the Pew Research Center, 51 percent of newspaper readership in 2015 was print-only, with just 17 percent exclusively digital — a remarkable finding given frequent predictions of print's demise going back many years. The ongoing importance of print was also reflected in advertising revenue. In 2014, newspapers reported that print accounted for $16.4 billion of the ad money they received. Digital ads brought in just

$3.5 billion — a total that had barely changed since 2007, when newspapers earned $3.2 billion in digital ad revenues. The newspaper industry has stopped reporting ad revenue totals. But according to an extrapolation by the Pew Research Center based on numbers reported by publicly traded newspaper companies, print and digital ad revenues likely fell by another 7.8 percent in 2015, which Pew called the "greatest decline since the recession years of 2008 and 2009."[23] Worldwide, spending on print advertising was expected to drop by 8.7 percent in 2016 — again, the largest decline since 2009.[24]

So if print continues to pay the bills and digital is stuck in neutral, why not place a renewed emphasis on print? The answer is that the business model is unsustainable: the $16.4 billion figure in print ad revenues for 2014 was a small fraction of the $47.4 billion reported in 2005. Overall, combined print and digital ad revenues dropped from $49.4 billion in 2005 to $19.9 billion in 2014, down 148 percent.[25] Newspaper advertising revenue was lower than it had been since the 1940s. As the economist Mark J. Perry wrote, "It took 50 years to go from about $20 billion in annual newspaper print ad revenue in 1950 (adjusted for inflation) to $63.5 billion in 2000, and then only 12 years to go from $63.5 billion back to less than $20 billion in 2012."[26]

And when there is dramatically less money to pay for watchdog journalism, there are going to be fewer watchdogs. In 1978, in the midst of the golden age cited by Steve Coll, there were 45,000 full-time newsroom jobs at daily papers in the United States. That number kept climbing until 1989, when it reached 56,900. At that point growth stopped — not because of the internet, which was still in its gestational phase, but for other reasons, such as the rise of publicly owned newspaper chains, which cut back their reporting staffs in order to drive up profits. In retrospect, this was the final, decadent stage of the monopolistic greed described by A. J. Liebling; soon enough, newspaper owners would be eliminating jobs not so that they could make more money but so that they could lose less. Employment fell slightly, to 53,600 in 2005 — and then the tidal wave hit, driving that number down to 32,900 in 2014, a number that has continued to shrink.[27]

Given those dire circumstances, it is not unreasonable to worry that one-newspaper cities — even large ones — may, at some point in the not too distant future, become no-newspaper cities. The situation got especially dicey in 2009, the low point of the Great Recession, when prominent number-two papers either folded (Denver's *Rocky Mountain News*) or switched to much smaller, online-only operations (the *Seattle Post-Intelligencer*).[28] And it wasn't just number-two papers. The *Boston Globe* was losing so much money that year that its owner at the time, the New York Times Company, threatened to shut it down.[29] The Times Company itself was rumored to be running out of cash, imperiling the existence of its flagship newspaper.[30] Freedom Communications, the owner of the *Orange County Register*, filed for bankruptcy several years before Aaron Kushner bought the company.[31] As the economy improved, the crisis facing newspapers eased a bit — or at least the rate of deterioration slowed slightly. But who's to say what will happen when the next recession comes along?

So far, every attempt to move the newspaper business into a money-making digital future has either failed or fallen short of expectations. If for-profit newspapers are to be saved, what's needed is the time and patience that only a wealthy, civic-minded owner can bring. Someone like Jeff Bezos. Or John Henry. Or — briefly — Aaron Kushner.

THERE IS A SCENE in *Citizen Kane*, Orson Welles's 1941 *roman à clef* about the newspaper baron William Randolph Hearst, in which Charles Foster Kane's former guardian, Walter Parks Thatcher, upbraids the younger man for squandering a fortune on the *New York Inquirer*, the newspaper he'd bought with his inherited wealth.

"Well, I happened to see your financial statement today, Charles," Thatcher says. "Now tell me honestly, my boy. Don't you think it's rather unwise to continue this philanthropic enterprise — this *Inquirer*, that's costing you a million dollars a year?"

"You're right, Mr. Thatcher," Kane replies. "I did lose a million dollars last year, I expect to lose a million dollars this year. I expect to lose a million dollars next year. You know, Mr. Thatcher, at the rate of a million dollars a year, I'll have to close this place in" — he pauses and smiles — "sixty years."[32]

The title of this book suggests that what we're witnessing is not entirely new but, rather, is a modern spin on an old story: rich men — and nearly all of them have been men, though Katharine Graham of the *Washington Post* was a notable exception — who run newspapers as fiefdoms, engaging in a form of journalism that is quirkier and more personal than the bland products produced by corporate chains.

The moguls never went away entirely, of course. In recent decades there has been a long parade of wealthy individuals who got into the news business for reasons that combined ego, public-spiritedness, and the genuine belief that perhaps they could succeed where others had failed. Among them: Mortimer Zuckerman, who used his real estate riches to buy the *New York Daily News* and *U.S. News & World Report*; Richard Mellon Scaife, heir to the Mellon fortune, whose *Pittsburgh Tribune-Review* advanced various anti-Clinton conspiracy theories; and Philip Anschutz, who bought Hearst's first paper, the *San Francisco Examiner*, with his telecommunications riches and attempted, with limited success, to build it into a national chain.[33] We'll meet a few more in the pages ahead.

But there is a difference between new-age moguls like Jeff Bezos, John Henry, and Aaron Kushner and the press barons of the past. Men like Joseph Pulitzer, Hearst, E. W. Scripps, and, more recently, Rupert Murdoch either made or expanded their fortunes in the newspaper business. They were press lords in the true sense of the term, larger-than-life figures who built their wealth and influence through their papers. The same was also true of their more buttoned-down peers, such as Adolph Ochs and his descendants at the *New York Times*, the Meyer-Graham family at the *Washington Post*, and the Taylor family at the *Boston Globe*.

By contrast, the new moguls are outsiders. The hope is that they'll apply the wealth and knowledge they acquired in other walks of life to keeping their newspapers running — and perhaps figuring out a sustainable business model, which has eluded every newspaper owner since the rise of the internet. Money helps, of course, especially at a time when newspapers face an existential threat. But though the *Post*, the *Globe*, and the *Register* all benefited from their owners' infusions of cash, none of these men has the desire or, in Kushner's case, the capacity to run his paper at a loss — as a "philanthropic enterprise," as Mr. Thatcher put it. Charles Foster Kane is not walking through that door.

Then there is the uncomfortable notion that wealth entitles someone to gain access to powerful media institutions, especially the ultimate access that comes with ownership. Again, there is nothing new about that. The veteran media critic Jack Shafer has argued that rich people like to buy media organizations because doing so imbues them with a panache and prominence that they would otherwise lack. "Plutocrats the world over delight in owning media properties," Shafer wrote, "and for good reason: Money can buy a lot, but unless you own a publication you're just one of the world's 1,426 billionaires — human cargo on a private jet, a delegator, an employer of lobbyists, another yakker in the opinion chorus."[34] But in an era when the rise of the 1 percent and widening income inequality have moved to the foreground of the public conversation, the idea that our great newspapers have become yet another aspect of civic life reserved for millionaires and billionaires is not universally welcome.

In an essay for the *Nieman Journalism Lab* in late 2015, the Los Angeles–based critic Maria Bustillos lamented this trend, writing that "controlling media is not an appropriate ambition for a businessman to have in a democratic society. . . . Media should never be permitted to become a mere megaphone for the exclusive use of the rich to impose their views on the rest of us."[35]

Although I understand Bustillos's concerns, I think it's a matter of who the owner is and how he conducts himself. There are good and bad publicly owned newspaper companies, and there are good and bad wealthy private owners. Given their track records so far, Jeff Bezos and John Henry give every appearance of having acquired their newspapers for the right reasons. So did Aaron Kushner, even if his dreams collided with reality. The *Washington Post* and the *Boston Globe* are iconic newspapers, the locus of perhaps the two best movies about journalism ever made: *All the President's Men*, about the *Post*'s role in exposing the Watergate scandal, and *Spotlight*, about the *Globe*'s reporting on pedophile priests within the Catholic Church. The *Orange County Register* has been both good and bad over the years, but it serves a county of more than 3 million people. The fate of these papers is of paramount importance.

Overall, a wealthy owner who really cares about his newspaper is about as much as we can hope for. At best, Jeff Bezos and John Henry will not only transform their papers into thriving enterprises, but will show the way for other newspapers. At worst, their readers will be better served than they would have been by slash-and-burn corporate raiders seeking to maximize profits for a few years before selling off their hollowed-out papers and moving on. But it's going to take a lot of experimentation and a lot of mistakes before they get it right. That's why it's worth examining Bezos's and Henry's strategies. That's why it's worth explaining why Kushner failed.

In *Citizen Kane*, just before Kane and Thatcher square off over the *Inquirer*'s annual million-dollar losses, Thatcher explodes at an absurd front-page story headlined "Enemy Armada Off Jersey Coast." He angrily throws a copy of the paper onto Kane's desk.

"Is that really your idea of how to run a newspaper?" Thatcher demands.

"I don't know how to run a newspaper, Mr. Thatcher," Kane calmly replies. "I just try everything I can think of."

CHAPTER ONE

THE SWASHBUCKLER

Jeff Bezos Puts His Stamp on a Legendary Newspaper

THE NATION'S CAPITAL was still digging out from the two feet of snow that had fallen over the weekend.[1] But inside the gleaming new headquarters of the *Washington Post,* a celebration was under way.

Among the speakers at the dedication festivities — held on Thursday, January 28, 2016 — was Jason Rezaian, the *Post* reporter who had just been released by the Iranian government. "For much of the eighteen months I was in prison, my Iranian interrogators told me that the *Washington Post* did not exist. That no one knew of my plight. And that the United States government would not lift a finger for my release," said Rezaian, pausing occasionally to keep his emotions in check. "Today I'm here in this room with the very people who proved the Iranians wrong in so many ways."

Also speaking were publisher Frederick Ryan, executive editor Martin Baron, Secretary of State John Kerry, and the region's top elected officials.[2] But they were just the opening act. The main event was a short speech by the host of the party: Jeffrey Preston Bezos, founder and chief executive of the retail and technology behemoth Amazon, digital visionary, and, since October 1, 2013, owner of the *Washington Post.*[3]

It was Bezos who had purchased the storied newspaper from the heirs of Eugene Meyer and Katharine Graham for the bargain-basement price of $250 million. It was Bezos who had opened his checkbook so that the *Post* could reverse years of shrinkage in its reportorial ranks and journalistic ambitions. It was Bezos who had moved the *Post* from its hulking facility on 15th Street to its bright and shiny offices on K Street, overlooking Franklin Square.[4] And it was Bezos who had flown Jason Rezaian and his family home from Germany on his private jet.[5] Now it was time for Bezos — a largely unseen, unheard presence at the *Post* except among the paper's top executives — to step to the podium.

Like Fred Ryan and Marty Baron, Bezos was wearing a lapel pin that announced #JasonIsFree, the Twitter hashtag that had, upon Rezaian's release, replaced #FreeJason. "We couldn't have a better guest of honor for our grand opening, Jason, because the fact that you're our guest of honor means you're here. So thank you," Bezos began. Next he praised Secretary Kerry.

And then he turned his attention to the *Post*, combining boilerplate ("I am a huge fan of leaning into the future"), praise ("I'm incredibly proud of this team here at the *Post*"), and humility ("I'm still a newbie, and I'm learning"). For a speech that lasted just a little more than seven minutes, it was a bravura performance.

Bezos called himself "a fan of nostalgia," but added, "It's a little risky to let nostalgia transition into glamorizing the past. The past, the good old days, they take on a patina as time goes on. They become in our mind even better than they really were. And that can be paralyzing. It can lead to lack of action." Next he invoked tradition, picking up on something Baron had said. "Important institutions like the *Post* have an essence, they have a heart, they have a core — what Marty called a soul," Bezos said. "And if you wanted that to change, you'd be crazy. That's part of what this place is, it's part of what makes it so special. I've gotten a great sense of that in the last couple of years. I kind of somehow knew it a little bit from the outside even before I got here."

And, finally, he offered some humor aimed at charging up the troops: "Even in the world of journalism, I think the *Post* is just a little more swashbuckling. There's a little more swagger. There's a tiny bit of *badassness* here at the *Post*." Bezos paused while the audience laughed and applauded, then continued: "And that is pretty special. Without quality journalism, swashbuckling would just be dumb. Swashbuckling without professionalism leads to those epic-fail YouTube videos. It's the quality journalism at the heart of everything. And then when you add that swagger and that swashbuckling, that's making this place very, very special."

The event closed with a digital ribbon-cutting that was even cheesier than it sounds, followed by a promotional video in which Marty Baron referred to the *Post* as "the new publication of record" — playing off a comment Bezos had made in November 2015 on *CBS This Morning* in which he said that "we're working on becoming the new paper of record."[6] And it was over.

The vision Bezos outlined for his newspaper that day was simultaneously inspiring and entirely at odds with the wretched state of the news business. Of course, the *Post* is different — but in large measure because of Bezos's vast personal wealth and his willingness to spend some of it on his newspaper. All was optimism and hope.

That said, people at the *Post* emphasized in conversations with me that Bezos was operating the paper as a business, not as an extravagant personal plaything. Although he had bolstered the newsroom, its staffing remained well below the level it had reached during the peak of the Graham era. But almost alone among owners of major newspapers, he had shown a willingness to invest now in the hope of reaching profitability in the future.

The *Washington Post*'s revival under Bezos is not just the story of one newspaper. Of far more significance is what it might tell us about prospects for the newspaper business as a whole. Thus everyone is watching Bezos closely to see whether he can apply the lessons he learned at Amazon to an entirely different — and arguably more difficult — challenge.

Bezos's *Post* has invested an enormous amount of effort in building the paper's digital audience. In 2014, Matthew Hindman, a professor of media and public affairs at George Washington University, identified a number of steps that newspapers should take to increase online traffic. Significantly, the *Post* has taken every one of them: it has boosted the speed of its website and of its various mobile apps; it has lavished attention on the design and layout of those digital platforms; it is developing personalized recommendation systems; it is publishing more content with frequent updates; it regularly tests different headlines and story treatments to see which attract more readers; it is fully engaged with social media; and it offers a considerable amount of multimedia content, with a heavy emphasis on video.[7]

Any newspaper can take those steps, though each of them may require more resources than a financially strapped owner can afford. In fact, the *Post* is utterly unique. Bezos is unimaginably wealthy; his net worth reached nearly $91 billion in July 2017, briefly making him the world's richest person, ahead of Microsoft founder Bill Gates.[8] Then there is the *Post* itself — a metropolitan newspaper that throughout its history had perhaps more in common with papers like the *Los Angeles Times*, the *Boston Globe*, and the *Philadelphia Inquirer* than with truly national papers like the *Times* and the *Wall Street Journal*. By virtue of its being in Washington, though, the *Post* is the hometown newspaper for the federal government, which automatically gives it national cachet. Taking advantage of its location, Bezos has explicitly given the *Post* a national mandate, resolving many years of indecision over whether the paper should place greater emphasis on national or local news. Owners of large regional newspapers elsewhere don't have that choice — it's already been made for them.

Still, in broad strokes, the main strategies Bezos is pursuing are applicable to any newspaper: invest in journalism and technology with the understanding that a news organization's consumers will not pay more for less; pursue both large-scale and elite audiences, a strategy that could be called mass and class; and maintain a relentless focus on journalistic excellence.

One of the most significant milestones of the Bezos era came in October 2015, when the *Post* moved ahead of the *New York Times* in digital traffic. According to the analytics firm comScore, the *Post* attracted 66.9 million unique visitors that month compared with 65.8 million for the *Times* — a 59 percent increase for the *Post* over the preceding year.[9] And the good news continued. In February 2016, according to comScore, the *Post* received 890.1 million page views, beating not just the *Times* (721.3 million) but the traffic monster *BuzzFeed* (884 million) as well. The only American news site that attracted a larger audience than the *Post* was CNN.com, with more than 1.4 billion page views.[10] As the Year of Trump wore on, traffic at both the *Post* and the *Times* continued to increase. In October 2016, for instance, the *Post* surged to 99.6 million unique visitors, but came in second among newspapers, behind the *Times*, which attracted 104.1 million. The *Post* slightly outpaced the *Times* in total page views, by about 1.19 billion to a little less than 1.15 billion.[11] By the spring of 2017, with the election over, digital traffic at both papers had dropped slightly. In April, the *Times* recorded nearly 89.8 million unique visitors and the *Post* 78.7 million. Among news sites, they were outranked only by CNN.com, with 101.2 million.[12]

Not surprisingly, the *Post*'s growth in online readership has been accompanied by a steep drop in paid print circulation. As is the case with virtually all newspapers, the *Post*'s print edition has shrunk substantially over the years and will almost certainly continue to do so. In September 2015, the *Post* reported that its weekday circulation was about 432,000 — just a little more than half of its peak, 832,000, which it reached in 1993. Sunday circulation, meanwhile, slid from 881,000 in 2008 to 572,000 in September 2015.[13] Given the newspaper business's continued reliance on print for most of its revenues, the Graham family clearly would have faced a difficult challenge if the decision hadn't been made to sell the paper.

Indeed, under Graham family ownership, the size of the *Post*'s newsroom had been shrinking for years. Under Bezos, it has been growing. As of March 2016, the *Post* employed about 700 full-time journalists, an expansion of about 140 positions. That was approximately half the number employed by the *New York Times*, but it was enough to allow the *Post* to deploy reporters both nationally and internationally to a degree that had not been possible in recent years. By the end of 2016, with readership surging and the *Post* reporting a profit, the paper was planning to hire perhaps as many as sixty more journalists. In addition, from the time that Bezos bought the paper through April 2015, the number of engineers working alongside journalists in the newsroom grew from four to forty-seven — a total that continued to increase over the following year.[14] Those engineers were involved in a dizzying array of projects, from designing the paper's website and apps, to building tools for infographics and database reporting, to developing an in-house content-management system and analytics dashboard.

Then there were the intangibles. Bezos had the good sense to retain Marty Baron, hired by Katharine Weymouth, the last of the Graham family publishers. Baron is widely regarded as one of the best editors working today. (A headline in *Esquire* asked, "Is Martin Baron the Best Editor of All Time?" The answer in the story that followed: Yeah, pretty much.)[15] Baron's public profile was raised by the Oscar-winning movie *Spotlight*, which told the story of how he and a team of reporters at the *Boston Globe* proved that the pedophile-priest scandal within the Catholic Church was far more widespread than had been previously known.[16] In addition, the *Post* won national attention — and Pulitzer Prizes — for its coverage (along with the *Guardian*) of Edward Snowden's revelations about the National Security Agency and lapses within the Secret Service. In 2016, the *Post* won a Pulitzer for its reporting on civilians who had been fatally shot by police officers — reporting that was based on a database the paper built.[17] The paper's principled and very public advocacy on Jason Rezaian's behalf served as a reminder of the *Post*'s importance as a journalistic institution.

"I think that he brought a sense, as he did in Boston, of a sort of omnipresence," said David Beard, a journalist who worked with Baron at both the *Globe* and the *Post*. "He can't possibly read 700 articles a day and be working hard to free Jason Rezaian. But he does manage to grapple with and understand quite a lot of the content."[18]

A larger audience, more journalists, a growing reputation for excellence — all of these developments had served to restore the *Post*'s luster to a level not seen since the glory days of the 1970s and '80s, the *Post* of the Pentagon Papers and Watergate, of Woodward and Bernstein, of Ben Bradlee and Katharine Graham. It was a time when the *Washington Post* and the *New York Times* were synonymous in the public consciousness as exemplars of top-flight journalism and when newspapers were admired, glamorous, and — very much contrary to the situation that exists today — highly profitable.

Bezos, who rarely speaks to journalists — even his employees at the *Post* — was not interviewed for this book. He did not respond to multiple email requests, phone calls, and letters sent over a period of months to him and to several public relations executives at both Amazon and the *Post.* But in his remarks at the dedication, he said he bought the *Post* because of its importance as an institution — and he emphasized that transforming it into a profitable enterprise would make it stronger journalistically as well. "The people who meet with me here at the *Post* will have heard me many times say we're not a snack-food company. What we're doing here is really important. It's different," he said. "This needs to be a sustainable business because that's healthy for the mission. But that's not why we do this business. We're not just trying to make money. We think this is important."

LONG BEFORE JEFF BEZOS proclaimed the badassness of his newspaper, long before Katharine Graham was defending her inheritance from the depredations of the Nixon administration, long before Philip Graham was handed the publisher's reins by his father-in-law, Eugene Meyer, at the tender age of thirty, there was a *Washington Post.* The history of the *Post* is often recounted as though it did not exist before Meyer rescued it from bankruptcy in 1933, just as the *New York Times* begins in the popular imagination with the humble Tennessean Adolph Ochs's purchase in 1896. In fact, the origins of both papers extend back into the raucous and often disreputable world of newspapers in the nineteenth century — a world in which a *Times* editor and owner, Henry Raymond, once manned a Gatling gun to keep an anti-draft mob away from his newspaper building during the Civil War.[19]

There is no evidence that any of the *Washington Post*'s publishers ever resorted to a Second Amendment remedy to defend his or her First Amendment rights. Nevertheless, the *Post*'s early years were colorful and entertaining, even if the paper's journalistic reputation was less than sterling. The pre-Graham years have been well documented by the longtime *Post* journalist Chalmers Roberts in his book *The Washington Post: The First 100 Years.*

The *Post* was founded in 1877 by a thirty-eight-year-old New Hampshire native named Stilson Hutchins. Like many if not most publishers of his era, Hutchins was smitten by politics more than journalism, and his main interest in establishing the *Post* was to advance the cause of the Democratic Party. The newspaper scene in Washington was crowded — there were already five Monday-through-Saturday papers and four Sunday papers. But they were all so pedestrian that serious news consumers eagerly awaited the arrival of the New York papers by train each evening.[20]

Hutchins succeeded in making the *Post* part of the fabric of the community — so much so that in 1884, when the Washington Monument was completed, one of the paper's reporters secretly inscribed his initials on the monument's aluminum cap. Hutchins also launched what may have been the first salvo in the long-running rivalry between the *Post* and the *New York Times,* publishing an editorial in 1878 calling the *Times* "a radical Republican sheet" and "a bitter, savage and proscriptive organ of the bitter, savage remnant of the ultra sectional part of Eternal Hate in the Northeastern states." Such florid language, unfortunately, reflected Hutchins's regressive views on race: the *Post,* unlike the *Times,* supported the return to white supremacy in the South as well as the resegregation of the District of Columbia.[21]

Hutchins sold the *Post* in 1889 to a pair of forty-two-year-old natives of rural Ohio — Frank Hatton, a Democrat, and Beriah Wilkins, a Republican. It was under their stewardship that the *Post* reached its pre-Meyer peak of journalistic credibility, such as it was. It was also under Hatton and Wilkins that a curious moment in the newspaper's history played out — the debut of a John Philip Sousa march simply called "The Washington Post." As Sousa told it, Hatton and Wilkins approached him about performing at an event for young authors that the *Post* was sponsoring. "One of them said it would be a great thing if I would write a special march for the occasion, to which I agreed," Sousa said. Some 20,000 people were in attendance outside the Smithsonian Institution on June 15, 1889, when what would become one of Sousa's most famous works made its debut.[22]

The *Washington Post–New York Times* rivalry got another boost in 1900 when Wilkins (Hatton had died in 1894) published a nasty riposte to a condescending item in the *Times* describing the nation's capital as "amiable and inefficient." The *Times*: "When a New Yorker first comes to Washington he is struck with the uniform politeness of the population, from Cabinet officers to bootblacks. After he has been here a few days he longs for the rudeness of New York." The *Post*: "No doubt. The pig returns to his wallow."[23]

Hatton and Wilkins's *Post* was progressive enough to express outrage when "a well dressed and fashionable young woman" was sent to a workhouse for fifteen days after she was caught smoking in public, and it was properly outraged by the antisemitism of the Dreyfus affair. But the *Post* sided consistently with capital against labor, and it was overly cautious on race beyond its pro forma opposition to lynchings and support for legal if not de facto equality.[24]

The heights scaled by the *Post* during the years of ownership by Hutchins, Hatton, and Wilkins might best be described as foothills. The situation, however, was about to get much worse. For in 1905, the *Post* was acquired by John Roll McLean, who, along with his son, managed to drive the paper into journalistic and financial bankruptcy in less than three decades. The elder McLean, a former professional baseball player from Cincinnati, was "a dreadful man," in the words of Alice Roosevelt Longworth. He was a dreadful publisher as well. Among other things, he cut back on coverage of the national political conventions to save money but sent reporters on the road with the Washington Senators in order to capitalize on the popularity of their star pitcher, Walter Johnson.[25]

But the sins of the father paled in comparison with those of the son, Edward Beale "Ned" McLean, spoiled as a child and frequently inebriated as an adult. In describing his uninspiring stint covering the Republican National Convention in Chicago in 1908, his less than loving wife, Evalyn, wrote that "he would not have recognized a piece of news — not even if the man who bit the dog likewise bit Ned McLean." McLean's *Post* took Germany's side before the United States entered World War I, then scurried to change its position; McLean was also an enthusiastic fanner of flames in the Red Scare that followed.[26]

Even if Ned McLean had never met Warren Harding, he likely would have run his inheritance into the ground. But his friendship with the lackluster president and his corrupt inner circle greatly accelerated the process. McLean played a minor role in the Teapot Dome scandal, falsely claiming to have lent $100,000 to Secretary of the Interior Albert Fall so that Fall could lie about the actual source of the money: bribes from oil interests. Fall would become the first cabinet member to go to prison, while McLean and the *Post* lost what was left of their reputation. Toward the end, McLean fell apart in ways that anticipated the much better known breakdown of a future *Post* publisher, Phil Graham: he took up with a woman he met at a Santa Monica party held by William Randolph Hearst's mistress, Marion Davies, tried to sell the *Post*, and, with his alcoholism raging out of control, was declared mentally incompetent. Ned McLean spent his final years in a hospital in Towson, Maryland, dying in 1941 at the age of fifty-five.[27]

The modern history of the *Washington Post* began in 1933, when Eugene Meyer bought the paper out of bankruptcy for $825,000. Meyer, a wealthy patrician, had sought to acquire the paper in 1929; the *New York Times* owner at that time, Adolph Ochs, had told him the *Post* was worth $5 million. Four years later, the Depression and McLean's continued incompetent ownership had driven down its value to less than one-fifth of Ochs's estimate. Meyer bought the *Post* in secret, even going so far as to deny to the Associated Press that he was the new owner. The reported reason for the subterfuge was that Meyer's wealth was well known, and if his interest had been revealed, the price would have increased.[28]

The *Post* under Eugene Meyer was not particularly energetic, though it was far more professional than it had been under either the elder or the younger McLean. Meyer was more interested in the editorial pages than he was in news, reflecting a sense then prevalent at many newspapers — the *New York Times* standing as a notable exception — that national and international news was a commodity you could get from wire services, whereas the opinion section was where a publisher could truly make his mark. The Meyer era was not a long one. In 1946, he convinced his new son-in-law, the brilliant, energetic, and erratic Phil Graham, to take over as publisher. Meyer himself left the paper so that he could accept an appointment from President Truman to become president of the World Bank. Meyer stepped down from that position in 1947, but by then Graham was firmly in charge, and Meyer did not interfere — though, crucially, he continued to subsidize the money-losing operation.[29]

In 2013, several months before he sold the paper to Jeff Bezos, Donald Graham — son of Phil and Katharine Graham — spoke with journalists who were compiling an oral history about what it was like during the years that the *Post* was teetering on the financial brink. "I grew up around the dinner table with people who were publishing an unprofitable *Washington Post.* It was no fun," he said. "They had the same people who ultimately were hailed worldwide as great journalists, but they couldn't do a damn thing because they weren't making any money."[30]

In that respect, the economic struggles of Eugene Meyer and Phil Graham were something of a prelude to the challenges facing newspaper owners today, including Jeff Bezos. From the moment Bezos took charge of the *Post,* his ultimate intentions became a source of endless speculation. How long would he keep sinking money into the paper before pulling the plug? Would he walk away if the *Post* failed to break even during the next few years? "He has never mentioned a deadline or anything like that," Marty Baron told me.[31] Good thing. Even though the *Post* announced at the end of 2016 that it had attained profitability, it was by no means out of the woods. Like all newspapers it still had to overcome larger forces such as declining print circulation and a precipitous drop in the value of digital advertising. In fact, the road to sustainability has always been difficult for newspaper owners. Consider that from the time Eugene Meyer acquired the *Post* in 1933 until Phil Graham purchased the *Washington Times-Herald* in 1954, the *Post*'s status as a profitable news organization was never entirely secure, and was at times downright tenuous.[32]

Phil Graham's struggles with mental illness and Katharine Graham's journalistic triumphs are well known. It is perhaps of greater importance, though, that during those years the Graham family, through hard work and sometimes through luck, built the *Post* into the kind of dynamo that had the resources necessary to challenge the powerful and hold them to account. As David Halberstam put it in *The Powers That Be,* his classic 1979 tale of the *Post* and other dominant news organizations, "It was a curious irony of capitalism that among the only outlets rich enough and powerful enough to stand up to an overblown, occasionally reckless, otherwise unchallenged central government were journalistic institutions that had very, very secure financial bases."[33]

During the early years of Meyer ownership, the *Post* was the number-three paper in Washington, trailing the *Times-Herald,* which attracted a working-class readership, and the *Star,* which served the city's ruling elite. An afternoon tabloid, the *News,* had an audience as well. The *Post*'s circulation rose from 50,000 at the time Meyer purchased it to 130,000 in 1941, but it was still losing money. Nevertheless, its reputation had improved to the point that *Time* magazine that year called it "the Capital's sole big-league newspaper."[34]

Graham was convinced that the *Post* needed to eliminate the *Times-Herald* if it was to survive. He lost out on a chance to acquire it in 1949, but—with a Bezos-like focus on long-term investment—he moved the paper from its fifty-six-year-old plant on E Street to a new $6 million facility on L Street. The *Post* began buying up television and radio stations as well. It was finally able to purchase the *Times-Herald* in 1954 for $8.5 million, plus another $1 million to compensate *Times-Herald* employees who'd be losing their jobs. The move nearly doubled the *Post*'s weekday and Sunday circulation, which had been around 200,000.[35]

Sam Kauffmann, the racist, antisemitic co-owner of the *Star,* predicted the *Post* would hang onto no more than 5,000 of its new readers. In fact, it kept most of them. And with the *Post*'s circulation concentrated in the morning, it was in a stronger long-term position than the larger *Star,* which, like afternoon papers across the country, would eventually be damaged beyond repair by the rise of television.[36] Years later, Donald Graham referred to the acquisition of the *Times-Herald* as "the day that saw to it that the *Washington Post* would survive for the next sixty years."[37]

Phil Graham's widow, Katharine Graham, the daughter of Eugene Meyer, became the publisher in 1963 following Phil's suicide—a tragedy that followed a long and very public psychological breakdown involving bizarre behavior, a scandalous affair, and threats to wrest full ownership of the *Post* from his wife and children. Tentative and unsure of herself at first, she proved to be an intrepid leader. In the first half of the 1970s, she made two bold moves that helped solidify the *Post*'s financial position.

The more significant of those moves was her decision to take the Washington Post Company public, which put more cash at the paper's disposal. Without it, she believed, she would have to sell one of the paper's television stations, but the change did not come without some cost to the paper's journalistic culture. The executive editor, Ben Bradlee, resigned from the company's board so that his salary would not be revealed, and the paper would forever after face the pressure of meeting the relentless demands for profits from the company's shareholders.[38]

Indeed, as newspaper after newspaper fell into the hands of publicly traded companies in the 1970s, '80s, and '90s, cost-cutting in order to rack up ever-higher profits led to diminished journalistic capacity many years before the internet-fueled collapse of the past decade. In 1996, the journalist James Fallows decried the "counting-house mentality" of such ownership, which led to downsized newsrooms and cuts in spending "to satisfy quarterly earnings demands."[39]

Public ownership can also make it difficult for management to invest in needed innovations. Faced with the question of whether to spend on a faster, more attractive mobile app or to return more money to shareholders, too many newspaper executives choose the latter — and may in fact have to choose the latter in order to meet their fiduciary responsibilities. The situation never got quite that dire under Graham family ownership. As with the Sulzbergers, who controlled the *New York Times*, the Grahams put together a complicated structure guaranteeing that they would hold a majority of the voting shares — an arrangement that occasionally proved unpopular with outside shareholders but that nevertheless preserved a viable level of funding for news.[40] In addition, the investor Warren Buffett, legendary for his focus on the long term, became the Post Company's largest shareholder and a trusted adviser to the Grahams, a relationship that benefited both parties.[41] But Jeff Bezos and John Henry, who are the private, sole owners of their newspapers, have the freedom to spend in ways that were lost to the Grahams once they'd made the decision to go public.

KATHARINE GRAHAM'S OTHER CRUCIAL MOVE was to endure a strike in 1975 in order to get the *Post*'s printing costs under control. So arcane were the work rules that when an advertiser submitted a finished ad (known in the post-hot-lead, pre-computer age as "camera-ready"), a union compositor still put together an equivalent ad, even though it would be discarded as soon as he was finished with it. In deciding to put a stop to such practices, Graham was fortunate in the viciousness of her opposition. At one demonstration, a leader of the union, Charlie Davis, carried a sign that read "Phil Shot the Wrong Graham," a reference to Phil Graham's suicide. On the night that the pressmen went on strike, some of them beat the night foreman and started a fire in an attempt to sabotage the machinery. Because of those actions they earned the enmity of the Newspaper Guild, which represented the reporters. With the paper's journalists crossing the picket line, the *Post* was able to resume publishing after just one missed day, enabling them to break the strike. The benefits of being able to modernize production were immediate, as income grew from about $13 million a year to $24.5 million in 1976 and to $35.5 million in 1977.[42]

Not all observers were sympathetic to the Grahams. Ben Bagdikian, a former *Post* national editor who spent much of his long, distinguished career after leaving the paper as an academic and a harsh critic of corporate journalism, wrote an article in the *Washington Monthly* attributing the strike to Katharine Graham's earlier decision to go public. "The idiosyncratic publishers, whose integrity led them to ignore narrow economic arguments in favor of quality, and who as a result created America's great newspapers, are disappearing," Bagdikian wrote. "They were being replaced by profit-maximizing conglomerate owners. It is a forecast of trouble for independent journalism in the country's most important news companies."[43] Graham recorded her response in a note to Ben Bradlee: "I am really embarrassed to think this ignorant biased fool was ever national editor. Surely the worst asps in this world are the ones one has clasped to the bosom."[44]

The *Post*'s rivalry with the *Washington Star* played a small role in the strike as well, a tidbit of interest mainly because of who owned the *Star* at that time: Joseph Allbritton, a Texan who had acquired the paper from the Kauffmann family in 1974. Katharine Graham wrote that Allbritton declined to help the *Post* during the strike because, in her view, the only way the *Star* could stay in business was for the *Post* to fail. Allbritton sold the *Star* to Time Inc. in 1978, which closed it in 1981 even though Katharine Graham, Donald Graham, and Warren Buffett had made overtures to set up a joint operating agreement under which both papers would be published.[45]

The Allbritton family's ambitions remained entangled with the *Post* for many decades to come. Years later, two *Post* journalists, John Harris and Jim VandeHei, were rebuffed when they proposed setting up a separate political website under the paper's umbrella. They took their idea to Joseph Allbritton's son, Robert, who helped them launch *Politico* in 2007.[46] With its hyperkinetic insider's approach to covering politics, the site quickly established itself as a serious rival to the *Post* on one of its signature beats, although *Politico* was often criticized for emphasizing the superficial horse race aspects of politics. Joseph Allbritton also backed a site cheekily named TBD.com (for "to be determined"), edited by the former washingtonpost.com editor Jim Brady and the future *Post* media blogger Erik Wemple, which covered local news in the Washington area in conjunction with a television station the Allbrittons had owned since acquiring the *Star.* Fortunately for the Grahams, Allbritton lost patience with it within months of its 2010 launch, and in 2012 the site was shut down.[47] Another Allbritton connection: About a year after Jeff Bezos bought the *Post,* he hired Frederick Ryan, a former Reagan administration official, to replace Katharine Weymouth as publisher. At the time that the move was made, Ryan was president and chief operating officer of Allbritton Communications and had served as *Politico*'s first chief executive.[48]

The *Post* and *Politico* make for a fascinating contrast. Both companies are ensconced in brand-new headquarters on either side of the Potomac; *Politico* occupies part of an office tower in the Rosslyn section of Arlington, Virginia. The missions of the two organizations are very different. The *Post* is a general-interest newspaper with a substantial print presence. *Politico* is aimed at people in the professional political community, and though it publishes a small print product (daily when Congress is in session; weekly otherwise), it's mainly digital. Yet if the ancient rivalry between the *Post* and the *New York Times* is mostly journalistic and symbolic, the *Post*'s rivalry with the Allbritton family has involved serious competition over whose news organization will prove to be more financially successful in the long run.

Like most successful business leaders, Katharine Graham could be ruthless. Phil Graham had been more interested in being a player in Washington's political circles than in publishing a great newspaper; his widow's ambitions were grander. Her most crucial move was to shift the charismatic Boston Brahmin Ben Bradlee from *Newsweek,* then a *Post*-owned property, to the newspaper, where in 1968 he rose to the executive editor's position. Graham's elevation of Bradlee strained friendships, but it was the one essential move she needed to make in order to establish the *Post* as the equal of the *New York Times.*[49]

The *Post*'s true coming of age arrived in the form of the Pentagon Papers — a secret history of the Vietnam War assembled on behalf of the federal government by the Rand Corporation and stolen by a Rand employee named Daniel Ellsberg. In 1971, the *New York Times* began publishing the Pentagon Papers, and Bradlee wanted them, too. Ben Bagdikian managed to obtain a copy. Then came the crucial question of what to do with it. Bradlee wanted to publish the papers and reportedly threatened to resign if Graham ruled otherwise. But the *Post* was in a difficult position — a federal appeals court had stopped the *Times* in its tracks, and the *Post* would be violating that court order, although it wouldn't necessarily be breaking the law since Washington was within the jurisdiction of a different federal appeals court. Against the advice of the *Post*'s lawyer, Graham gave the word: publish. The case was soon heard by the Supreme Court, which ruled six to three in favor of the *Times* and the *Post.*[50] From that moment on, the *Post* and the *Times* were generally spoken of as the two leading American newspapers.

If the Pentagon Papers proved that the *Post* could be an equal partner with its ancient rival, the *Times,* the Watergate scandal showed that the *Post* could on occasion surpass the *Times* — and everyone else. The story of how two young reporters, Bob Woodward and Carl Bernstein, helped bring down a president has been told on so many occasions that I need not repeat it here. But Watergate defined a high-water mark for the press in America, inspiring an idealistic generation of young people to go to journalism school. And the *Washington Post* was the leading symbol of that era. The *Post* may not have been as comprehensive as the *Times,* but how could the faceless men who ran the Gray Lady compete in the public imagination with Jason Robards, Robert Redford, and Dustin Hoffman?

The Pentagon Papers and Watergate also showed how important a tough owner with integrity could be. With both stories, and especially with Watergate, Graham made decisions that were unassailable journalistically yet could have resulted in the end of Graham ownership. The Nixon administration threatened to challenge the licenses of the *Post*'s television stations;

moreover, a finding that the company had broken the law by publishing the Pentagon Papers would have endangered the paper's public stock offering.[51] And even though the Supreme Court decided that the government could not stop the *Times* and the *Post* from publishing the Pentagon Papers, there was nothing in its ruling to prevent the government from prosecuting the papers for violating Wilson-era national security laws after the fact. Indeed, the Nixon White House began to explore such a prosecution, though the effort quickly fizzled.[52]

Jeff Bezos faced none of these challenges before the bizarre presidential campaign of 2016 got under way. The one story that might have gotten the *Post* in legal trouble because of its potential national security implications, the Edward Snowden leaks, had pretty much played out by the time Bezos took control. Bezos commanded financial resources that the Grahams never had. His backbone before 2016 had not been similarly tested. But he has said that he's prepared. In his message to *Washington Post* staff members the day that the purchase was announced, Bezos alluded to an infamous moment during Watergate when Nixon henchman John Mitchell barked at Bernstein that "Katie Graham's gonna get her tit caught in a big fat wringer" if a particularly damaging story were published.[53] Bezos wrote, "While I hope no one ever threatens to put one of my body parts through a wringer, if they do, thanks to Mrs. Graham's example, I'll be ready."[54] As we shall see, it was not long before Bezos would be put to the test.

The *Post*'s run of great journalism and greater fortune continued after Watergate. In the mid-1970s, the paper launched its Style section, a showcase for arts, culture, and features starring writers such as Sally Quinn, the future second wife of Ben Bradlee, and Tom Shales. The uncertain progress of Style in its early days occasioned perhaps the greatest response an editor ever gave to a meddling publisher: "I can't edit this section unless you get your fucking finger out of my eye." Incredibly, David Halberstam reported, Graham "loved" Bradlee's impudent response.[55] But the glory days gradually began to recede into the rhythms of a newspaper that continued to excel but that no longer conjured up the excitement of standing up to — and bringing down — the president of the United States. How could it?

Carl Bernstein left the paper and for years led a life that was both personally and professionally tumultuous, punctuated by the publication of his well-received books about Pope John Paul II and Hillary Clinton. Bob

Woodward, who remained at the *Post*, was promoted to the editing ranks, where he presided over the worst scandal in the history of the Pulitzer Prizes: a story about an eight-year-old heroin addict written by a young reporter named Janet Cooke. The story turned out to have been fabricated, and the Pulitzer awarded to Cooke was revoked. Woodward returned to the reporting ranks, where he occupied himself mainly with writing best-selling books on subjects ranging from the death of the comedian John Belushi to the Supreme Court to President George W. Bush's decision to go to war in Afghanistan and Iraq.[56]

THERE IS A COMMON PERCEPTION that people in the newspaper business made little effort to adapt to the internet, thus contributing mightily to the predicament in which they find themselves today. In reality, executives at papers like the *New York Times* and the *Boston Globe* have been innovating online since the mid-1990s. It's just that everything they tried proved unsuccessful, at least economically. More than anything, the not unreasonable idea that a newspaper's content could be made available for free on the web and supported by advertising turned out to be wrong. The rise of Craigslist, which decimated the market for classified ads, and the shrinking value of online display ads in an ever-expanding digital universe could not have been predicted in the early days of internet news.[57]

Such was the case with the *Washington Post* as well. The paper's first major venture into online publishing came in 1994, when the *Post* launched a paid service called Digital Ink on a long-forgotten network, ATT Interchange. The *Post* switched to the open web in 1996, starting washingtonpost.com, which has been the paper's online home ever since.[58]

After Digital Ink, the *Post*'s digital operations were renamed Washingtonpost.Newsweek Interactive and were headquartered on the opposite side of the Potomac River in Arlington, Virginia. WPNI, as it was known, was responsible for the online presence of not just the *Post* and *Newsweek* but other Graham properties as well, including *Slate* (an online-only politics and culture site acquired by the Washington Post Company from Microsoft), *Foreign Policy*, and broadcast operations.[59] Those properties continued to reside with Graham Holdings, a company headed by Don Graham, after the *Post* was sold to Bezos.[60]

Post executives hoped to develop a new revenue source through online hyperlocal journalism. "Hyperlocal" is a word that means different things to different people. Most, though, agree that it involves a heavy focus on community affairs, from local government meetings to youth sports. WPNI's experiment in hyperlocal was called *Loudoun Extra,* which covered Loudoun County, Virginia, about twenty-five miles west of Washington. With a population of about 310,000,[61] the county was on the large side for a hyperlocal site. The project did not go well. Although *Loudoun Extra* was overseen by Rob Curley, a respected digital news pioneer, the site failed to attract much traffic. The *Wall Street Journal* pronounced it a "flop" in June 2008, about a year after its debut. In an interview with the *Journal* and in a post on his own blog, Curley blamed the site's woes on poor integration with washingtonpost.com and on a lack of outreach to the community. He wrote that "both of those problems were my fault. Completely."[62]

The *Loudoun* experiment may also have been harmed by tensions between Curley and Jim Brady, then the editor of washingtonpost.com and now the founder and publisher of *Billy Penn,* a mobile-first local news service in Philadelphia. Curley has a reputation for being difficult to work with, a reputation I learned about through a number of confidential conversations with people, most of whom were commenting on his stint as the editor of the *Orange County Register* from 2014 until early 2016. Brady chose his words carefully when I asked him about his own relationship with Curley. "He's a talented guy, for sure," Brady said. "He got put into a situation that assured that he and I were going to bump heads. And we did. And I think there was a little bit of a battle over control of the future of the site because there was a bit of a battle over very different styles. We seem to have made some peace with it. I still trade messages with him on Facebook every so often. But it was a tough time. The time he was there was time that we didn't innovate as much as we should have because there was too much of a power struggle going on there, which I'm just as much to blame for as he is."[63] Curley declined to comment on the record, but I have no reason to believe he harbors any animosity toward Brady.

In any case, online-only hyperlocal probably wouldn't have worked out as a profitable enterprise for the *Washington Post* any more than it has for other large news organizations. The *Boston Globe,* under New York Times Company ownership, started dozens of free sites in the suburbs and in the city's neighborhoods called *Your Town.* The sites began to wither away after John Henry bought the paper and were quietly folded in 2014 after six years of operation.[64] Hyperlocal journalism thrives in the form of dozens of independent grassroots sites, both for-profit and nonprofit, some with paid staffs, some with volunteers. But such projects have not proved to be a reliable source of revenue, especially as part of larger organizations. As one membership group for hyperlocal publishers puts it, "Local doesn't scale."[65]

Like all newspaper owners during the early years of the internet, Donald Graham made questionable calls. But the one monumental decision that sealed the Graham family's fate unfolded in April 2005, the day after Mark Zuckerberg, then the twenty-year-old founder of a tech start-up called Thefacebook, ended up in the men's room of a fancy restaurant, sitting on the floor and crying miserably over a mess he had gotten himself into.[66]

As told by David Kirkpatrick in his book *The Facebook Effect*, Graham took an interest early on in the company that would become Facebook. Originally Thefacebook was aimed at colleges and universities, and the service reminded Graham of a handwritten book of comments that he and other members of the *Harvard Crimson* used to keep. "I vividly remembered that every time any of us would walk into that room we would read every word written in those ledgers and write our own comments," Graham said. "I have often thought about the power of those comment books and wondered whether there was some way to replicate them in a place like this," meaning the *Post*. Zuckerberg was looking for investors, and Graham offered $6 million for a 10 percent share, which would have given Thefacebook a value of $60 million.[67]

It was an extraordinary offer, and Graham and Zuckerberg reached what both men believed was a handshake deal. But unbeknownst to Zuckerberg, his company president, Napster cofounder Sean Parker, kept shopping for a better deal — and got one from Accel, a Silicon Valley–based venture capital firm. Zuckerberg's bathroom breakdown took place in the midst of a dinner with Accel executives at which Zuckerberg, still not legally old enough to drink alcohol, ordered a Sprite rather than share in the $400 bottle of wine that Accel executive Jim Breyer had bought. Zuckerberg was despondent at the prospect of having to tell Graham that he wanted to break their agreement.[68]

Zuckerberg's misery did not stop him from going for the gold. During a phone call with Graham the next day, Graham tried to talk Zuckerberg into sticking with their deal, telling him that Accel would seek a much greater hands-on role in Thefacebook than the *Post* would. "Mark, does the money matter to you?" Graham asked. In the end, Graham let Zuckerberg do as he wished, telling him, "Mark, I'll release you from your moral dilemma. Go ahead and take their money and develop the company, and all the best." Accel ultimately invested $12.7 million for 15 percent of the company, giving Thefacebook a value of $98 million. Despite what had happened, Zuckerberg and Graham remained close, with Graham later serving as a member of Facebook's board.[69]

I asked Jim Brady, the former washingtonpost.com editor, whether he thought there was anything Don Graham could have done differently that would have ensured continued Graham ownership of the *Post*. Just one, Brady replied: holding Zuckerberg to his promise. "That would be the only thing," he said, "but I also think on some level that's so who Don is."[70] The consequences of being who Don is were devastating. In 2012, just before Facebook went public, it was estimated that the *Post*'s share might have been worth $7 billion, a time when Facebook itself was worth about $100 billion.[71] In April 2017, Facebook's market capitalization was hovering around the $410 billion mark,[72] which would have made the *Post*'s share all that more valuable. Don Graham could have been his own Jeff Bezos. Or as Graham himself said not long before he sold the *Post*, "If we were a $20 billion market cap business instead of a $4 billion market cap business, we'd be doing better."[73]

The final years of Graham ownership were difficult ones for the *Post*. Len Downie Jr., who had succeeded Ben Bradlee as executive editor in 1991, retired in 2008. Don Graham's niece Katharine Weymouth, several months into her new position as the *Post*'s publisher, replaced Downie with Marcus Brauchli, previously the top editor of the *Wall Street Journal*. Brauchli and Weymouth soon found themselves in the midst of an ethical dilemma over a series of paid, off-the-record "salons" Weymouth intended to organize to bring together *Post* journalists, top government officials, and corporate lobbyists. Weymouth backed away from the idea while Brauchli issued some confusing statements regarding how much he knew about the plan.[74] Their relationship deteriorated after that, with Weymouth reportedly expressing open hostility toward Brauchli.[75] In late 2012, Weymouth replaced Brauchli with Marty Baron, the editor of the *Boston Globe*, a move that turned out to be as inspired as Katharine Graham's hiring of Ben Bradlee had been two generations earlier.[76]

During those years the *Post* got much, much smaller. In 2008, with losses mounting, 231 employees took early-retirement buyouts. At its peak, the *Post* employed more than 1,000 full-time journalists.[77] Between 2003 and 2008, that number fell from around 900 to fewer than 700.[78] As I noted earlier, the staff had been cut to about 560 before Bezos purchased the paper and was back at about 700 in early 2016 — suggesting that despite Bezos's willingness to invest in the *Post*, he does not intend to expand the editorial staff to the size it was during the Graham-era heyday.

Toward the end of the Graham family's ownership, when technology-fueled decline and the Great Recession were endangering newspapers everywhere, the *Post*'s financial situation grew especially grim. Revenues at the Washington Post Company, including its television stations and other ventures, fell by 10 percent, to $3.15 billion, during the first three quarters of 2011. Profit was down 72 percent, to $55 million. The company's debt rating was downgraded twice. And the stock price fell from a high of $942 in 2004 to less than $400.[79]

Despite these problems, Don Graham, in messages to shareholders and employees, said that the *Post* had managed to return to the black during the years immediately leading up to the sale. In the Washington Post Company's 2012 annual report, Graham wrote that the *Post* had recorded its third straight profitable year. And in his remarks to *Post* employees on the day that the sale to Bezos was announced, he said that cost-cutting had enabled the *Post* to reestablish its profitability. "As the *Post* fell to tens of millions of dollars in losses in 2009, I wasn't sure the paper could be profitable again soon," Graham said. He praised Katharine Weymouth "and her outstanding team" for returning the paper "to cash-flow profitability the next year, and it remains there, making your job and Jeff's far easier."[80]

The story Graham told was one of a newspaper that faced challenges but was not in a dire situation. Indeed, in the spring of 2013 Graham sounded as though his family might be able to keep the *Post* indefinitely. "We are uniquely structured so we didn't give a damn what we made for any given quarter or any year," he said. "That remains the strength of the place. As a business, the Washington Post Company can be genuinely, no kidding, long-term-minded. If somebody said to me there's a way out for newspapers but you're going to have to lose $100 million a year to get there four to five years from now I would sign up for it in a minute."[81]

Several months later, Graham shocked the media world when he announced that his family was leaving the newspaper business, ending an eighty-year run that spanned four generations. It was truly the end of an era — and the beginning of a new one, which would be presided over by a geeky retail and technology savant based nearly 3,000 miles away.

CHAPTER TWO

THE *CRUX* OF THE MATTER

John Henry's Culture of Experimentation

THE SCENE AT BOSTON COLLEGE in September 2014 contained enough cognitive dissonance to induce vertigo.[1]

Some two decades earlier Cardinal Bernard Law had invoked the wrath of the Almighty in denouncing the *Boston Globe* for its coverage of the pedophile-priest scandal. "We call down God's power on the media, particularly the *Globe*," Law said at the time.[2] Ten years later Law was on the run following a series of reports in the *Globe* that revealed the full extent of the cardinal's role in covering up that scandal.

On this late summer's evening at Boston College, though, the interactions between the *Globe* and the Catholic Church couldn't have been warmer. The occasion was the formal unveiling of *Crux*, a website devoted to "all things Catholic." The project had been launched by the *Globe* in the hope of attracting a national and international audience of English-speaking Catholics. The *Globe* had left nothing to chance, right down to the location. Boston College is, after all, a well-known Jesuit school that has long served as a center of Catholic life in Greater Boston.

The star panelist that evening was Cardinal Seán O'Malley, who'd been brought in to clean things up after Law fled the country. O'Malley thanked the *Globe*'s owner, John Henry, and his wife, Linda Pizzuti Henry, the paper's managing director. He praised his fellow panelist John Allen, a journalist and author recruited from the *National Catholic Reporter* to write for both *Crux* and the *Globe*. And he expressed the hope that *Crux* would help foster "a better understanding of Catholicism."

O'Malley's presence was uncontroversial. He was no supporter of Law, and he had worked diligently to deal with his church's long-standing refusal to come to terms with predator priests. The same could not be said of another panelist, Mary Ann Glendon, a professor at Harvard Law School and a former US ambassador to the Vatican. An outspoken Catholic conservative, Glendon had ripped into the *Globe* in late 2002, just weeks before Law stepped down. "All I can say is that if fairness and accuracy have anything to do with it," she said, "awarding the Pulitzer Prize to the *Boston Globe* would be like giving the Nobel Peace Prize to Osama bin Laden."[3] Toxic words. At Boston College, though, no such rhetoric was heard.

Among those in the audience that evening were several members of the Spotlight Team who had brought down Law. Of course, they not only won the Pulitzer that Glendon had said they didn't deserve, but were about to become famous: the movie *Spotlight* would be released the following year and would go on to win the Academy Award for Best Picture. Cardinal O'Malley himself would later praise *Spotlight* as an "important film" and acknowledge the media's role in exposing church officials' "crimes and sins."[4]

John Allen offered what was essentially a mission statement for *Crux*. The goal, he said, was to provide "an intelligent, thoughtful, serious presentation of the Catholic Church." In response to questions about how Catholics could move beyond divisions within the church, he replied, "I think we're less polarized than tribalized." His goal with *Crux*, he added, was to help those factions understand each other. "Friendship is the magic bullet when it comes to tribalism," he said. "I want to create a space where all these tribes can become friends."

It all sounded so promising. A year and a half later, though, the *Globe* ended its support for *Crux*. In a memo to the *Globe*'s staff, the paper's editor, Brian McGrory, and its managing editor for digital, David Skok, wrote that the decision had been made because the website wasn't making enough money. "We simply haven't been able to develop the financial model of big-ticket, Catholic-based advertisers that was envisioned when we launched *Crux* back in September 2014," they said.[5]

The *Globe*'s decision did not mean the end for *Crux*. Ownership of the site was transferred to Allen, who continued to publish in partnership with the Knights of Columbus.[6] But it did mean the end of an important experiment for John Henry and the *Globe*. At its peak, *Crux* employed about a half-dozen journalists, including a Vatican correspondent. The site was led by a longtime *Globe* editor, Teresa Hanafin. The cognitive dissonance of that evening at Boston College notwithstanding, there was nothing wrong with the journalism; in fact, it was quite good. But without a workable business model, Henry's hopes of generating revenue for the *Globe* — or even of putting *Crux* on sustainable footing — had proved to be elusive.

Not that Henry was walking away from the larger idea that *Crux* represented. In the fall of 2015, he launched a much more ambitious project, *Stat,* to cover health and life sciences.[7] But *Crux* stands as something of a paradigm for Henry's ownership of the *Globe*: a noble experiment begun with great optimism, uncertainty over how it could bring in enough revenue to survive, and then, finally, a strategic retreat.

At the beginning of 2017, the *Globe* was in the midst of substantial change. The size of the newsroom staff was being reduced, as it had been a number of times both before and after Henry bought the paper. Editorial and business employees were getting ready to abandon the paper's hulking 1950s-era headquarters in Dorchester, off the Southeast Expressway, and move to a smaller space in downtown Boston sometime later in the year, with printing operations being transferred to a facility in the exurbs. And Brian McGrory was preparing to release the results of a reinvention report, months in the making, to which dozens of staff members had contributed.[8]

The *Globe* of 2017 may no longer be the 800-pound gorilla of New England journalism. Of course, even a 600-pound gorilla is pretty big. But if it keeps shedding pounds year after year, there will come a point at which its capacity to hold powerful institutions accountable will be seriously compromised. The question now, as it had been since 2013, was whether Henry would be able to apply his wealth and his financial acumen to saving a great metropolitan newspaper in the face of external forces that were threatening the existence not just of the *Globe* but of every large regional paper in the country.

JOHN HENRY IS A NONTRADITIONAL NEWSPAPER OWNER. Like Jeff Bezos and Aaron Kushner, he had no previous experience in the business. He made his money elsewhere, and he inspired optimism when he bought the *Globe,* because of his deep pockets as well as his background as a successful investor.

In two respects, though, Henry harked back to the earliest *Globe* traditions. First, like Charles Taylor, who was brought in to save the *Globe* a year after its founding in 1872, Henry acquired the paper essentially free of charge. In fact, by the time he sells the paper's outmoded headquarters in Dorchester, he may well have turned a profit. After purchasing the *Globe,* the *Worcester Telegram & Gazette,* and their websites for $70 million, Henry turned around and sold the Worcester paper for an estimated $7 million to $15 million.[9] Two separate attempts to sell the Dorchester plant had fallen through as of May 2017, but by one estimate the second of those deals, if it had been completed, would have brought in $80 million.[10] It's true, of course, that Henry had also spent a considerable amount of money on the *Globe.* As just one example, it cost him around $75 million to purchase the paper's new printing plant in Taunton, a small city about thirty-five miles south of Boston.[11] But if you're trying to turn around a declining business, it's certainly better to begin with no upfront costs.

The second Taylor parallel: Henry is the principal owner of the Boston Red Sox — a relationship that the *Globe*'s newsroom has to negotiate every day but that, again, is nothing new in the long history of the paper.

The *Globe* was founded by a half-dozen prominent businessmen. According to Louis M. Lyons's authorized history of the *Globe,* they committed $150,000 to the new venture. No doubt there was a need: although Boston at that time was home to ten newspapers, it was nevertheless considered a journalistic backwater. The *Springfield Republican,* in Western Massachusetts, was in Lyons's view "the most distinguished journal in New England."[12] In 2017, the *Republican,* owned by the Newhouse chain, remained one of the better daily papers in the region.

And here is where the first John Henry parallel comes in. The *Globe* did not get off to a good start. Within months, fire and an economic depression had wiped out most of the founders' $150,000. The only one of the original investors who stuck with it was Eben D. Jordan of Maine. Jordan was the founder of Jordan and Marsh, a department store whose name was later shortened to Jordan Marsh and whose pages and pages of Sunday ads kept the *Globe* and other papers solvent for many decades. Jordan identified a possible savior: Charles H. Taylor, the twenty-seven-year-old owner of a successful monthly magazine called *American Homes.* Taylor was reluctant. He had just been elected clerk of the state legislature, and taking the publisher's job would have meant a substantial cut in pay. But he was eventually persuaded to try his hand at rescuing the *Globe.* He began in 1873, with the paper on track to lose $60,000.[13]

Within a few years, Taylor owned the *Globe*—and, like Henry, he acquired it without putting any of his own money into it. In 1877, the paper was down to its last $632.47. Taylor himself mortgaged his house for $5,000, but that was a pittance compared with the $100,000 in debt the business had accrued. With bankruptcy looming, the company was renamed and reorganized. The new Globe Newspaper Company issued 1,250 shares of stock at $100 each, with 1,243 of those shares going to Taylor. Taylor promptly transferred all but three of his shares to the *Globe*'s newsprint supplier and to Eben Jordan. The transaction left Taylor as the "nominal owner," as Lyons described it, even though he had put no capital into it. Over the next few decades he was able to purchase enough shares to become the owner in fact as well as on paper, and he and his descendants remained in charge of the *Globe* until 1993.[14]

As for the second Henry parallel: Taylor bought the city's three-year-old American League baseball team in 1904 and handed it over to one of his sons, John I. Taylor, who had worked for the *Globe* but who had little interest in the newspaper business.[15] It was under John Taylor's ownership that the team became the Red Sox (he scooped up the name after Boston's National League team, the former Boston Red Stockings and the future Boston Braves, stopped wearing red socks) and began future Boston Braves, stopped and began the construction of Fenway Park.[16] In an unfortunate bit of timing for Taylor, the Americans, as the future Red Sox were called, won the first World Series ever in 1903, the year before his father bought the team, and did not win again until 1912, the year after the Taylors had sold it.[17] But the Taylors did manage to avoid the infamy of Harry Frazee, who, while he owned the Red Sox, sold Babe Ruth's contract to the New York Yankees, kicking off eighty-six years of futility popularized by the *Globe* columnist Dan Shaughnessy as the "Curse of the Bambino."[18] Those decades of losing finally came to an end in 2004, by which time the team's ownership group was led by none other than John Henry.

The Taylor and Henry eras were not the only occasions when the fortunes of the *Globe* and the Red Sox were intertwined. For a number of years the New York Times Company held a minority stake in the Henry-led Fenway Sports Group, which owned the Red Sox, a soccer team in Liverpool, and 80 percent of New England Sports Network (NESN), the cable channel that carries Red Sox and Boston Bruins games. The Times Company gradually extricated itself from that investment, cashing out its last remaining shares in 2012.[19] Over the years, the parent company's financial interest in the Red Sox may have created an occasional uncomfortable moment for journalists at the *Globe*. But that was minor compared with John Henry's very visible presence as the top executive of both institutions. Still, there has been no evidence of Henry's meddling in the *Globe*'s coverage of the Red Sox.

The most substantive dilemmas have arisen not over whether the Red Sox have won or lost a game but, rather, when the team has made news as a major business in the city with its own interests and priorities. Non-sports stories involving the Red Sox include a disclosure, and, as a reader, I have detected no sign that the paper is holding back on tough coverage. For instance, in September 2013, shortly after Henry announced he would buy the paper, the *Globe* ran a story on a controversial deal with the city that allowed the Red Sox to close two public streets near Fenway Park on game days so that they could sell concessions. The story included the tidbit that the Boston Finance Commission had criticized the deal as one that would "give away rights to a public street without reasonable public notice, without public advertisement, and without utilizing a public process."[20]

But Boston being Boston, what the Red Sox do on the field matters, too. In October 2011, the *Globe* ran an investigative report by Bob Hohler on the epic collapse of the Red Sox that season. The story included the revelation that three of the team's starting pitchers availed themselves of chicken and beer during games, and it contained derogatory information about manager Terry Francona's personal life that was widely suspected to have been leaked by a high-ranking Red Sox official, perhaps even someone in Henry's ownership group.[21] Needless to say, such a story would have raised all kinds of questions if Henry had owned the *Globe* at that time.

Perhaps no sportswriter in the city is more caustic than Dan Shaughnessy, who loves nothing better than to kick the home team when it's down. Henry would have to demolish the wall between the *Globe*'s business and news sides in order to take action against Shaughnessy — and there have been no signs that he is so inclined. Brian McGrory has said that, under Henry's ownership, Shaughnessy has "the safest job in New England."[22] Still, it has to be awkward.

"Of course it's awkward," Shaughnessy replied when I put that question to him. "It's a big bowl of awkward." But, he added, "I don't deal with John.

I can't speak for what it's like for him, but I think it's impressive that I'm still there and that I'm allowed to do what I do. And I think that's a good thing for everybody."[23]

The one time Shaughnessy's independence was questioned during the Henry era occurred in September 2015, after NESN had announced that it was pushing out the popular Red Sox announcer Don Orsillo. Shaughnessy reported in an online-only article that pro-Orsillo signs would be confiscated by Fenway Park employees as fans filed in. That piece of news was removed from the *Globe*'s website as the evening wore on, and there was no mention of it in the next day's print edition. There was a brief public clamor over the deletion.[24] But Shaughnessy himself dismissed it as a rapidly changing story that hadn't been "properly vetted" and that wouldn't have been published at all in pre-internet days.[25] I have no reason to doubt Shaughnessy's explanation. But the fact that the editing of his story became a story in itself shows how sensitive the *Globe* has to be in response to any suggestion that it is doing its owner's bidding.

As for Shaughnessy's interactions with Henry, they have been few. "We've exchanged a couple of hellos," Shaughnessy told me. Every February, Henry traditionally takes questions from the press at the Red Sox' spring training facility in Fort Myers, Florida. "I pitched a few questions into that, and he answered them professionally," Shaughnessy said. "It was a group thing. We haven't had any one-on-one at all." Overall, he added, he was pleased that Henry had bought the paper. "To have billionaire smart owners with deep pockets coming in and trying to figure it out, I think that's good for everybody," Shaughnessy said. "I applaud that kind of initiative on behalf of the industry."[26]

CHARLES TAYLOR GREW UP in Charlestown, a small city that later became part of Boston. Like many newspaper proprietors of the eighteenth and nineteenth centuries, Taylor got his start by working in a print shop, in his case at the age of fifteen. He served in the Civil War and was discharged after suffering an injury. He was all of seventeen when he returned to civilian life.[27]

Taylor liked to be referred to as *Colonel* Taylor. But despite his wartime service, that title was based more on ego than on genuine accomplishment. He began referring to himself as such after a stint in 1869 as military secretary to Governor William Claflin. No doubt it sounded impressive during his successful campaign for the state legislature, to which he was elected as a Republican from the suburb of Somerville.[28] Then, in 1890, Taylor won a battlefield promotion after William E. Russell was elected governor. The *Globe* had gushingly referred to Russell as a "candidate without a flaw," and Russell rewarded Taylor by making him an honorary member of his military staff. As a consequence of this arduous duty, the publisher was known as General Taylor for the rest of his life.[29]

Under Taylor's guidance, the *Globe* grew as a business but did little to distinguish itself from its undistinguished competition. At the time that the *Globe* made its debut, the *Boston Herald* — a bitter rival for many decades and, as of 2017, still an independent daily — accounted for more than half of the 170,000 newspapers sold in the city every day. The *Herald* printed morning and evening editions and, according to Lyons, was "a newsier paper than the rest." Perhaps more important in explaining its success, it cost two cents at a time when everyone else was charging four.[30]

Five years in, with his control of the *Globe* now unquestioned, Taylor struck back. He cut the price of the paper from four cents to two; added Sunday and afternoon editions to what had been a morning-only paper; switched the political orientation from Republican to Democratic in order to pursue a working-class readership; and introduced features that appealed to women and children. The *Globe* championed the cause of Irish independence, supported organized labor, and campaigned for the right of Catholic priests to be allowed into hospitals in order to administer last rites. Because of its populist orientation and sympathy for Irish causes, the *Globe* became known as "the maid's paper." It was a formula that worked: circulation rose to 100,000, and by 1890 it was the dominant paper in the city.[31]

The *Globe*, the *Herald*, and their competitors were crowded together in downtown Boston on a stretch of Washington Street known as Newspaper Row. It was a colorful scene where horse-drawn delivery trucks filled the street and handwritten news bulletins were hung in the windows. At its peak, eleven papers made their homes on Newspaper Row, though the best of them — the *Christian Science Monitor*, which in its early days devoted some of its coverage to state and city news — was located elsewhere in the city. Newspaper Row fizzled out in the 1950s when the *Herald* and the *Globe* moved to massive new facilities with easy highway access.[32] Like many papers, the *Herald* and the *Globe* have since reversed course. The *Herald* moved to offices in Boston's newest neighborhood, the Seaport District, in 2011.[33] The *Globe*'s new downtown offices, on State Street, are just a few blocks from the former Newspaper Row.

The *Globe* can take credit for a number of firsts. Among other things, it was the first to publish full-page ads and the first to bestow bylines on its reporters. It was also the first to take a story over the phone. On February 13, 1877, Alexander Graham Bell delivered a lecture at the Essex Institute in Salem, Massachusetts, showing off the telephone he had invented by talking with his assistant, Thomas Watson, who was in Boston. A *Globe* reporter named Henry M. Batchelder had covered the lecture, and afterward he asked Bell if he could transmit his story to a colleague who would station himself on the receiving end in Watson's office. Bell agreed. It was a landmark moment, but the clueless editors published Batchelder's story on an inside page.[34]

If the *Globe*'s failure to understand the importance of Bell's invention was a journalistic misdemeanor, other lapses bordered on the felonious. The *Globe*'s editorial voice in the late nineteenth century was muted compared with those of some of its peers. Its editorials were pseudonymously signed by "Uncle Dudley" — a play on a popular saying of the day, "Take it from your Uncle Dudley." Though Lyons wrote that the Uncle Dudley essays took "an affable, informal, philosophical approach," J. Anthony Lukas, in his book on Boston's desegregation crisis, *Common Ground*, argued instead that they were characteristic of the *Globe*'s self-satisfaction. "Fat and prosperous, genial and complacent, the *Globe* grew increasingly disinclined to offend any segment of its hard-won readership," Lukas said. "As the years went by, the *Globe*'s fairness descended into timidity, its benevolence into sanctimony."[35]

That timidity played itself out in various ways. When the muckraking journalist Lincoln Steffens wrote an article for *Metropolitan Magazine* in 1914 on local corruption, the Boston press — including the *Globe* — gave it little play. The root of the problem, Lukas observed, was that even though the paper's Yankee executives were appalled by crooked Irish American politicians like John F. Fitzgerald and James Michael Curley, they didn't dare say so because they didn't want to offend their Democratic working-class readers. This fear of their own audience extended to national politics as well. In 1896, General Taylor refused to endorse William Jennings Bryan, a populist who had won the Democratic presidential nomination. The *Globe* did not endorse a candidate for public office again until 1967, when it supported Kevin White's mayoral candidacy over that of Louise Day Hicks, a conservative whose coalition included a considerable number of white racists. The *Globe* also proved to be gutless during the long ordeal of Nicola Sacco and Bartolomeo Vanzetti, political radicals who were convicted of robbery and murder under dubious circumstances and executed in 1927. The *Atlantic Monthly*, then based in Boston, published a devastating analysis of the case by the future Supreme Court Justice Felix Frankfurter, and the conservative *Herald* won a Pulitzer Prize for an editorial questioning the verdict. But the *Globe*, as Lukas put it, remained "a timorous bystander."[36]

Into this void entered the *Boston Post*, whose energy made it the city's leading newspaper during the first half of the twentieth century. Under the ownership of Edwin Grozier, a protégé of Joseph Pulitzer who acquired the paper in 1891, the *Post*'s circulation grew from 20,000 to 600,000, making it for a time the largest-circulation broadsheet in the country. Grozier loved promotions, and one of them persists to this day: *Post* Santa, now *Globe* Santa, a charitable endeavor whereby readers donate money for the purchase of Christmas toys for poor children. And despite a sensationalistic approach, the *Post* was capable of good journalism — as in 1919–20, when it exposed the get-rich-quick artist Carlo Ponzi, whose scheme of promising impossibly high returns while paying off his early investors with money raised from new victims was forever after associated with his name. The *Post* won the 1921 Pulitzer Prize for Public Service for its coverage of the Ponzi story — the only Boston paper to win that most prestigious of Pulitzers until the *Globe* won the first of its three in 1966.[37]

The *Post*'s vigor in covering the Ponzi case was an exception to the overall somnolence of Boston's newspapers. Although Edwin Grozier's only son, Richard, proved to be exactly the kind of risk-taking publisher that was needed during the Ponzi matter, he suffered from mental illness and within a few years had withdrawn to his family's home, in Cambridge.[38] When the pacifist reformer Oswald Garrison Villard surveyed the city's newspaper scene in his 1944 book *The Disappearing Daily*, he pronounced Boston a "journalistic poor-farm," and the *Post* a "particularly low but successful scarlet woman of journalism." Villard admired only one Boston paper — the *Christian Science Monitor*, to which he devoted an entire chapter. And he was harsh in his assessment of the *Globe*: though he described General Taylor's successor, William O. Taylor, as having "inherited his father's kindly heart," he denounced the paper as "sadly subservient to the great advertisers."[39]

In the early 1950s, Joseph Kennedy, father of the future president, attempted to buy the *Globe* and the *Post*, the latter of which had fallen upon hard times. It was a both-or-nothing deal. With the Taylors refusing to sell the *Globe*, the *Post* was acquired by John Fox, a successful financier who used his pages to engage in vicious redbaiting. He also harmed the *Post*'s relationship with its traditionally Democratic readership by endorsing Dwight Eisenhower for president in 1952. Much worse, he essentially extorted $500,000 from Joseph Kennedy in the form of a loan that was apparently never paid back in return for supporting John F. Kennedy's 1952 Senate campaign.[40]

What finally destroyed the *Post* was Fox's failure to add a television station to his holdings. The TV license he sought was instead obtained by the Boston Herald-Traveler Corporation, which published the morning *Herald* and the afternoon *Traveler*. The *Post* folded in 1956. Fox never returned to prominence, and for a time performed as a pianist in jazz clubs around the city. When he died, in 1984, he was broke and forgotten, living in a Beacon Hill boarding house.[41]

The *Herald*'s move into television, meanwhile, represented an existential threat to the *Globe* — and set the stage for one of the great battles in Boston newspaper history. It was a fight from which would emerge the modern *Globe*, making the *Herald* a perpetual also-ran.

THE PUBLISHER of the *Herald* and the *Traveler* in the mid-1950s was Robert "Beanie" Choate, said to be the model for the newspaper editor Amos Force in Edwin O'Connor's novel *The Last Hurrah*. For some time Choate had been pushing the Taylor family to merge the *Globe* with his papers. Choate meant business. So intent was he on eliminating the last vestiges of newspaper competition in Boston that at one point he tried to use his influence to prevent the *Globe* from obtaining financing for a new printing plant.[42]

As Lukas described it, in January 1956 Choate invited the *Globe*'s new publisher, William Davis Taylor, grandson of the General, to meet with him for lunch at the Somerset Club on Beacon Hill. Several other *Globe* and *Herald* officials joined them. On the menu: broiled scrod and Taylor fricassee. "If you build, we'll build," Choate told his adversary. "If you go to ninety-six pages in your first section, we'll go to ninety-six pages. It's like the arms race. Let's stop now, let's put the two papers together." Taylor refused. Choate responded that the consequences would be severe. "You fellows are stubborn," Choate said. "Worse than that, you're arrogant. You better listen to us or we'll teach you a lesson. I'm going to get Channel 5, and with my television revenues I'll put you out of business."[43]

The Herald-Traveler Corporation already owned two radio stations in the city. Under rules set by the Federal Communications Commission, or FCC, to limit cross-ownership, the company should have been prohibited from adding a television station. But Joseph Kennedy wanted a Pulitzer Prize for his son Jack's book *Profiles in Courage* in order to boost his nascent bid for the presidency, and he had something to trade. The Pulitzer judges were notably unimpressed with *Profiles,* declining even to name it a finalist in the 1957 biography category. So Joe Kennedy and his friend Arthur Krock, a *New York Times* columnist, intervened with the Pulitzer Advisory Board, which had the power to override the judges. Kennedy dispatched an intermediary, a local judge named Francis Xavier Morrissey, to visit Beanie Choate, the only Bostonian on the Pulitzer board. Choate told Morrissey that the price of his vote was the license for Channel 5. Jack Kennedy got his Pulitzer. Choate got his television station.[44]

The *Globe* during those years was badly in need of a shake-up. In 1960, the journalist Peter Braestrup conducted a study of Boston's newspapers and discovered that not much had changed since Oswald Garrison Villard's visit several decades earlier. Braestrup quoted a local journalist who said the *Globe*'s editors were so cautious that they "tend to think twice before printing the weather report." Braestrup also quoted an anonymous *Globe* editor to devastating effect: "We don't go in for crusading or exposés. Maybe we should do more. But if the District Attorney or someone else launches an investigation, we cover it in full. Of course, if a DA is crooked, or if law enforcement officers don't move in, there's a problem." To which Braestrup added, "The problem is, essentially, that the *Globe* hates sticking its neck out."[45]

But even as Braestrup was writing up his findings, the *Globe* was in the midst of a generational change that would transform the sleepy paper. William Davis Taylor, known as Davis, had succeeded his father, William O. Taylor. More significant, Thomas Winship, who'd been covering Washington for the *Globe*, was brought home to help his father, Laurence Winship, the paper's editor since the late 1930s. Within a few years Tom was named the editor. The younger Winship had learned the value of activist journalism during a stint at Phil Graham's *Washington Post*, and under his leadership the *Globe* became far more energetic. The *Globe* hired a slew of young reporters who were turned loose on the city. Pulitzers became a regular occurrence. Uncle Dudley was banished. In 1974, *Time* magazine recognized the *Globe* as one of the ten best papers in the country.[46]

Winship's place in Washington was taken by Robert Healy, the son of a *Globe* mailroom employee who had himself joined the paper as a copyboy right out of high school in 1942. It was Healy who turned out to be the key to the *Globe*'s survival. For his dual assignments were to cover the nation's capital and to do everything he could to relieve the *Herald* of its television license.[47]

In carrying out the second of those two tasks, Healy had a secret ally: US Representative Thomas P. "Tip" O'Neill, the future speaker of the House. In the late 1950s, O'Neill thought he might run for governor someday, and he was afraid that his ambitions would be thwarted if the Republican *Herald* became too powerful. He began feeding information to Healy showing that the FCC had acted corruptly in awarding the television license to Choate. Thanks to O'Neill, Healy received telephone records obtained by government investigators showing that there had been improper contact between Choate and the FCC chairman, George McConnaughey. There was much more to the story, including years of legal proceedings as well as the *Globe*'s first Pulitzer — awarded for the revelation that President Lyndon Johnson's choice for a federal judgeship, the aforementioned Francis Xavier Morrissey, had lied about his professional credentials.[48]

"O'Neill's intercession on behalf of the *Globe*, and its subsequent rise to become the state's leading newspaper, altered the course of Massachusetts politics and journalism — and gave O'Neill a powerful ally, and protective friends, in the news business back home," wrote John Aloysius Farrell in his 2001 biography, *Tip O'Neill and the Democratic Century.* As Healy said of O'Neill, "He did right for the *Globe* and all right in the *Globe* through the years."[49]

The saga finally came to an end in 1972, when the FCC stripped the *Boston Herald Traveler* of its television license and awarded it to a community group. The *Herald Traveler,* faced with extinction, promptly merged with the *Record American,* a Hearst-owned tabloid. Throughout the 1970s, the *Boston Herald American* struggled for a niche, at first positioning itself as a respectable conservative broadsheet more or less in keeping with the *Herald Traveler*'s roots, then switching to the *Record American*'s tabloid format. The *Herald American* reached a sensationalistic apotheosis of sorts under editor Don Forst when the psychiatrist for President Ronald Reagan's would-be assassin, John Hinckley, was criticized during Hinckley's trial. Forst's gigantic front-page headline: "Hinck's Shrink Stinks."[50] The paper continued to lose money, though. It nearly collapsed in 1982, but was saved at the last minute by the newspaper baron Rupert Murdoch, who shortened the paper's name back to the *Boston Herald.*[51] Murdoch's *Herald* enjoyed some success, combining aggressive local news coverage with a lurid approach, a lottery-style game called Wingo, and a good sports section. In 1994, Murdoch sold it to Patrick Purcell, his longtime protégé, who remained the publisher of a vastly smaller though still feisty *Herald* as of 2017.[52]

Although the Kennedys were at first adversaries of the *Globe,* Healy later became as close to them as he was to O'Neill. It was Healy who revealed that Ted Kennedy would run for his brother Jack's Senate seat, and it was Healy who negotiated with President Kennedy over the news that Ted had been expelled from Harvard after he was caught cheating. (A subdued story about the matter was published below the fold on page one.)[53] Under Tom Winship and Healy, who eventually became the number-two editor, the *Globe* was often criticized for being too close with Boston's Democratic establishment. Future editors, especially Matt Storin in the 1990s and Marty Baron in the 2000s, devoted quite a bit of effort to excising bias from the news pages, though the *Globe*'s reputation as a liberal paper persists.

The *Globe*'s endless struggle with the *Herald*'s broadcast ambitions played itself out in one last, faint echo in 1988, when Murdoch, who then owned the *Herald*, purchased Channel 25. Ted Kennedy, by then a leading member of the Senate, quietly slipped a provision into a bill that made it almost impossible for the FCC to grant a waiver to its rule prohibiting someone from owning both a daily newspaper and a TV station in the same market.[54] At the time, I was a reporter for the *Daily Times Chronicle*, which served Woburn and several surrounding communities north of Boston. I remember covering a local appearance by Kennedy as he was dogged by the *Herald* reporter Wayne Woodlief. "Senator, why are you trying to kill the *Herald?*" the persistent Woodlief asked him several times.

Murdoch chose to sell off Channel 25, thus saving the *Herald*; he repurchased the TV station after selling the *Herald* to Purcell. But the *Herald* columnist Howie Carr remained bitter. He told me years later that Kennedy's actions were worse than O'Neill's, since O'Neill was just trying to help one of several papers rather than destroy the *Globe*'s only daily competitor. "I think Tip was just trying to get an ally," Carr said, "whereas Ted was trying to kill the paper in order to deliver the monopoly to his friends."[55]

The liberal reputation the *Globe* developed during the Winship era was cemented during Boston's school desegregation crisis of the mid-1970s, when the *Globe* wholeheartedly supported federal judge Arthur Garrity's order to bus children to different neighborhoods in the city to achieve racial balance. It was a terrible time in Boston, as white racism ran rampant and bullets were fired into the *Globe*'s headquarters and at one of the paper's delivery trucks.[56] The *Globe* took the right moral stand, and its coverage earned the paper its second Pulitzer for Public Service.[57] Winship in those years enjoyed a reputation as one of the finest editors in the country. But it was also during those years that the *Globe* became known as the paper of Boston's suburban liberal elite and the *Herald* that of the urban white working class, a dichotomy that has persisted to this day.

THURSDAY, JUNE 10, 1993, will go down as a momentous occasion in Boston newspaper history. For it was on that day that the *Boston Globe* made a startling announcement: the paper would be sold to the New York Times Company. With Murdoch still at the helm of the *Boston Herald*, the sale — which was finalized that October — meant that neither of Boston's two remaining daily papers would be locally owned.[58] Just as the competition between Washington and New York had long played out in the pages of the *Post* and the *Times*, so, too, had Boston become accustomed to looking up at New Yorkers — especially in the bitter rivalry between the Red Sox and the Yankees, a rivalry felt far more keenly in Boston than in New York. And now the Yankees owned the *Globe.*

The Times Company paid $1.1 billion, an enormous price for its new property given that the company's entire stock market valuation was $2.2 billion. Wall Street was underwhelmed. Within a few weeks, the Times Company announced that it would spend $100 million to buy back its shares, the price of which had started to fall as soon as the sale was announced.[59]

What brought an end to 120 years of Taylor ownership was, quite simply, the proliferation of heirs. Trusts set up for the benefit of General Taylor's and Eben Jordan's descendants were due to expire in 1996, and they controlled 68 percent of the votes at Affiliated Publications, the company the Taylors had set up as the *Globe*'s corporate umbrella. By the early 1990s, there were well over a hundred heirs, many of them with no connection to or interest in the newspaper business. If *Globe* publisher William O. Taylor II, the son of Davis Taylor, and his inner circle had failed to act while they still controlled the company, the fear was that the paper would be sold off to a chain owner that would be more interested in quarterly profits than in journalism.[60]

Not that all was sweetness and light. Conversations between the two sides had actually begun the previous October, but they broke down over questions of independence. There were secret negotiations at Boston's Ritz-Carlton, with those taking part referring to the *Globe* with the code names "Bean" and "Charles," and the Times Company as "Apple" and "Hudson." By the time the details were finally worked out, Bill Taylor had an understanding that he would report directly to the Times Company chairman, Arthur O. "Punch" Sulzberger, rather than to one of his underlings and that the *Globe*'s management team would be left in place for five years. "We feel it's a good deal for all our shareholders, it protects a valuable franchise, and it ensures editorial quality for many years to come," Taylor said.[61]

The five-year agreement ensured that change would come slowly. The editor during those early years of Times Company ownership was Matthew Storin. Tom Winship had retired in 1984 and was succeeded by Michael Janeway, a cerebral *Atlantic Monthly* alumnus who'd served as the paper's Sunday editor. Janeway's time was not a happy one; he stayed just long enough to convince Storin, his managing editor, to leave. In 1992, Storin — by then the managing editor of the *New York Daily News* — was lured back to serve as executive editor under Jack Driscoll, who had replaced Janeway and was getting ready to retire. Storin became the top editor just a few months before the *Globe* was sold.[62]

It was during these years that I reported on the *Globe* as the media columnist for the *Boston Phoenix*, the city's alternative weekly. Matt Storin was measured and thoughtful in my encounters with him, though my sources in the newsroom told me that he occasionally displayed a fearsome temper. He kept a life-size cardboard cutout of Ivana Trump in his office, a memento of his days in New York. Storin improved the paper by ordering tough coverage of politicians who had once gotten an easy ride from the *Globe*, like the Kennedy family and John Kerry, and by competing harder on breaking news with the smaller but more nimble *Herald*. The paper itself was redesigned and made more attractive. But it was Storin's misfortune to preside over a double dose of newsroom scandal in the summer of 1998.

The first blow landed in June, when the columnist Patricia Smith suddenly resigned after an internal investigation revealed that she had fabricated people and stories. Smith was the *Globe*'s highest-profile African American, and it did not go unnoticed that the paper's most prominent columnist, Mike Barnicle, a well-connected Irish American, had for years thrived despite facing credible accusations that he'd faked some columns and plagiarized others. Indeed, Barnicle's legendary predecessor, George Frazier, became enraged when Barnicle once borrowed the form (if not the substance) of Frazier's classic "Another Man's Poison" collections of one-liners while Frazier was dying in the hospital. According to Frazier's biographer, my Northeastern University colleague Charles Fountain, Frazier screamed, "Why that little son of a bitch. I'll fix him."[63]

Within weeks of Patricia Smith's departure, the *Herald* caught Barnicle ripping off a series of quips from a book by the comedian George Carlin —

a book Barnicle claimed he hadn't read. After video surfaced of him endorsing said book on a local television show, Storin insisted Barnicle resign, but that got negotiated down to a two-month suspension as the *Globe* came under pressure from Barnicle's powerful friends and supporters. Then, in August, I reported in the *Phoenix* that Barnicle had copied parts of a 1986 column about the Louisiana politico Earl Long from a biography written by A. J. Liebling. Barnicle's employment ended that afternoon amid yet another incident: *Globe* editors said they could not confirm the existence of two boys with cancer he had written about in 1995.[64]

Although no one on the corporate side of the New York Times Company said anything publicly, one powerful *Times* journalist pronounced himself appalled at the *Globe*'s initial decision merely to suspend Barnicle — especially given that an African American woman had just been removed for essentially the same transgressions. "Editors have to be able to trust what reporters and columnists write and say," he wrote. "Journalists do not make things up or present others' writing and thought as their own." The author: Howell Raines, editor of the editorial page. Less than five years later Raines would be forced to step aside as executive editor of the *Times* after it was revealed that another young African American reporter, Jayson Blair, was himself a serial fabricator and plagiarist.[65]

The Times Company, meanwhile, was beginning to loom larger in the life of the *Boston Globe*.

In late 2015, Matt Storin and I met at an Irish pub in Bath, Maine, down the coast from his home, to which he had retired following a long post-*Globe* career in communications and teaching at his alma mater, Notre Dame. He told me that he welcomed it when the Times Company bought the *Globe*. On the other hand, he said Times Company executives made it clear that the *Times* was in one category and the *Globe* was in another.[66]

"I felt that when they bought us, OK, here come some fresh ideas," Storin told me. "I was probably naive about the fact that, well, this isn't going to affect me because we're part of a noble tradition of editorial independence. And basically that continued. Except that, gradually, we began to see that we were acolytes to their altar." By way of example, Storin said, *Globe* and Times Company executives would periodically meet at Blantyre, a luxury hotel in the Berkshires. "We were made to feel pretty good, not like aliens, though even in the beginning you knew you weren't as important as the

Times paper," Storin said. "But at the meetings at Blantyre it was just *Times* business executives and *Globe* editorial. They weren't going to talk about the *Times* newspaper as much. They were going to talk about the *Globe* newspaper."

From the Times Company's perspective, the purpose of the *Globe* was to make money while still putting out a respectable journalistic product. Storin and I both recalled seeing an analysis during those years showing that the Times Company had modest profit expectations for the *Times* but expected much higher margins from a string of smaller papers that it owned, mainly in the South. The *Globe* and the *Worcester Telegram & Gazette,* which the Times Company bought in 1999, were somewhere in the middle in terms of profit expectations. Increasingly, the *Globe* was treated as merely a division within the company. And the idea that the *Globe* could remain a benevolently run local institution with the Taylor family in charge was becoming anachronistic. In 1997, Bill Taylor retired and handed off the publisher's reins to his younger second cousin Benjamin Taylor, a popular executive who'd spent much of his career in the newsroom.[67]

Ben Taylor's time in the publisher's office would prove to be brief. The Taylor era came to an end in July 1999, when Arthur Sulzberger Jr., who had succeeded his father as chairman, removed Ben Taylor and installed Richard Gilman, a senior vice president at the Times Company. It was not clear why Sulzberger acted when he did. Although ad revenue and circulation were down at the *Globe,* Ben Taylor said the paper had achieved a 25 percent profit margin for three consecutive years. Most likely it was just a sense that the moment had come for New York to assert itself. The five-year agreement leaving the Taylors in charge had expired a year earlier, the dust from the Smith and Barnicle scandals had settled, and Sulzberger may simply have wanted to exert more influence on his second-largest newspaper.[68]

An equally significant break with the past occurred in mid-2001, when Storin retired and Martin Baron, the executive editor of Knight Ridder's *Miami Herald,* was announced as the new editor of the *Globe.* Baron arrived in the middle of a difficult year. To comply with budget cuts ordered by New York, Storin had merged the paper's Sunday Focus and book sections, folded a weekly supplement covering New Hampshire, and accepted about sixty early retirements in the newsroom, which was then in excess of 500 people. Storin later said he realized at the time that the lucrative decades the newspaper business enjoyed from the 1960s through the '90s were coming to an end. "I well remember when, almost by default, we grew and prospered year to year in a way that sometimes we didn't even understand," Storin told me in 2007. "I had ridden that baby right up to the top of the roller coaster, and it was starting to hit a downward trough during the time I was there. In all honesty, I could see what was coming. Could I see all of this? No. But I could see that it was going to be a tough slog from then on."[69]

Storin had urged management to promote one of his deputies to the top spot, and the Times Company considered other outside candidates (including a future *Times* executive editor, Bill Keller) before settling on Baron. Even then, though, Baron was considered a rising star. Under his guidance the *Miami Herald* had won a Pulitzer for its coverage of Elián González, a young Cuban refugee who had washed up on shore in late 1999, and had undertaken its own recount of the Florida ballots following the contested 2000 presidential election. (The *Herald*'s verdict: George W. Bush won.) Baron had also gotten rave reviews for his performance in high-ranking editing positions at the *Los Angeles Times* and the *New York Times*.[70]

Within days of his arrival, Baron made a crucial decision that would help define the *Globe*'s place in the public imagination for the next generation. Just before he arrived, the columnist Eileen McNamara wrote about the case of Father John Geoghan, a Catholic priest accused of sexually abusing dozens of children. The survivors' lawyer, Mitchell Garabedian, had accused Cardinal Law of helping to cover up Geoghan's crimes; McNamara wrote that the truth might never come out because the documents in the lawsuit Garabedian had filed were sealed.[71]

Baron, coming from Florida, which had a more progressive public-records law, could not understand why the *Globe* couldn't obtain the documents, and he pushed his new staff to get them. The *Globe* was not the only news organization to report on Law's possible involvement in the pedophile-priest scandal. In particular, one of my *Phoenix* colleagues at the time, Kristen Lombardi, wrote a groundbreaking series of deeply reported articles starting in early 2001.[72] But the *Globe* cracked the case wide open the following year, obtaining the documents that had been sealed and publishing literally hundreds of articles on multiple priests.[73] Law was forced to step down and leave the country, and the *Globe* won its third Pulitzer for Public Service. The 2015 film *Spotlight,* named after the paper's investigative Spotlight Team, may be the best movie about journalism since *All the President's Men* two generations earlier.

THE GLOBE'S COVERAGE of the Catholic Church was accountability journalism at its most meaningful, and it came at a propitious moment. The *Globe* had covered a similar story involving pedophile priests in the early 1990s, the one that provoked Cardinal Law to "call down God's power on the media." Yet, over time, the story faded away. What changed, as Clay Shirky argued in his book *Here Comes Everybody,* was that by 2002 the *Globe* was online, enabling readers to share the paper's coverage nationally and internationally — a simple gesture, multiplied over and over, that shook the church worldwide. "The act of forwarding a story to friends and colleagues had gone from tedious to all but effortless," Shirky wrote. "Even more important, forwarding the story to a group was as easy as forwarding it to an individual, and any of the recipients could forward it to others as easily as the original sender had done."[74]

But the sharing power of the internet was exceeded only by its power to destroy economic value. At the time that Baron took charge, the *Globe* still had bureaus across the country and around the world. After the terrorist attacks of September 11, 2001, which occurred just as Baron was settling in, the *Globe* dispatched reporters to Afghanistan to cover the war against Al Qaeda and the Taliban. Even the *Boston Herald* sent a reporter. During those years the *Globe* also had a correspondent stationed in the Middle East. In 2002, that position was held by Anthony Shadid, who was accidentally shot while reporting from the region; Baron flew to Israel so that he could be by his reporter's side, an early sign that the *Globe*'s new editor had the right values.[75] Like major metropolitan newspapers everywhere, the *Globe* was a full-service newspaper, covering the city, the region, the nation, and the world. (Shadid would move on to a distinguished career at the *Washington Post* and the *New York Times,* and died of an apparent asthma attack while on the ground in Syria in 2012.)[76]

Within a few years, though, the *Globe* — again, like most major metros — had pulled back dramatically, closing all of its bureaus except its

Washington office. It is sometimes said that the two most popular sports in Boston are politics and revenge. In deference to the former, the *Globe* still operated a Washington bureau as of 2017, and staff members traveled the country covering the 2016 presidential campaign. Beyond that, wire services provided most of the *Globe*'s national and international coverage. By choosing as he did, Baron was able to preserve the *Globe*'s essential mission, which was to cover regional and local news. But the move put a cap on the ambitions of *Globe* journalists, who had to leave for other news organizations if their goal was to report from somewhere other than Boston or Washington.

Marty Baron was a different sort of editor for the *Globe*: the first outsider, the first Jew, bilingual (he is fluent in Spanish). Though he rarely raises his voice, he is direct, and his demeanor is that of someone who does not suffer fools gladly. In his early years at the *Globe* he developed a reputation for working impossibly long hours and doling out criticism more often than praise. Within the newsroom, staff members joked that Baron's motto appeared to be "the joyless pursuit of excellence."[77] In recent years Baron has lightened up. When Gabriel Sherman of *New York* magazine asked him in 2016 about *Spotlight*, Baron responded, "I would say it's incomplete in terms of who I am. A small minority of people say I have a sense of humor."[78] It's a line I've heard Baron use to good effect at several speaking appearances. But it is nevertheless safe to say that *Globe* journalists, though they respected Baron, found him a little intimidating during his first few years at the helm.

That respect later grew into something approaching affection. Whether the Times Company had originally overpaid for the *Globe* or not, there was no question that the paper had made a lot of money for New York over the years — money that disappeared after 2005, when the business crisis afflicting newspapers took a downward turn from the chronic to the acute. In April 2009, just days after the *Globe* had eliminated some fifty newsroom positions, the Times Company made a stunning demand: in order to cover losses that it said could reach $85 million for the year, the *Globe*'s unions would have to give back $20 million in pay and benefits that they had already agreed to. Half of that would come from the largest union, the Newspaper Guild, whose members included the paper's journalists. And if those cuts couldn't be achieved, the *Globe* would be shut down.[79]

With the future of the *Globe* in doubt, Baron led by example. Despite the strife, which was marked by heated rhetoric and a rally by employees at the historic Faneuil Hall,[80] the paper itself maintained its standards, a reflection of Baron's steady leadership. The Guild eventually agreed to the concessions, and the Times Company responded by putting the *Globe* up for sale. There was some interest, including an offer from a group led by Stephen Taylor, an ex–*Globe* executive and a member of the former ruling family; Ben Taylor was part of the group as well. But the Times Company pulled the paper off the market later in the year, saying the *Globe*'s numbers had "significantly improved."[81]

After the wreckage had cleared, the Times Company appeared to ease up on the throttle. In late 2009, Christopher Mayer, a well-liked veteran *Globe* executive, was named publisher, succeeding Steven Ainsley, a Times Company veteran who had succeeded Richard Gilman several years earlier.[82] Then, when Marty Baron left for the *Washington Post* in December 2012, Mayer replaced him with Brian McGrory, a popular columnist and former metro editor.[83] McGrory turned out to be an inspired choice, but he might not have gotten the job if there had been a New York–directed nationwide search as there had been when Matt Storin retired. Nor did the company renew its efforts to sell the paper in a serious way. In late 2010, a local entrepreneur named Aaron Kushner stepped forward and said he wanted to buy the paper, a bid I will examine in some detail in the next chapter. But there was no indication that the Times Company ever seriously considered selling to Kushner.

In February 2013, the Times Company announced that, once again, it would attempt to sell the *Globe*.[84] Then, on April 15, two young immigrants carried out a terrorist bombing at the scene of the Boston Marathon. Three people were killed near the finish line, and an MIT police officer was subsequently murdered. Scores of bystanders were seriously injured. It was the biggest story to hit Boston in many years. And the *Globe* excelled, providing day after day of riveting coverage. For many of us, it was a wake-up call, reminding us what an indispensable civic institution the *Globe* still was, especially given the diminished state of Boston's other news organizations.

Boston's renewed affection for the *Globe* set the stage for what was to come: a return to local ownership and a sense that Boston in the twenty-first century would be more than just a franchise town, more than an outpost of giant corporations that did their real business elsewhere. No longer would out-of-state owners be dictating how the city's leading news organization would be run. We would tell our own stories.

If only John Henry could figure out the business end.

BY EARLY 2016, it seemed pretty obvious that *Crux* had not lived up to expectations. The quality was excellent; as a lifelong non-Catholic, I found John Allen's coverage of Francis's papacy engaging and insightful. The site was attractive. A regular column on spirituality written by Margery Eagan (a colleague of mine at the public broadcasting station WGBH) won an award from the Religion Newswriters Association.[85] But the few ads on the site, which tended toward Catholic-specific appeals to join the priesthood or become a missionary, couldn't have been bringing in much money. And the site was free, so there was no other source of revenue.

Before Henry bought the *Globe*, the paper had begun a free website called *BetaBoston* to cover the local innovation economy. Under Henry the *Globe* launched two more — *Crux* and *Stat*. During an interview in February 2016, I asked Henry whether he believed those projects could generate enough money to sustain themselves and to throw off enough revenue to help fund the *Globe* as well. "Less so than I did a year or two ago," he replied. *Crux*, he said, "sounds like a great idea. It *is* a great idea." But, he added, during its brief life it hadn't come close to paying its way.[86]

Brian McGrory and David Skok's memo came a month later. The ownership of *Crux* was transferred to John Allen, and *BetaBoston* was subsumed into the *Globe*'s website. Within months, *BetaBoston* had disappeared altogether, although McGrory told me that the site's coverage of the city's technology and innovation sectors had helped ramp up the *Globe*'s own reporting in those areas.[87]

Did *Crux* fall short of expectations? Yes, but it was an experiment, and experiments often don't work out. Given that the newspaper business is often (and rightly) criticized for its hidebound ways, Henry deserves credit for being willing to try something radically different — and for walking away from it as soon as it became clear that it wasn't working. In recent years, "fail faster" has become a catchphrase for how to encourage innovation, and Kathleen Kingsbury, a Pulitzer Prize–winning editorial writer who succeeded Skok as managing editor for digital, referred to it when I asked her about *Crux*. "I would love to have more of a culture of being able to take risks and failing. And I think that *Crux* is a great example of that," Kingsbury told me. "It was something that we tried and it didn't work. So we moved on. And that's actually something we need to do more of."[88] (Kingsbury announced in June 2017 that she would leave the *Globe* to become deputy editorial page editor of the *New York Times*.)[89]

Yet, many months later, *Crux* was still around. It may not have lived up to the *Globe*'s expectations, but it quite literally did not fail. As of early 2017, John Allen was continuing to operate it as a standalone site. The staff was smaller than it had been previously, with the number of full-time editorial employees dropping from about a half-dozen to three. But *Crux* had a presence in the Vatican, a stable of freelance contributors, and an audience that Allen told me was growing.

Allen praised the *Globe* for transferring the ownership of the site to him free of charge and for continuing to host it on its web servers until he could make other arrangements. "I have nothing but deep gratitude for the *Boston Globe*," he said.[90] Still, Allen believed that things could have turned out differently. He said *Crux* was initially given a three- to five-year horizon, which got cut back because of the *Globe*'s deteriorating finances. He also thought the sponsorship model he had worked out with the Knights of Columbus and other Catholic organizations was something that traditional news organizations have to be willing to embrace. He acknowledged the possibility of conflicts over a sponsor's agenda. But, he asked, "What do you think advertising is? You have to be upfront from the beginning about what the nature of this relationship is. This is the new world."

In fact, the *Globe* had accepted grant money to fund some of its reporting on public education and to pay for a classical music critic who was hired to fill in for the regular critic while he was away on a fellowship.[91] More such partnerships are likely to develop, and they always present potential conflicts with the funders' interests — conflicts that should not be a significant problem for a news organization committed to transparency and independence. Still, it would have been awkward in the extreme for the *Globe* to take money from Catholic organizations given its history. What if they threatened to abandon *Crux* the next time the Spotlight Team came calling?

Not long after the *Globe* parted company with *Crux*, I asked Henry for his own postmortem on why it hadn't worked out. "I was new to the business," he replied, "and at that point thought that good journalism could attract adequate ad revenue in an area that wasn't being covered seriously enough. We were never able to achieve any scale." Why didn't the *Globe* attempt the route Allen had taken, with a smaller staff and sponsorships? "At the *Globe* we try to do too many things," Henry said. "I contributed to that. We need to concentrate on our core business — what our local readers rely on us for."[92]

Crux represented just a small investment that, in the end, told us little about the fate of the *Globe*. By the time 2017 began, Henry had been in charge for more than three years. His plan for putting his newspaper on a more sustainable footing was still not entirely clear. Some ideas had been tried and cast aside. Some ideas had yet to be put into effect. And the newsroom was being cut.

"Until revenues stabilize in this industry, cuts are going to continue or there will be bankruptcies," Henry told me. "In general, as long as newspaper revenues decline you're going to have cuts. Either that or you're going to have to find philanthropists. I don't see large annual losses as something that's sustainable. For American journalism to be sustainable you've got to address reality."[93]

Henry's ideas for addressing reality would, he hoped, stop the decline and end the need for repeated rounds of cutting. After taking a chance on *Crux*, expanded print sections, and a disastrous attempt at bringing in a new vendor to handle home delivery, Henry was pursuing a simpler agenda: reducing operating expenses by moving the *Globe* out of its inefficient Dorchester plant and asking readers to pick up a larger share of the costs through high-priced digital subscriptions. If it worked, the *Globe*'s future would be secured. If not, then the *Globe* would find itself in the same position as nearly every other large regional newspaper — reducing its budget in order to stay ahead of falling revenues, thus risking further decline by offering its dwindling readership fewer and fewer reasons to keep on paying.

CHAPTER THREE

UNREQUITED LOVE

Spurned in Boston and Maine, Aaron Kushner Looks West

MY CELL PHONE RANG. On the line was Aaron Kushner, the entrepreneur who was the public face of the group that had purchased the *Orange County Register* nearly three years earlier. It was March 2015. I was heading out to Southern California the following week to ask people why Kushner's stewardship of the *Register* had run off the rails and whether there was still a chance that he could set things right. I had hoped to interview Kushner as well, but my multiple attempts to connect with him had failed. And here he was, finally, talking to me as I stood in a loud, freezing-cold subway station in Boston.

He told me that he'd read what I'd written about him, making it clear that he was disappointed.[1]

I reminded him that I was hardly alone — that media observers of all stripes had criticized him after it became obvious that his ambitions for the *Register* were no match for reality. Besides, I said, others had been much harsher than I had been, and I wanted to give him a chance to make his case.

He agreed to see me. I still have the interview listed on my calendar. It never took place. Interviews get canceled all the time, of course. This particular cancellation, though, was accompanied by a bit of drama, which I'll get to shortly. First, though, some background on what had intrigued me about Kushner and why his stewardship of the *Register* was such a failure.

From mid-July 2012 until Jeff Bezos and John Henry scooped up the *Washington Post* and the *Boston Globe* a little more than a year later, Aaron Benjamin Kushner was perhaps the most celebrated and scrutinized newspaper executive in the country. His plan was highly idiosyncratic: to turn back the clock by rejecting nearly two decades of dogmatic certainty that the future was digital and that readers would not pay for news. Kushner, who'd become wealthy by launching a dot-com and, later, by running a greeting card company, had been seeking to break into the newspaper business for several years, trying and failing to acquire the *Boston Globe* and the *Portland Press Herald* of Maine. So when Kushner finally was able to take charge of a major daily newspaper, he went about it like a man who'd just been freed from a long confinement.

Kushner's emphasis on print over digital was counterintuitive. But after years of wretched news for newspapers, a lot of media analysts bit back on their skepticism during the early months of Kushner's stewardship. He was a young man — just thirty-nine years old when he and his partners bought the *Register*'s parent company, Freedom Communications. He was smart, apparently rich, and supremely confident that he had a better way of doing business. Why not give him a chance?

Kushner went on a hiring binge, nearly doubling the 180 to 200 full-time journalists the *Register* had employed.[2] He purchased a second daily, the venerable *Riverside Press-Enterprise,* and launched a third, the *Long Beach Register.* Then, even as the wheels were coming off, Kushner made his most audacious move, launching yet another paper, the *Los Angeles Register,* in competition with the mighty *Los Angeles Times.*

The great dismantling commenced almost immediately. The Long Beach and Los Angeles papers were quickly abandoned. And in the fall of 2014, Kushner stepped aside as publisher, handing the reins to a casino executive named Richard Mirman. Kushner said the decision was his, insisting that he had recruited Mirman because he was too busy with his responsibilities running Freedom.[3] But it was obvious to everyone that the *Orange County Register*'s all-too-brief return to its glory days had come to an end.

The week after Kushner and I talked, I found myself in the cafeteria of the *Los Angeles Times,* interviewing folks about the Southern California media scene in general and the *Orange County Register* in particular. A reporter came up to us with breaking news: Kushner was out. I was supposed to interview him the next day. Given everything that had happened in the preceding months, Kushner's resignation from his executive positions at Freedom was not exactly a surprise. But was it too much to hope that it could have been put off until, oh, the following week?

Kushner and I exchanged several emails as I attempted to salvage our interview, but ultimately he demurred. I tried several more times over the next year. In September 2016, I contacted him once more, sending him an email telling him I was making my final attempt. To my surprise, he said yes. We spoke twice, the second time at his request. Maybe the passage of time had had its effect, because he proved to be more introspective about what had gone wrong than I had expected.

But not *too* introspective. Kushner is nothing if not confident about his own abilities and insights. He told me that he had concluded it all would have worked out just fine if he'd expanded the paper gradually rather than all at once. "If we had known going in we had ten years to get subscriber revenue to where we wanted it to go, and therefore we're going to meter out the investment in improving the quality of the newspaper over a ten-year timeframe, not a ten-month timeframe, my guess is that it would have actually worked exactly the way we wanted it to," he said.[4] Kushner may have been right about the timetable. It was his spending rather than his emphasis on print that brought his tenure at the *Orange County Register* to an abrupt end. Kushner had spent several years trying to buy a newspaper. In retrospect it is startling how quickly it all fell apart.

We'll hear more from my interview with Kushner later in this chapter and in chapter 7. First, though, some background on how he ended up in Southern California in the first place — and why it turned so bad so quickly.

FOR KUSHNER, the *Orange County Register* was something of a consolation prize. The truly beloved object of his affection was the *Boston Globe*, the largest daily paper in New England, which the New York Times Company had owned since 1993. The internet had transformed the *Globe* from a profitable asset into dead weight; the Times Company, which had problems of its own, had tried to sell the paper in 2009, only to pull back. By the time Kushner came along, it seemed likely that the *Globe* could be bought for the right price, even though the Times Company's public stance was that the paper was no longer for sale.

The news that Kushner wanted to purchase the *Globe* was broken by the paper's smaller tabloid rival, the *Boston Herald*, in October 2010. According to the report, a group headed by Kushner was meeting with business leaders and preparing a bid for the *Globe* and the *Worcester Telegram & Gazette*, which the Times Company also owned. The *Herald* cited reporting by the *Portland Press Herald* that, five years earlier, Kushner had purchased a greeting card company in Maine "and sacked nearly half its employees just days before Christmas." No doubt there were a few people at the *Globe* who jumped when they saw that.[5]

Kushner was not well known in Boston's notoriously insular business, political, and media circles. He was raised in Georgia and had earned a bachelor's degree in economics and a master's in organizational analysis at Stanford University. He'd also been a member of Stanford's gymnastics team, a powerhouse that won two national titles and was a runner-up during Kushner's senior year. After graduating from Stanford, he moved to Chicago to take a job with the Boston Consulting Group. He launched a website called ChangeMyAddress.com, which simplified the task of updating your address on the web after you'd moved. In 1999, Kushner sold it to Imagitas, which was based in Newton, Massachusetts; Kushner moved to the Boston area in order to take a job as the company's vice president. The service eventually morphed into MyMove.com, which was still operating as of 2017.[6]

For someone whose wealth derived from cashing in during the dot-com boom, what Kushner did next was puzzling. In 2002, he and a business partner acquired Marian Heath, a greeting card company in Wareham, Massachusetts. Kushner became the chief executive. The venture was not entirely new to the Kushner family, as his grandfather and great-grandfather had also worked in the greeting card business. Still, it seemed notable that a young man like Kushner, who achieved early success in the burgeoning internet economy, would be interested in a field tied to a physical, printed product such as greeting cards — and that, later, when he entered the newspaper business, he took the stance that news executives should double down on print.[7]

In a supremely self-confident interview published in *Boston* magazine in early 2011, Kushner spoke with Katherine Ozment about his interest in greeting cards. "At the time it was a very contrarian thing," Kushner told Ozment. "E-greetings were incredibly popular, and there were a lot of people who actually were saying that physical paper greeting cards were going to disappear, similar to how people are saying today that physical newspapers are going to disappear. And I believed, as I still believe, that there are things that simply cannot be replaced digitally."[8]

But Ozment found, as the *Portland Press Herald* had previously, that

Kushner brought a slash-and-burn management style to the greeting card business. He had wanted to expand Marian Heath, whose market share trailed industry leaders Hallmark and American Greetings by a considerable margin. One of the ways he intended to do that was by buying up smaller competitors and folding them into his operation. Among those competitors was Renaissance Greeting Cards, which was based in Maine. As Ozment described it, Kushner downsized the company right after he bought it, carrying out his task in a particularly insensitive manner. Renaissance employees who arrived at work one morning in December 2005 were met by people with clipboards. Some staff members were told to report to the cafeteria and others were sent upstairs. The upstairs group got to keep their jobs; those in the cafeteria were laid off. Of Renaissance's seventy-seven employees, thirty-four lost their jobs that day.

There were signs that Marian Heath was not all that flush during Kushner's time at the helm, which seems significant given the financial difficulties Kushner would later encounter even before he had finished building up his Southern California newspapers. Ronnie Sellers, a founder of Renaissance, had left long before Kushner bought the company. But he stayed in the business, and by the time Ozment interviewed him, he was in charge of a greeting card company in South Portland, Maine. Sellers told Ozment that his sales doubled as frustrated wholesale buyers stopped doing business with Marian Heath. "I was hearing from sales representatives who rep our line and also rep Marian Heath, and they told me that Marian Heath wasn't paying them, or was paying them very late," Ozment quoted Sellers as saying. "Artists and licensors who had sold content to Marian Heath also told me that they weren't getting paid their royalties on time. Some of these were owed substantial amounts of money. I assumed, therefore, that it was likely that Marian Heath was running short of cash, and that the grand plan that Aaron orchestrated may have run aground."

In his interview with Ozment, Kushner denied any talk of financial trouble, called the layoffs at Renaissance part of the "incredibly painful transitions" that had hit the greeting card business, and said Marian Heath's continued existence was evidence of his management prowess. "How anybody could think that we didn't love the business and understand the business and that I didn't have a great vision for the business and leadership for the business, I don't see how anybody could make that argument," he said.

Kushner left in 2009 because, he said, he and the financiers who had backed him disagreed on their "vision" for the company.

Married with three young children and living in the wealthy suburb of Wellesley, Massachusetts,[9] Kushner found himself casting about for what to do next. The *Globe* was in the midst of turmoil marked by union unrest created by a Times Company demand that employees give back some $20 million in agreed-to pay and benefits and by the subsequent failed attempt to sell the paper. Kushner, the dot-com entrepreneur–turned–greeting card magnate, was about to embark on a journey of several years that would ultimately take him to three states in his quest to buy something that very few people other than he wanted: a daily newspaper.

THERE IS NO EVIDENCE that executives at the New York Times Company ever seriously entertained Aaron Kushner's offer to buy the *Globe*. For one thing, Kushner's timing was wrong. The Times Company pulled the *Globe* off the market in October 2009 after shopping it around for several months, announcing that the paper's financial situation had "significantly improved." The *Globe* did not officially go back on the market until early 2013.[10] Kushner made his move in late 2010 and early 2011, a brief window during which people at the Times Company may have genuinely believed they could make a go of it.

Of course, Kushner could have made an offer that the Times Company would not refuse. But that didn't happen. When the *Globe* was finally sold to John Henry in 2013, the price was shockingly low — just $70 million — but it was for cash. By contrast, indications are that Kushner's offer, estimated at $200 million, was complicated and highly leveraged. I learned that Times Company executives considered Kushner's proposal but concluded it was not something they were willing to pursue. The *Globe*'s own February 2013 report that the paper was once again for sale said simply that Kushner had "made no headway" with the Times Company.[11]

Kushner attracted prominent investors and supporters. Among them were Benjamin and Stephen Taylor, cousins whose family had sold the *Globe* to the Times Company in 1993 and had been involved in efforts to buy it back in 2009. Ben Taylor, the last member of his family to serve as publisher, declined my request for an interview.[12] But in early 2011, the *Globe* reported that the two Taylors had agreed to "provide money and advice" to Kushner, with Ben Taylor saying, "He has some good ideas about how to grow the business. I've gotten to know him, and I feel he has a good sense of the vital role a newspaper like the *Globe* plays in the community."[13]

Another Kushner supporter was Ben Bradlee Jr., son of the legendary *Washington Post* executive editor and a formidable journalist in his own right. Bradlee, a former top editor at the *Globe* who helped shepherd the Spotlight Team's reporting on the pedophile-priest crisis, had retired to write a well-regarded biography of the Red Sox legend Ted Williams called *The Kid*. In 2011, Bradlee met Kushner for lunch. Bradlee was impressed with what he heard. "The idea was for him to meet people who had been at the *Globe* and who he perceived as influential," Bradlee told me. "He was new — he'd been living in Wellesley, but I'm not sure how well he knew Boston. He was looking for investors. So I agreed to introduce him around to people. And I did link him up with some important investors — probably most importantly the Taylors. They were of symbolic importance rather than how much money they put in."[14]

I asked Bradlee what impressed him about Kushner's plan. His answer: Kushner's emphasis on print at a time when it seemed that the promise of digital journalism was never going to evolve into a sustainable business model. "By this time, obviously, newspapers were in free fall," Bradlee said. "He seemed to be still a believer in print, which attracted me, perhaps naively. And he seemed to link that to baby boomers, and the growing baby boomer demographic, which he believed was still going to be tied to print. So I think he was hopeful that the baby boomer cohort, as it aged, having grown up with print, would still want to remain there. Which made sense to me since I was having trouble myself with the shift to digital."

Despite all that, Bradlee said, Kushner was unable to line up a serious conversation with Times Company people. For one thing, although Bradlee said he did not probe too deeply, it seemed clear to him that Kushner was not putting much of his own money on the table. For another, Bradlee believed Kushner may have assumed too high a profile. "I think that they considered him a pain in the ass because he was getting a lot of press," Bradlee told me. "He kept popping up as an interested buyer, and the *Times* didn't want to sell back then. So I think they saw him as this relatively obscure gadfly who didn't have the necessary pedigree that the *Times* thought probably a Boston buyer should have. So I'm not sure they ever took him seriously. I do recall that he was told by them, probably through an intermediary rather than a direct contact, that no, it just wasn't for sale. And he finally gave up."

Not everyone who met Kushner shared Ben Taylor's and Ben Bradlee's views that his ideas for reviving the *Globe* were plausible. One particularly outspoken skeptic was Alex Jones, a journalist and media scholar who retired in 2015 as director of the Shorenstein Center on Media, Politics and Public Policy, part of Harvard's John F. Kennedy School of Government. Like Bradlee and Taylor, Jones had been schmoozed by Kushner. Unlike them, Jones was appalled. "He was so arrogant about believing that the people who were in the newspaper business didn't have a clue what the fuck they were doing," Jones told me. "There's no question there are plenty of fools in the newspaper business. But there was a kind of dismissiveness, you know?"[15]

Jones's criticism was rooted more in a sense that Kushner hadn't thought his plan through than in any specifics. For instance, Jones thought Kushner's idea of generating revenue while at the same time helping nonprofit organizations (which I will explain in more detail later on) was "a clever scheme." Nor was Jones necessarily put off by Kushner's emphasis on print. Rather, what struck Jones was Kushner's ignorance about what he was getting into and his overweening confidence that he knew how to solve problems that people in the news business had been struggling with for years. "The fact that he had no experience whatsoever in newspapers did not trouble him," Jones told me, oozing sarcasm. "He was smart, he was a successful businessman — he said — and he had spent a great deal of time analyzing and studying and figuring out what would work and what would not. I don't know where he got his information about the *Boston Globe* from. I don't know, really, where his ideas came from except from his obviously fertile and inventive mind."

After several meetings, Jones said, the two parted company. Jones was noncommittal and had no intention of getting the Shorenstein Center involved — which, he suspected, was what Kushner wanted. "He got kind of fed up with me because I was reluctant to say this was the most brilliant scheme I've ever heard of," Jones said. "I'll tell you what he wanted. He wanted me to be a conduit to approach other people and for me to vouch for him. And I said, 'I'm not going to vouch for you. I don't know you. And

I think what you have in mind is a very risky proposition. I'm not going to basically take my reputation and the trust people have in me and suggest that they should trust you.'"

When I shared the highlights of Jones's brutal assessment with Kushner, he responded with bland equanimity, saying that he admired Jones. "There's certainly no shortage of people who are very happy to say anything negative about what we were doing in Orange County," he said. "You know I certainly have strongly held beliefs. You have to. So some people often can mistake strongly held beliefs for arrogance. Others recognize it for what it is. If you don't have strongly held beliefs in what you want to try, how are you ever going to even get the opportunity to try it? In any case, just so we're clear — we are on the record — I have never said that other people in the newspaper industry were anything other than smart, well intentioned, and working on different approaches."

The criticism that Kushner lacked a detailed plan for running the *Globe* is something that has come up over and over. Katherine Ozment, in her *Boston* magazine profile of Kushner, wrote that she pressed Kushner several times without success. "We will take the things that the *Globe* does really well and expand upon them and layer on additional things that they haven't yet been able to do and do those," he told her.[16]

It appears that Kushner's plan may have consisted of little more than spending money he didn't have in order to fund a wildly ambitious expansion that would bring in new revenue. Needless to say, that didn't work when he tried it in Southern California. But to the extent that Kushner really did have an idea of how to revive the *Globe*, it is contained in the twenty-nine pages of a report I obtained called *The 2100 Trust Business Summary*. (The "2100" represents the year, the idea being that Kushner was focused on the long-range future.)[17] Every page of the report, dated September 20, 2010, is marked "Confidential." It's an outdated proposal for an acquisition that never took place. Still, parts of it offer a preview of what Kushner tried to do with the *Orange County Register*.

What I found in the plan offered considerable evidence of what Alex Jones (and others) have called Kushner's arrogance — assertions that he would succeed, with very little in the way of evidence as to how he would get there. Take, for instance, the beginning of the executive summary:

> We intend to purchase a major metropolitan newspaper and digital media business that is central to its community. We believe we can elevate its role to being essential.
>
> To do so sustainably, we have a clear plan to double its paid circulation and cash flow based on conservative operating assumptions and five specific growth initiatives, with a healthy queue of growth opportunities beyond those five.
>
> We are going to make a lot of money. But that is not why we have worked so hard to make sure that we are successful. This is about our children. This is about the narratives that we weave through every aspect of our lives and how we relate to the challenges we will face in the years to come. This is about how we elevate our schools, our hospitals, our non-profits, our local businesses, our government. This is about who brings us together as a community. This is about what our community looks like without the paper. This is about what our community could look like with the paper filling even half of its potential.[18]

There are, needless to say, a few warning signs here. As the report makes clear later on, the author or authors are referring to the *Boston Globe.* By writing that they intend to "elevate its role to being essential," they are saying, obviously, that the *Globe* was not essential in 2010. But despite years of downsizing that had affected the entire newspaper business, the *Globe* was still the largest news organization in New England. The New York Times Company had spared it from the more devastating cuts that had hit many other newspapers. The editor, future *Washington Post* executive editor Martin Baron, was even then among the most respected in the business.

This wouldn't matter if it were only an expression of opinion. Neither Kushner nor anyone else was under any obligation to like the *Globe* or to believe it couldn't be better. What matters is that an assumption about the paper's business prospects — that paid circulation could be doubled and that "we are going to make a lot of money" — flowed directly from the notion that the *Globe* was no longer "essential" and that Kushner was somehow going to change that. Needless to say, that should have been a huge, flashing hazard light to anyone thinking about becoming an investor.

Another curiosity: The report lists Baron and Christopher Mayer, then the publisher, as members of the "experienced, sharp and fast moving team" that would run the *Globe* under Kushner's leadership, and it includes thumbnail biographies that sing their praises. In a chart of key players, Baron's and Mayer's names appear together, with a notation that says, "One is on board, the other is expected."[19] According to both men, though, it just wasn't true. "I never indicated I would be part of his team. I never saw his plan. I have no idea what he's referring to," Baron told me. "Perhaps he made an assumption since we knew each other."[20] Added Mayer: "I was never part of his team, and I never saw his plan. I don't believe we've ever even met each other in any context."[21] When I asked Kushner what he meant by "One is on board, the other is expected," he replied, "I know we hoped and expected that both would stay. But of course, ultimately, you can't know that until after you own a business and negotiate compensation and all the other things that go along with an executive being happy in deciding to stay."

Parts of Kushner's plan were reasonable. For instance, the confidential report says: "Unlike every other newspaper in the country, our primary revenue stream is no longer advertising. The core driver of our business is actually direct subscriber revenue." The report goes on to say that all of the paper's digital content would be moved behind a paywall within five years.[22] In fact, Chris Mayer at that time was working toward exactly that model. Under Mayer's watch, the *Globe* raised the price of its print edition substantially, which resulted in fewer papers being sold but more revenue. He also ended the practice of publishing the digital *Globe* on the paper's free Boston.com website, moving the paper's journalism to a new, subscription-based BostonGlobe.com site.[23] Within a few years, most newspaper executives had come around to the belief that the advertising model no longer worked and that their prospects depended on persuading their readers to pick up a substantial share of the cost. Mayer and the *Globe* had begun moving in that direction a half-dozen years earlier.

Despite referring to the *Globe* in the opening lines as a paper that was not "essential," the report later on sings the praises of its business practices, noting that it reached at least 50 percent of adults in the market area every week.[24] But if the *Globe* was already doing so well, how did Kushner expect to double circulation?

I could go on. There are references to "doubling coverage" by adding 200 full-time and 150 part-time newsroom employees at a time when the *Globe*'s editorial staff was somewhere in the range of 300 to 350 (presaging the 150 or so staff reporters Kushner added to the *Orange County Register*), "quadrupling" the investigative reporting team, and adding about twenty-eight pages to the paper on a daily basis. "Within 24–36 months we will roughly be the third or fourth largest newsroom in the country," the report says.[25]

But let me focus a bit on Kushner's plan for nonprofits, which was, in fact, an intriguing if flawed idea that he tried out at the *Register* and that John Henry, in a more modest form, implemented at the *Globe*. Starting with the proposition that total newspaper advertising in the United States was $45 billion in 2009 (it was actually less than $28 billion, according to the Pew Research Center),[26] the report claims that donations to nonprofits greatly exceeded that, with a total of $300 billion nationwide. Nonprofits also employed some 14 percent of people in the *Globe*'s market area, the report says, adding, "If we are serious about being essential to our subscribers and the community as a whole, developing cost effective programs for non-profits is a fabulous way to grow."[27]

So how did Kushner propose to tap into the nonprofit market? He outlined four ideas, two of which would be implemented immediately. The first was to send a $50 voucher each quarter ("a handsome, physical $50 check," in case you were wondering) to all seven-day subscribers, which they could donate, in turn, to the nonprofit of their choice to be spent "anywhere in our [that is, the *Globe*'s] business." The idea was to increase the perceived value of a subscription while at the same time pulling nonprofits into the *Globe*'s ecosystem. As with Kushner's proposal to add 350 full- and part-time employees to the newsroom, this was extremely ambitious: it would provide $100 million a year to nonprofits, whereas the largest grantor in the region, the report claims, provided $75 million. Of course, much of the sting would be removed by specifying that the money be spent "in our business."[28]

So how would the *Globe* benefit from giving each of its subscribers $200 a year to donate to nonprofits? Nonprofit organizations might choose to provide home subscriptions to the *Globe* as a paid benefit for their employees. That, in turn, would trigger vouchers that the nonprofits could use to advertise in the *Globe*. The idea was that the nonprofits would spend money on subscriptions for their employees but then receive an advertising benefit in excess of that. "Bottom line," the report says, "these are sticky subscriptions and because we are starting from such a low base of subscribers relative to the size of our market, every 2,000 subscribers is literally 1% growth." Kushner's other immediate plan for working with nonprofits was to get the *Globe* involved in funding after-school programs; in later years, the *Globe* would provide support for teachers and volunteerism.[29]

In fact, when Kushner tried out the nonprofit idea at the *Orange County Register* — he called it the Golden Envelope program — it did not go well. Subscribers were given $50 to donate to nonprofits, which could be used in exchange for free advertising. *Register* ad salespeople were then reportedly told to push the nonprofits into buying ads above and beyond the free space they were getting from the vouchers. It didn't work. "On one side," an unnamed *Register* source told the alternative newspaper *OC Weekly*, "we had people saying this is our commitment to help out nonprofits. On the other side, you had people saying, 'Money, money, money.' A lot of nonprofits were offended — how is that building community?"[30]

Kushner didn't deny the accuracy of the *OC Weekly* article when I asked him about it, saying that nonprofits should, in fact, buy ads in local newspapers. "The reality for newspapers and for nonprofits is that a huge slice of what should be a really important revenue base and support base for newspapers is almost completely absent in every newspaper," he said. "And ultimately it's a vicious downward cycle where the nonprofits in a particular community really depend on the newspaper's health and coverage and advertising to grow their enterprises. Yet — there are a few exceptions, but they're really few and far between — the nonprofit community invests almost no money in their newspapers."

Several years later, John Henry and his wife, Linda Pizzuti Henry, who chairs the Boston Globe Foundation, the *Globe*'s charitable subsidiary, did in fact implement a version of Kushner's plan. Called GRANT, for "Globe Readers and Non-profits Together," it was a modest effort to build goodwill with the nonprofit community by letting readers vote on which organizations deserved free advertising.[31] Certainly there was no evidence that the *Globe* was trying to use the program to bring in more revenue for itself.

Kushner's very public efforts to buy the *Globe* eventually faded away. The next time he popped up was in early 2012, when he set his sights north in an attempt to buy Maine's largest daily newspaper, the *Portland Press Herald*. He nearly succeeded.

I MET TOM BELL AND GREG KESICH in a fifth-floor conference room in the modernistic downtown tower where the *Portland Press Herald* had rented space during the previous few years. Bell, a blunt-talking staff reporter, was president of the News Guild of Maine Local 31128. Kesich, more diplomatic, was the editorial page editor and vice president of the local. At the time of our interview, in December 2015, the *Press Herald* — the largest newspaper in Maine — was facing an uncertain future under a new owner, a fact of life that had been true for most of the preceding decade. The principal topic of our conversation that afternoon, however, was Aaron Kushner, and how the union had stopped him from buying the paper in 2012, not long after he'd given up on acquiring the *Globe.*

"He struck us as very — immature?" said Bell, groping for the right word. "I think he behaved as if we had no options. He was coming at us in a kind of 'take or leave it' — not even 'take it or leave it,' but 'this is what you're going to have to take.' So right off the bat that put us in a very defensive posture."

Kesich agreed. "He seemed immature and kind of cocky at the same time, acting as if he had all the cards," he said. "We ended up spending about a week with him negotiating."

Bell: "We liked him less and less."

Kesich: "Every day we liked him less and less. Initially we were trying to find some ways to make agreements. And at the end we decided we could not make any agreement that would deliver this guy to our newspaper. We couldn't ask the members to approve any contract with him. And so we really purposely agreed to nothing, I think."[32]

The story of how Aaron Kushner nearly bought the *Press Herald* and its affiliated media properties has not often been told. It's kind of a semi-forgotten way station between his failed attempt to buy the *Globe* and his tenure at the *Orange County Register.* Nevertheless, it's worth recounting in some detail, as it offers clues to what he had in mind for the *Globe* as well as why things went wrong so quickly at the *Register.*

The deep funk into which the *Press Herald* had sunk by the time Kushner came along was unusual in some of its details but otherwise fairly typical of what had happened to newspapers everywhere.

The *Press Herald* was born in 1921 when a Maine media entrepreneur named Guy Gannett bought and merged the *Portland Daily Press* and the

Portland Herald; he also acquired papers in Waterville and Augusta, the state capital. The Gannett family (pronounced "GAN-nett"; the large Gannett chain is "gan-NETT") operated those and other papers as well as television stations for many years. The *Press Herald*'s Sunday edition was known as the *Portland Sunday Telegram* until 1968, when its name was changed to the *Maine Sunday Telegram*.[33]

In 1998, the company, by then known as Guy Gannett Communications, sold its Maine newspapers to the Seattle Times Company. The choice may have seemed odd, but the family that owned the *Seattle Times* had Maine ties: Alden Blethen, a Maine native who had worked as a lawyer in Portland, moved west and bought the *Times* in 1896.[34] Officials of Guy Gannett Communications were said to be reluctant to sell the newspaper but believed they had no alternative because of the terms of the Gannett family trust[35] — an echo of the complications that had forced the sale of the *Globe* five years earlier.

As is invariably the case with such newspaper sales, all was hope and optimism when the deal was finalized. "We don't see any major, dramatic changes," Seattle Times Company publisher Frank Blethen was quoted as saying. "We practice a pretty aggressive brand of independent journalism, and our whole idea is to raise the bar journalistically. We have to run a business and get a return, but one of our key phrases is that we make money to print newspapers, not the other way around."[36]

But the good times gradually gave way to a familiar story of decline and then collapse. The Seattle Times Company had borrowed $213 million to purchase its Maine properties. With the newspaper business crumbling and the Great Recession hitting hard, the Blethens found themselves unable to get out from under the deal they had made. By 2008, the Maine papers had gone through four rounds of layoffs over the course of a year, closed their statehouse bureau in Augusta, and cut back on pages. There was even talk that the *Press Herald* might shut down.[37] Finally, though, the Blethens found a buyer in the person of Richard Connor, a native of Bangor, Maine, who headed a group called MaineToday Media. Connor, who was also the publisher of Pennsylvania's *Wilkes-Barre Times Leader*, said he expected to run the papers at a profit, but warned that he might have to cut 100 of the 500 or so full-time jobs at the papers.[38]

Given the state of the newspaper economy, that was not an unreasonable position for Connor to take. Unfortunately, the Connor ownership proved to be disastrous. Connor resigned at the end of 2011 after presiding over a debacle that resulted in the *Press Herald*'s downtown buildings being sold, more than 160 jobs being eliminated, and the company being sued by a North Carolina paper company for some $124,000 in unpaid bills. Connor was also criticized for his sloppy finances, especially with regard to allocating expenses incurred by his Pennsylvania and Maine properties, as well as blurring the lines between news and advertising. By January 2012, Kushner's 2100 Trust was reportedly prepared to make a major investment in MaineToday Media. And within days, it was reported that Kushner and his partners intended to become the majority owners.[39]

The company that Kushner sought to buy comprised several properties, as it still did as of 2017. Although the *Portland Press Herald–Maine Sunday Telegram* was by far the largest newspaper in the group, it also included the *Kennebec Journal* of Augusta, the *Waterville Morning Sentinel*, the Maine Today.com arts-and-entertainment website, and several smaller publications. Among the players on Kushner's team were Chris Harte, a longtime newspaper executive and member of the Harte-Hanks newspaper family. Harte had served as president of Guy Gannett's newspapers in the 1990s before the sale to the Seattle Times Company. His role was especially prominent; in stories about the pending deal, he was described as the lead investor. Harte did not respond to my several requests for an interview. But at the time he told the *Bangor Daily News*, "We have a lot of ideas about how we can continue the process that's been going on for years, trying in tough times to make sure the paper stays important for all of these communities." He added that he would not serve as chief executive and that the unnamed publisher — presumably Kushner — would be "fantastic." Another investor was Jack Griffin, a former president of Time Inc., who had worked in a variety of executive positions at media companies.[40]

The tone of news coverage at the time was that the Harte-Kushner-Griffin group had, in fact, bought the papers and that the only thing left to do was cross a few *t*'s and dot a few *i*'s. Indeed, Tom Bell and Greg Kesich told me that for a while in early 2012 it did seem like a done deal. "They were acting as if they were going to take over," Bell said. "They had people embedded in different departments kind of watching the managers and in some cases telling the managers what to do. They were acting like they'd already bought the place." But Kushner and company had not yet reached out to the Newspaper Guild. That proved to be their undoing.

Once talks between the union and the would-be owners began, Kushner emerged as the lead partner. And according to Bell and Kesich, they had no problem with that — at least at first. "We didn't actually intend to stop Aaron Kushner initially," Kesich said. "The paper was heading towards bankruptcy. We went into negotiations with him, and he had a partner with him at the table, with an open mind to figure out how can we make this work."

Bell and Kesich told me that Kushner sought fifty changes in the union contract, including major items such as a longer work week at the same pay and a doubling of how much employees would pay for health insurance — reductions that would have followed years of cuts under previous owners, including the loss of their pension benefits. The union officials pushed back. Harte, who had been attending the negotiations but said little, stopped showing up. And Kushner, Kesich said, "kind of scolded us. He said, 'I just want you to know you've lost Chris.' Our administrative officer muttered, 'I guess my voodoo doll must be working.' That was how badly he was reading the room — that we were supposed to be really upset that we lost this guy who never said a word."

Then, too, the union officials said that Kushner's business plan made no sense to them. It was, in essence, the plan he had outlined for the *Globe* and that he implemented at the *Orange County Register.* "He was going to hire more reporters and increase the quality of the print product, and he was going to charge more for it," said Bell. "He was very dismissive of the web."

Bell and Kesich came to believe they had to stop the sale. So they issued a demand of their own: that the contract remain in force if the company declared bankruptcy. It was, they said, the key moment, because it was tantamount to saying that they preferred bankruptcy to Kushner. Essentially that ended Kushner's attempt to buy the company.

Kesich recalled that Kushner was still trying to line up additional investors even after his exclusive buying period had come to a close. But *Press Herald* staff members had other ideas. As Bell and Kesich described it, people started talking, and before long they had lined up an angel investor: Donald Sussman, a billionaire Maine businessman who at first agreed to help with finances and then decided to go all in and buy a majority stake in

MaineToday Media. Bell and Kesich were personally involved in the negotiations, and they referred to Sussman by the code name "Batman" so word wouldn't get out. By February, they had a deal. "It was the longest of long shots," Kesich told the *Guild Reporter.* "We got a message to him that the paper was in trouble and that we were a forward-looking, progressive union that was determined to save it."[41]

When I asked Kushner what had happened in Portland, he replied that the union "found an owner who didn't believe that any changes were necessary at all in the newsroom or with the union contract, and they went with him. Who's to say whether that ended up being a better choice or not? There's no way of knowing. But that was their prerogative."

The Sussman ownership was not without some awkwardness. At the time, Sussman was married to Democratic congresswoman Chellie Pingree, which led to accusations of liberal bias in the news pages. Maine conservatives "went bonkers," recalled Michael Socolow, an associate professor of journalism at the University of Maine.[42] But it also led to something of a renaissance for the Maine papers — a renaissance that took place even as the broader newspaper economy continued to deteriorate.

Among the people who were part of that renaissance was Lisa DeSisto, the chief executive officer of MaineToday Media. DeSisto and I had worked together in the early 1990s at the *Boston Phoenix.* She later served in various business-side positions at the *Boston Globe* and helped launch the paper's Boston.com website in the mid-1990s. She joined MaineToday in late 2012 in response to an overture from Sussman's team. Under Sussman, DeSisto told me, newsroom staffing at the *Press Herald* and the company's other two daily papers had risen from 100 to 150. But that wasn't all. Digital resources were added, investments were made in the company's circulation and content-management systems, local business coverage was restored, and — this being Maine — a weekly section called Source was launched to cover the sustainable food and lifestyle movement. In total, Sussman invested $13 million in improving the papers. "It was an act beyond anything of which I've ever seen in terms of his commitment and investment," she said.[43]

Unfortunately, the Sussman era proved brief. In 2015, Sussman sold MaineToday Media to Reade Brower, who owned four weekly newspapers in Maine. DeSisto told me that Sussman had taken on a large amount of debt when he bought MaineToday and that the Brower transaction left the properties with a clean slate. Then, too, Sussman and Pingree would soon announce that they were getting divorced, which may have played a part in his decision to get out. All except eight of the company's 390 employees were offered jobs with what was essentially a new company, so any fears that there would be massive layoffs were not realized. But there was clearly a sense that what had been a special time in the recent history of the *Press Herald* was coming to an end.[44]

"My take on the whole thing is that this billionaire politically connected person came in and basically saved the place," Michael Socolow said. "Sussman not only kept it on an even keel, he improved it." But, he added, "It's very clear he was a reluctant newspaper owner."[45]

For their part, Greg Kesich and Tom Bell told me that they saw the three years of Sussman's ownership as something of an opportunity lost — that though the *Press Herald* improved, little was done to reinvent the business for the digital age. When we met, they were in the midst of what they expected would be difficult negotiations with the new ownership. "He doesn't have the kind of deep pockets that Sussman had to float a newspaper," Kesich said of Brower.

"We're still not profitable," Bell said. "The paper never really changed much in the way it delivers news or is organized. And then Sussman sold it, and now we're heading down the same path we were when Kushner was circling. We're facing another big downsizing. The Sussman era allowed us to hire a bunch of reporters and improve the quality of the journalism and gave us a few years — three years. But we didn't get our act together as a business and put us on a sustainable path to the future, because we're in big trouble right now."

Months later, it did not appear that the Brower ownership would turn out to be as onerous as Kesich and Bell had feared. Brower seemed committed to local newspapering. In August 2016, he and a partner rescued Vermont's *Rutland Herald* and its sister paper, the *Barre-Montpelier Times Argus*, which were on the brink of financial collapse. "I don't have a cut and slash personality," Brower said when the sale agreement was announced. "I believe that you can't save your way to prosperity."[46]

When I caught up with Greg Kesich later that fall, he told me that though some downsizing had been implemented (among other things, Tom Bell had taken a buyout), Brower had invested in a new press and seemed committed to stability. "The real problem is not the philosophy of the owner," Kesich said, "but the laws of gravity and the long-term effect of declining revenue."[47] Which, needless to say, is a problem that no newspaper owner has been able to solve.

AFTER HIS RETREAT FROM MAINE, Aaron Kushner was forced to deal with the reality that his ambition of owning a large daily newspaper had been handed two major setbacks. His bid to buy the *Boston Globe* had not been taken seriously. And his near success in acquiring the *Portland Press Herald* had fallen apart. He and his partners then tried to buy the Media General chain of newspapers, but the legendary investor Warren Buffett purchased it instead.[48]

In 1871, the great editor Horace Greeley wrote to an aspiring newspaper reporter who was seeking his advice on how to advance his career. Greeley's counsel: "I believe that each of us who has his place to make should go where men are wanted, and where employment is not bestowed as alms. Of course, I say to all who are in want of work, Go West!"[49]

In Southern California, the land of hope and dreams, yet another daily newspaper, the *Orange County Register*, was for sale. It had slid into bankruptcy in 2009, and after it emerged a year later, it fell into the hands of several Wall Street investment companies. They wanted to get out. Aaron Kushner's chance to own and publish a newspaper had finally arrived.[50]

Celebrity Cult against
TBS (Costa Mesa) useful
adjunct the the deep
state hard right RNC.
Prosperity gospel hook to
brainwash multitudes,
Smoke & mirrors falderol that
sucks up $ from the
desperate & misdirects
their understanding of
who is oppressing them.
Pie in the sky when you die.
fabulous conventions, cruises
substitute for real life betterment

CHAPTER FOUR

THIS IS YOUR BRAIN ON THE INTERNET

Can News Break Free of the Distraction Machine?

FOR MORE THAN TWO DECADES, newspaper executives have been frantically, desperately trying to drag their publications into the digital future. And if you're tempted to say that the future has long since arrived, here is what I mean. The digital future is one in which a newspaper's online operations are profitable and sustainable, and in which print exists — if at all — as a high-priced luxury for those willing to spend the money. The digital present is one in which nearly twice as many adults get news from online sources as from print, but in which the aging, shrinking print audience is still responsible for three-quarters of a typical newspaper's revenue.[1] The online journalism of the twenty-first century, when well executed, is better than its print predecessors. Video, more photography, interactive infographics, and the like have all contributed to a richer experience. But the existential question for which we still don't have an answer is: Who will pay for it?

With digital having failed to replace print as a reliable source of advertising revenue, many newspapers have made a substantial bet that they can persuade their online readers to pay. This is a bet made not so much out of a sense that it's the smart thing to do as out of the conviction that it's their last remaining hope. If a newspaper's online readers won't cover most of the cost, then there is literally no one else left. Of course, a few papers will survive, and the *New York Times* and the *Washington Post* would seem well positioned to be among them. But the idea that we will have dozens of large regional newspapers like the *Boston Globe* and the *Orange County Register* spread across the country will recede into the past. Nonprofit news organizations may take up some of the slack. Public radio stations, in particular, could leverage their websites to offer more local coverage than they do now. Still, a large chunk of the accountability journalism we depend on for self-government will simply disappear.

Now, I will grant you that the digital media era has been brief and that it is way too early to reach any definitive conclusions about business models. Someday, perhaps, we'll discover ways to fund journalism that we haven't thought of yet.

But what if the financial challenges created by the internet run deeper than our inability to create a viable business model? What if all of these efforts are for naught? What if the kind of journalism we need most is not going to make the transition to a sustainable online future because of something inherent in the very essence of digital culture? The internet is literally changing our brains in ways that make it harder to absorb any complex writing in more than dribs and drabs. That has consequences for society, and thus for the business of news as well.

The downside of digital media is something I can feel even as I use it, even though I have long been an enthusiast when it comes to technological change. I followed the 1992 presidential election returns on Prodigy, a pre-internet online service, and wrote about the experience for the alt-weekly *Boston Phoenix.* I got an internet account that let me connect with a mainframe somewhere out in the ether so that I could use Gopher. (Text-only Gopher sites were similar to websites except that they lacked hyperlinks, which meant that you needed to drill down into a site to find what you were looking for and then return to the top before moving on to another site.) I still remember the excitement of installing Mosaic, the first graphical web browser, after another *Phoenix* reporter told me she'd read about it in the *New York Times.*

Digital technology made me more efficient. I spent an afternoon in 1996 at the library, poring through microfilm, looking for proof that a columnist who was praising the Republican presidential candidate Pat Buchanan had denounced him as an antisemite four years earlier. After several hours, I found it. Needless to say, just a few years later I would have been able to call it up in a few minutes.

The negative effects were more subtle. They weren't apparent right away — certainly not in the era of dial-in modems and America Online. It wasn't long, though, before the internet had become a gigantic distraction machine. The fast, always-on access ushered in with broadband was the first big change. The second was the rise of social networks, with the concomitant temptation to keep checking in.

Needless to say, the implications for journalism are enormous.

SEVERAL YEARS AGO I spent some time wrestling with Marshall McLuhan's impenetrable masterpiece, *Understanding Media.* The book is best known for his phrase "the medium is the message," by which he meant that when we consider the effects of advances in media technology, we should look at how the technology itself, rather than the content it carries, is changing us.[2]

McLuhan and others have observed that radio is not just an audio version of newspapers and that television is not just radio with moving pictures; rather, each development works on the human brain in different ways, leading to social and cultural changes that could not have been anticipated. Digital media combine text, audio, video, photos, and much more, but few would argue that they are linear extensions of newspapers, radio, and television. For that matter, they are the most powerful communication tools in history, but to say that they can do far more than the telegraph or the telephone doesn't begin to get at their true revolutionary impact. You could call the internet the most significant development since the printing press, but even that is insufficient. Virginia Heffernan, in her 2016 book *Magic and Loss: The Internet as Art,* may not have been exaggerating when she wrote: "The Internet is the great masterpiece of human civilization. As an artifact it challenges the pyramid, the aqueduct, the highway, the novel, the newspaper, the nation-state, the Magna Carta, Easter Island, Stonehenge, agriculture, the feature film, the automobile, the telephone, the telegraph, the television, the Chanel suit, the airplane, the pencil, the book, the printing press, the radio, the realist painting, the abstract painting, the Pill, the washing machine, the skyscraper, the elevator, and cooked meat. As an idea it rivals monotheism."[3]

McLuhan argued that our media are "extensions" of our human capabilities and that those capabilities wither as we become more dependent on our tools.[4] Similarly, the internet is changing our brains — and maybe not for the better.

Among the most penetrating observers of how the internet is rewiring the way we think is Nicholas Carr, a journalist and author. Carr is no Luddite; his beat is technology, and he maintains both a personal website and a blog.[5] But in his 2010 book, *The Shallows,* Carr attempts to come to terms with an alarming reality: the internet has changed us in ways that make sustained concentration and deep reading much more difficult. Paying homage to McLuhan, Carr writes, "As our window onto the world, and onto ourselves, a popular medium molds what we see and how we see it — and, eventually, if we use it enough, it changes who we are, as individuals and as a society."[6]

Carr cites studies showing that McLuhan's metaphor about our tools being "the extensions of man" is literally true. Consider, for instance, what happened to primates (and, after all, humans are primates) that were trained to use rakes and pliers to reach for pieces of food that would otherwise be out of their grasp. The parts of their brains responsible for controlling those tools grew. Even more telling, Carr writes, "the rakes and pliers actually came to be incorporated into the brain maps of the animals' hands. The tools, so far as the animals' brains were concerned, had become part of their bodies."[7]

In other words, our brains respond and change as they learn to use tools, whether they be pliers or digital media; those tools become McLuhanesque extensions of ourselves. The same holds true for old-fashioned books. Carr observes that the act of book-reading is unnatural in the sense that we need to remold the circuitry we were born with so that we can do it well. After books were introduced centuries ago, readers "had to train their brains to ignore everything else going on around them, to resist the urge to let their focus skip from one sensory cue to another," he writes. "They had to forge or strengthen the neural links needed to counter their instinctive distractedness, applying greater 'top-down control' over their attention." He adds, "The brain of the book reader was more than a literate brain. It was a literary brain."[8]

Now we are teaching our brains to respond to a very different type of intellectual environment, defined not by deep absorption in a book (or, for that matter, a long magazine or newspaper article) but by torrents of information we can't process without the help of Google, by distractions in the form of email and social media, and by hyperlinks enticing us to click while we are in the middle of reading something else. A 2003 study (and keep in mind that Facebook, the ultimate distraction, was not launched until a year later) found that more than 80 percent of those responding were spending more time reading electronic documents than they had previously and that they were "browsing and scanning" and "doing more non-linear reading."[9]

Given the data overload we have to deal with in the digital age, how could it be otherwise? As Virginia Heffernan says, the internet, far from ushering in the age of non-reading that some predicted, has instead led to the burden (and temptation) of constant reading. "It's hyperlexia that keeps people's eyes fixed on their phones and not on nature, art, friends, mates, children, or work," she writes. "And it's hyperlexia that leads to fatalities in driving-while-texting accidents."[10]

During the same year that *The Shallows* was published, Carr wrote an essay in which he discussed what his critique meant for journalism. He acknowledged that his sense of doom was nothing new — a French poet and philosopher, Alphonse de Lamartine, issued a warning in 1831 about the rise of the daily newspaper in apocalyptic terms that were similar to his own alarm about the internet. Nevertheless, Carr argued, digital media represented something uniquely disruptive. "Unlike the printed page," he wrote, "the Web never encourages us to slow down. And the more we practice this hurried, distracted mode of information gathering, the more deeply it becomes ingrained in our mental habits — in the very ways our neurons connect. At the same time, we begin to lose our ability to sustain our attention, to think or read about one thing for more than a few moments."[11]

Carr's solution, unfortunately, sounds more like a lament. He closed with a wan plea for news organizations to act as "a counterweight to the Net," writing: "They're going to have to find creative ways to encourage and reward readers for slowing down and engaging in deep, undistracted modes of reading and thinking. They're going to have to teach people to pay attention again. That's easier said than done, of course — and I confess that I have no silver bullet — but the alternative is continued decline, both economic and intellectual."[12]

From the vantage point of 2017, it's possible to identify news organizations that are trying to act as a counterweight to the distractions inherent in digital. A short list would include the *New York Times*, the *Washington Post*, the *Wall Street Journal*, good regional papers (including the *Boston Globe*), NPR and public radio stations in general, and public television staples such as the *PBS NewsHour* and *Frontline*. Yet the newspapers on that list have gone all-in on digital distribution. How could it be otherwise? All of them, some more than others, have embraced the idea of building traffic by supplementing their high-quality journalism with regular short updates, sometimes for important news, sometimes for trivia maximized for viral sharing. Now, I'm as likely as the next person to be taken in by clickbait, and newspapers have long been filled with odds and ends aimed at readers who want to kill a few minutes with something light and amusing. Online, though, clickbait becomes part of the larger digital torrent. We scan and skim, but we rarely engage fully with a piece of writing because, as Virginia Heffernan puts it, "digital literacy . . . involves chiefly the refusal to read."[13]

I don't mean to suggest that long-form, in-depth journalism is passing from the scene. In fact, publishers have discovered something surprising: readers prefer short *and long* articles to the medium-length stories that make up much of a typical newspaper's offerings. The dead zone is right around 700 words. "Too much reporting is 700-word articles that everyone else has got," according to Kevin Delaney, the editor-in-chief of the business-oriented website *Quartz*. Those medium-length articles, he has said, are too long to be shared but too short to appeal to readers looking for in-depth journalism.[14] For newspapers, a 700-word article is ideal because it fits nicely onto a page. But if readers sense that 700 words is too much for a one-dimensional story, yet not enough for explaining something in detail, then you have a situation in which the tail is wagging the dog: story lengths are being determined not to serve the needs of the audience but to conform to the industrial processes used to manufacture the newspaper.

The continued viability of long-form journalism does not contradict the concerns raised by Nicholas Carr and Virginia Heffernan. We remain bobbing about on a vast sea of information, sampling a little of this and a little of that. If we happen to stumble upon something that captures our interest, well, we'll read it. But spending ten or fifteen minutes reading a long article on your phone is very different from sitting down every morning with a newspaper, whether in print or online, in order to absorb the news of the day. Indeed, the scatteredness of digital media threatens the very notion of "the news of the day."

Now, it's possible that the ability to browse through and process large amounts of information quickly and efficiently will prove to be more valuable than the deep reading and sustained concentration that defined what it meant to be an educated, well-informed person in the pre-digital era. What Carr decries and Heffernan describes may just be the latest in a series of evolutionary adaptations that began when humans first drew pictures of hunting expeditions on the walls of caves. But these changes are bringing us a new type of journalism — a disintegrated type of journalism in the literal sense that it is not integrated with anything larger or more coherent. Instead, it consists of a seeming infinite number of disconnected bits. And the major challenge is trying to figure out which ones not to read.

A good news organization can provide tremendous value in this environment through what we used to call gatekeeping and by what we now often refer to as curating — making sense of all the news streaming by us by picking out the important stuff, placing it within a hierarchy (front page, section front, buried inside), and leaving out the rest. The people who run virtually every newspaper larger than a community weekly have staked everything on the notion that there is an audience that will pay not just for the journalism they produce but for their considered judgment regarding what to include and what to leave out. The great challenge for newspapers is that each generation will place less value on that sort of curation than did the generation before as they assemble their own news reports through their social media feeds and through what their friends are recommending and sharing.

When I visited the *Washington Post* in early 2016, among the people I met with was Julia Beizer, the director of product; at the time that we spoke, she was about to take a new position as head of product for the *Huffington Post*. Her job at the *Washington Post* was to swim against the tide that Carr described: to persuade digital readers to drop in on a regular basis and to become paid subscribers; to get them to suspend their skimming and scanning for a little while each day in order to engage deeply with one digital news source. I asked her if she had read *The Shallows*. She told me that she had. "You've got to know your enemy," she said, laughing. She added: "I take a very optimistic outlook on all of this. These are the early days. My children are two and four and know the difference between Android and iOS and can get around them much easier than any adult you have ever seen. So I think our brains are changing, absolutely. I also think it's OK. And I think where that goes is exciting."[15]

More substantively, Beizer told me she thought Carr was too pessimistic about our ability to absorb the shift to digital just as we absorbed the shift to the printed word centuries ago. "We ran a piece a couple months ago about how our brains have adapted to knowing that we can Google basically any fact," she said. "We have gained all this capacity, thinking that we don't have to remember something — we can just Google it. Now, one point of view you could have is that that is terrifying. We're outsourcing this critical function to the cloud, and how can we give up our own innate ability to remember things? Another would be to say we're making ourselves into superhumans. And I think I tend towards the latter. Our brains' ability to adapt to change has been well documented throughout history. I think this is just another time for us to do that."

I don't think Carr would disagree with any of that. In *The Shallows* he comes down firmly on the side of Plato, who disagreed with his mentor Socrates' mourning the rise of the written word and the decline of the oral tradition — and, thus, of memory.[16] The point of Carr's book — and Heffernan's — is that we need to look not just at what we've gained from the internet, but at what we've lost as well: wider than ever, but shallow, as Carr puts it; magic and loss, in Heffernan's elegant phrase.

What we may be losing is the central role in democracy that has historically been played by the type of journalism traditionally offered by newspapers. Rather than transitioning from print to an all-digital or mostly digital future, newspapers are breaking apart, their components reduced to just more stuff we have to sift through, reading what captures our fancy and discarding most of it in our never-ending struggle to keep up.

IT IS A STAPLE of every discussion about journalism and the internet. If only newspaper owners had thought about online media sooner, so this line of argument goes, they could have figured out a business model. In fact, anyone who was paying attention for the past forty years knows that is too simplistic. Newspapers were among the earliest adopters of digital technology.

On YouTube you can find a 1981 clip from KRON-TV in San Francisco on early efforts by the city's two daily papers at that time, the *Chronicle* and the *Examiner*, to publish their content online.[17] You may have seen it; from time to time the clip is recycled and becomes something of a viral sensation. It features a dignified, older-looking gentleman in a suit and tie named Richard Halloran, who owns what appears to be a Radio Shack TRS-80 computer. The reporter, Steve Newman, tells us that Halloran is dialing a local number that will connect him with a computer in Columbus, Ohio. At the same time, editors at the *Examiner* are "programming today's copy of the paper into that same Ohio computer." Next we see Halloran placing the receiver of his rotary-dial phone into a pair of acoustic couplers. "When the telephone connection is made," Newman says, "the newest form of electronic journalism lights up Mr. Halloran's television with just about everything the *Examiner* prints in its regular edition." Just about everything, that is, except photos, ads, or comics.

It's not exactly a reader-friendly experience; a close-up of Halloran's terminal (not actually a television, by the way) shows white type on a black background in all capital letters. The *Examiner*'s David Cole tells Newman, "This is an experiment," adding, "We're not in it to make money. We're probably not going to lose a lot, but we aren't going to make much, either." The report closes with the anchor offering some amusing information about how silly it all is: "It takes over two hours to receive the entire text of a newspaper over the phone," she says, "and with an hourly use charge of five dollars, the new telepaper won't be much competition for the twenty-cent street edition."

The experimentation continued. In the mid-1980s, the Knight Ridder chain introduced its own electronic news service called VideoTron. VideoTron was not a success, no doubt because of the same technical limits documented in the KRON report — slow computers, slower modems, high cost, no graphics. "It was just basic text. It was not fast. There was nothing great about it," *Washington Post* executive editor Marty Baron, then a business reporter at the Knight Ridder–owned *Miami Herald*, recalled in an interview many years later. "It was interesting, but it's not as if the general population was eating it up, saying, 'Oh, we've got to have this.'"[18] Starting in the early 1990s, as technology improved, newspapers tried offering some of their content on the burgeoning online services of the day — mainly CompuServe, Prodigy, and America Online. These services were slow, but they offered some graphics and were much more user-friendly than the text-based services of the 1980s.

Around the same time, a Knight Ridder executive named Roger Fidler developed an idea that was stunningly close to the tablets and smartphones of the 2010s. In the early 1990s, I attended a conference at Columbia University at which Fidler outlined his vision for a digital tablet on which we would read newspapers and magazines — something he had been thinking about for the previous dozen or so years. The screen would have the same resolution as a glossy magazine; the devices would be flexible so you could roll one up and take it with you; and they would be so cheap that newspapers would give them away to eliminate the money-burning tasks of printing and distribution. How far ahead of his time was Fidler? Even as of 2017, we were nowhere near achieving any of those three goals.

Fidler also anticipated the choice and interactivity that would come with digital newspapers. For instance, he said that a subscriber might purchase a subscription to the *New York Times*'s international news, the *Washington Post*'s political news, and her local paper's regional news. And the tablet would have interactive capabilities so that you could, for instance, click on a restaurant ad to make a reservation. "It was not quite like Roger had descended from another planet, but he was saying some things that were simply very hard to believe at the time," John Woolley, who worked with Fidler, said in 2012. "He had conjured up this idea of a tablet at a time when laptops were revolutionary. He was clearly a futurist. And he didn't care what anyone believed. He never backed down."[19]

I have no notes from that conference, so I'm relying largely on my memory, as well as a video that Fidler put together when he was head of the Knight Ridder Information Design Laboratory in Boulder, Colorado.[20] The prototype in the video was simultaneously retro in that the display looked exactly like a printed newspaper and futuristic in its capabilities, which included better, faster interactive graphics than we generally see today as well as sophisticated voice controls.

But keep in mind McLuhan's admonition that the medium is the message. Fidler envisioned a revolutionary leap forward in the way we interact with text, photography, graphics, audio, and video. What he did not envision was that the digital future would be altogether different from what had come before and that we would use it in ways he could not imagine. In his talk at Columbia, he said that we'd download the content we had paid for by plugging our devices into, say, our cable television box before going to bed. In the video, he also raised the possibility of something that looked like a credit card that you could take with you and use to load more content onto your device if you were away from home. What he missed was that digital newspapers would be distributed via the open web rather than a closed system controlled by publishers. Fidler could see into the future in ways that were remarkable. But in 1994, he did not mention what would turn out to be the most revolutionary change of all. Even though he brilliantly anticipated the technological revolution that was to come, he failed to foresee the cultural revolution that would accompany it.

"For most people a newspaper's like a friend," Fidler says in the video. "It's somebody you know who you have come to trust. Over the last fifteen years there have been many attempts to develop electronic newspapers, and many of the technologists who have been pursuing these objectives assume that information is simply a commodity, and people really don't care where that information comes from as long as it matches their set of personal interests. I disagree with that view."

In fact, Fidler was wrong. Most news turned out to be so generic that it is difficult to imagine anyone would ever pay for it. As I am wrapping up this chapter in late March 2017, one of the big news stories of the day is the fate of President Donald Trump's tax proposals following the Republican Congress's failure to repeal the Affordable Care Act — a major plank in Trump's platform. Entering "Trump taxes" at Google News brings more than 7.3 million results — the very definition of commodity news. More than twenty years after the narrator of Fidler's video assured viewers that people wanted "a specific newspaper with a branded identity," there are very few types of content that readers might be persuaded to pay for: certain types of local and investigative stories that no other news organizations are publishing; personalities that distinguish a paper from its competitors, such as popular columnists; and the intelligent judgment of editors regarding what news is the most important, what's less important, and what can be left out of the paper altogether.

It is that last possibility, the role of a good newspaper as a curator of what we need to know, that brings us back to the concerns raised by Nicholas Carr.

The value of curation was understood from the very beginning of the digital news era. In 1995, Arthur Sulzberger Jr., the publisher of the *New York Times,* and Neil Postman, a critic of media culture best known for his 1985 book about television, *Amusing Ourselves to Death,* shared a stage in Cambridge, Massachusetts, at an event hosted by the Nieman Foundation.[21] Postman spoke up for the traditional role of a newspaper as curator and convener. "A newspaper is a theory of what constitutes an informed person," Postman said. "A newspaper can make an essential contribution to the polity by functioning as a filter." Postman was pessimistic, though, saying the driving thrust of technology was to isolate people from each other, allowing us to indulge our personal interests and thus undermining any sense of a common culture. "Everything is moving us away from a sense of co-present community life," he said.

Sulzberger, by contrast, was the enthusiastic optimist that day, telling the audience, "He or she who has the best news should win this one. And that's pretty exciting." While acknowledging that the internet's early adopters were cheering the demise of media gatekeeping, he predicted that the ordinary citizens who were just starting to get online would welcome traditional curation. "Those people want order out of chaos," Sulzberger said. "People aren't going to want to explore all the corners. They're going to find the corners that help them and then they're going to stop."

The following January, the *Times* began publishing most of its content daily on the web. In an article that, looking back, is almost heartbreaking in its naive hopefulness, the paper declared, "With its entry on the Web, The Times is hoping to become a primary information provider in the computer age and to cut costs for newsprint, delivery and labor."[22]

Of course, the reason the internet dreams of Arthur Sulzberger and other news executives didn't come true was that the promise of digital advertising failed to become a reality. But I would argue that that specific failure is inextricably woven into the larger issues raised by Neil Postman, Nicholas Carr, and Virginia Heffernan. We're jittery, distracted, trying to take in too much information at once, sorting out (or not sorting out) fake from real news, and not engaging deeply with any of it. Our "theory of what constitutes an informed person," as Postman put it, is changing. And it's not at all clear what role newspapers will have in whatever new theory emerges.

ONE WAY NEWS ORGANIZATIONS could fight back against the scan-and-skim culture of the internet—to act as a "counterweight," as Carr suggests—would be to try to convince readers that they offer quality not available anywhere else. The idea behind charging for digital access is that readers should be willing to pay for good journalism that they can't get elsewhere and that isn't encumbered by intrusive ads. Presumably you will value something you pay for, and thus you will slow down and read it. Unfortunately, the prevailing model for digital advertising could be called anti-quality, as it rewards clicks and page views rather than deep engagement with the journalism those ads are supposed to pay for.

It is a loser's game, and it's only getting worse. As the cost of online advertising, much of it mediated by Google, continues to drop, news organizations must pursue more and more clicks and more and more page views, which leads, in turn, to a further decline in ad prices. The finite space of a print newspaper establishes something of a floor under the cost of ads. The infinite space of the internet has led to a race to the bottom for advertising, pitting news organizations against each other as well as every other type of digital media. The floor has been removed. Newspapers traditionally relied upon market inefficiencies to raise the money they needed to pay for journalism, as advertisers paid a premium to reach their target audience as well as readers who had no interest in what they were selling. With digital, there is no shortage of advertising opportunities, no artificial constraints to keep the price of ads from falling.

"The expense of printing created an environment where Wal-Mart was willing to subsidize the Baghdad bureau," wrote Clay Shirky in 2009. "This wasn't because of any deep link between advertising and reporting, nor was it about any real desire on the part of Wal-Mart to have their marketing budget go to international correspondents. It was just an accident. Advertisers had little choice other than to have their money used that way, since they didn't really have any other vehicle for display ads."[23] John Wanamaker, a pioneer in the rise of modern department stores and advertising, once put it this way: "I know that half of my advertising dollars are wasted. . . . I just don't know which half."[24] The internet has ruthlessly wrung out those inefficiencies. That may be good if you're a business owner trying to allocate your ad budget. But it's proved devastating for journalism.

Nicco Mele, the former senior vice president and deputy publisher of the *Los Angeles Times*, who's now the director of the Shorenstein Center on Media, Politics and Public Policy at Harvard's Kennedy School, explained at a Shorenstein seminar why a digital advertising strategy based on clicks simply doesn't work for news organizations that are built around original (which is to say expensive) journalism. "Google has fundamentally shaped the future of advertising by charging on a performance basis — cost per click," he said. "And that has been a giant, unimaginable anchor weight dragging down all advertising pricing."[25]

For example, Mele said that a full-page weekday ad in the *LA Times*, which would reach 500,000 people, costs about $50,000. To reach the same 500,000 people on LATimes.com costs about $7,000. And if that ad appeared on LATimes.com via Google, it might bring in no more than $20. "Models built on scale make zero sense to me," Mele said, "because I just don't see any future there." Yet it has led even our best newspapers to supplement their high-quality journalism with a pursuit of clicks for the sake of clicks.

A common name for this form of advertising is the CPM model, and it's been the prevailing system online since the earliest days of the commercial web. CPM stands for cost per thousand ("M" is the Roman numeral for 1,000), and it means that an advertiser pays a certain amount of money for every 1,000 impressions, or page views. Because the CPM model doesn't differentiate between an in-depth investigative article or feature story that you might spend twenty minutes with and a photo of a cute cat, some industry leaders are trying to move digital advertising in the direction of payment for high-quality content that readers actually value rather than mere clicks. A few news organizations, mainly at the smaller community level, have resisted CPMs, embracing instead a flat fee for ads based on size and placement, which is the traditional model used by print newspapers.[26] But CPM is the dominant system. Some are trying to change that.

In September 2014, I took a seat at the annual conference of the Online News Association, which was being held in Chicago. The speaker that morning was an energetic thirtysomething named Tony Haile, the founder of Chartbeat, an analytics firm based in New York that helps news organizations measure every click, unique visitor, page view, and numerous other data points that drive the modern newsroom. Haile was on a mission. As he explained to the crowd, Chartbeat's numbers were all too often being used for ill, with publishers pushing editors and editors pushing reporters for more clicks without regard to quality. The problem, he said, was that such measures not only were harming journalism, but were also hurting those news organizations' bottom line. It was the law of unintended consequences, and Haile explained to his audience that its negative effects were not limited to the news business.[27]

"Sometimes the simplest, most logical metrics just backfire in ways you couldn't even imagine," he said. As an example, he cited American hospitals, which in the 1990s adopted a measure that would help them hold themselves more accountable. "They chose the mortality rate," he said. "I mean, what better way for a hospital to judge how well it's doing than how many people are dying? Trouble was, the fastest way to improve your mortality rate was to stop admitting the sickest patients. It was to stop doing the experimental surgeries."

Haile left us in suspense regarding the fate of sick patients who were denied hospital care. Instead, he moved on to the point of his talk: using metrics to identify high-quality journalism and to persuade advertisers that quality was ultimately worth more than sheer volume. The best way of measuring the value of a piece of content, he said, was to calculate how much time readers spent with it. He explained that metrics had advanced to the point at which it was possible to measure more than clicks or how long someone spent on a page before clicking again — a fairly meaningless statistic, he said, since it often meant that the user had left without closing his browser. Unlike the early days of CPM-based advertising, when metrics were crude and numbers such as unique visitors ruled the day, Haile said, it had become possible to measure such activities as how quickly a user was browsing through a web page, which would indicate whether or not he was actually reading. Thus we had finally reached the point where news organizations could think about charging advertisers for how much time a reader actually spent with a piece of journalism. Indeed, the *Washington Post* already uses its in-house analytics tool Loxodo to measure such data points. "You can look at how far down users are scrolling. And you can even look at the speed at which they are scrolling," the *Post*'s chief technologist, Shailesh Prakash, told me. "So you want stories where users go deep into the story and they scroll slowly, because that shows engagement."[28] Haile's big idea is to transform that engagement into advertising dollars.

Creepy stuff for sure, and we can only hope that we don't reach the point at which such measurements can be associated with individual users. But Haile's remarks struck me as a promising alternative to the downward spiral of more page views bringing in ever-shrinking revenues. As Haile pointed out, the time-spent measure might also reintroduce the notion of scarcity, which had been lost in the transition from print to digital. The expensive industrial processes used to manufacture a print newspaper created scarcity in the form of limited competition — the barriers to entry were simply too high to allow more than one or two papers in a given area to thrive. A time-spent metric, Haile said, creates a different kind of scarcity. "The only unit of scarcity on the web is people's time and attention. It is zero-sum," he said. "If I'm spending five minutes on the *Guardian,* I'm not spending five minutes on the *New York Times.*"

Haile's data show that, in fact, readers value quality over clickbait — that though they may click on a viral headline such as "This Cat Stuck in a Grate Is All of Us" (an actual *BuzzFeed* offering from July 2016), the chances of their actually reading it are low.[29] In an essay for *Time* magazine, Haile wrote about what he dubbed the "Attention Web" and how it differs from the CPM-dominated media ecosystem we've grown accustomed to. A few of his findings were particularly worthy of note. In a study of 2 billion web visits over the course of a month, it turned out that 55 percent of those visits clocked in at fewer than fifteen seconds. In addition, topics that readers spent some time with tended to be more newsworthy and substantive than those they clicked on and then quickly fled. For instance, "Edward Snowden" and "Obamacare" did better than "hairstyles" and "nude." "For quality publishers, valuing ads not simply on clicks but on the time and attention they accrue might just be the lifeline they've been looking for," Haile wrote, adding, "This move to the Attention Web may sound like a collection of small signals and changes, but it has the potential to transform the web. It's not just the publishers of quality content who win in the Attention Web, it's all of us."[30]

We are still at the early stages of setting advertising prices on the basis of time spent rather than clicks. There is no guarantee that it will become anything more than a niche phenomenon, and there is no guarantee that it won't create perverse, unintended incentives, just as the CPM model did. But some publishers are trying it — including the *Financial Times,* the very sort of prestige newspaper that presumably could most benefit from charging for quality rather than quantity. Time Inc., Hearst, and Condé Nast have also dipped their toes in the water. "The only way you can actually look at the amount of value someone's placed on content is how much time they're spending with it," said Brendan Spain, the US commercial director of the *FT,* in an interview with the *International Business Times.*[31]

It is exceedingly unlikely that wide-scale embrace of the Attention Web would lead to the nirvana envisioned in the early days of online news, with lucrative multimedia advertising covering the costs of websites and with all-digital newspapers freed from the costs of printing and distribution. Nor is it realistic to think that a mere change in the business model could undo the neural changes taking place in our brains as we interact with digital media. Nevertheless, coming up with a way to reward deep engagement at least gives news organizations the right financial incentives.

IF THE INTERNET is more than a mere extension of text, radio, photography, and television, if it's more than just a better communications device than the telephone, if it's as important as monotheism, as Virginia Heffernan would have it, then what, exactly, is it? I would argue that its overarching cultural impact has been in the way it allows us to build and participate in communities that go far beyond anything available to us in the material world. "The virtual community," as Howard Rheingold called it in his 1993 book of that name, has proved to be a revolutionary force, sometimes for good, often for bad, but always in ways that are incredibly powerful.[32]

Communities built around journalism have not fared especially well. Early efforts to harness the wisdom of the crowd for reporting projects came to naught — perhaps because the technology to make it work wasn't available yet, perhaps because expectations of what online volunteers could contribute were overblown. And though there are examples of well-run comments sections, for the most part they are cesspools of pseudonymous hatred and stupidity. I would blame that mostly on the refusal of news organizations to invest in the systems and staff they need to manage comments properly. Still, in the early days a lot of us thought that most people would behave themselves and that those who didn't could be held to account by other commenters. That's not what happened.

Then there is Facebook, which has become the ultimate virtual community — the largest, most visited stop on the internet, swallowing up everything in its path. It has become the single most important force with which news organizations must contend. They can't ignore it. Consider that, as of 2016, Facebook claimed to have 1.65 billion active users per month — a time when the *Washington Post* and the *New York Times* were the only American newspapers with 100 million unique monthly visitors. More than a billion people were logging onto Facebook on a daily basis, and the average time spent per visit was around twenty minutes — a lifetime compared with the minutes or seconds reported by most news sites.[33] And so newspapers have entered into a delicate dance with Facebook, using the service in order to distribute their journalism but wondering where it will all lead.

People in the media business refer to this as publishing their content on "distributed platforms," by which they mean Facebook, Snapchat, Google, Apple News, Instagram, and Twitter — but mostly Facebook. Relying on Facebook carries with it risks as well as opportunities for news organizations. The algorithm that powers Facebook's newsfeed is a mystery, and it's almost impossible to know whether and how much of your journalism will be seen by your intended audience. Instant Articles, which reside on Facebook's own server and thus load, well, instantly, offer a much better user experience than most news organizations' own mobile platforms. But the advertising money is doled out on Facebook's terms, which could change, and most of the customer data stays with Mark Zuckerberg and company. As of mid-2016, the Facebook Live video service was creating a sensation, with multiple news organizations wanting to get in on the action. But Facebook has rolled out products before only to retreat, and there was little indication of the company's ultimate intentions.

"Social media and platform companies took over what publishers couldn't have built even if they wanted to," writes Emily Bell, director of the Tow Center for Digital Journalism at the Columbia Journalism School. "Now the news is filtered through algorithms and platforms which are opaque and unpredictable."[34] In a subsequent article accompanying a study by the Tow Center, Bell notes that Facebook and its ilk need to deal with ethical issues that traditionally have been the purview of news organizations rather than technology companies. "Platforms now must consider significant issues ranging from broad questions of free speech to how to preserve and maintain the integrity of archived material," she writes. "We have heard growing concern over the opacity of algorithmic and editorial systems that distribute a much more personalized version of news and information, but we do not yet have the right framework to regulate such systems."[35]

The problem is that Facebook's business is not tightly integrated with journalism. Facebook executives see news as just one more type of content that its users might want to look at, but it eschews any responsibility for transforming its customers into informed citizens. Sometimes it has tweaked its algorithm in ways that favor serious journalism, as it did in 2014, when *Upworthy* — at the time a notorious purveyor of viral fluff of the "What Happened Next Will Make You Cry" variety — saw its traffic plunge after Facebook took steps to weed out clickbait.[36] But sometimes it has harmed journalism. In 2016, for instance, Facebook tinkered with its algorithm to favor content shared by family and friends over news stories — a perfectly defensible decision given that its view of community encompasses far more than news. Nevertheless, it was disconcerting to news organizations that had grown dependent on Facebook as a primary means of distribution.[37]

Facebook has also tried to offer news content through its Trending Topics column, which comprises stories that its users are supposedly talking about the most. But that proved to be not quite the case when it was revealed that human editors were overriding the algorithm in order to add important stories that users didn't appear to care about all that much. Allegations were made that Trending Topics also excluded stories that would be of interest to conservatives. That led to a meeting between Facebook executives and Republican Senator John Thune and a promise to do better.[38] Which brings me back to Emily Bell's point about journalistic decisions being entrusted to technology companies not accustomed to dealing with such issues. There is nothing wrong with Facebook officials vowing to fix problems with Trending Topics and to eliminate liberal bias. But they should have politely — or impolitely — declined to chew it over with an elected official on the grounds that the First Amendment guarantees their right to freedom of the press, a right that belongs to Mark Zuckerberg just as surely as it does to Jeff Bezos.

It's useful to keep in mind that Facebook's practices are not aimed at harming news organizations or creating an ill-informed citizenry. Facebook's corporate goal is to sell advertising and to make as much money as it can from that advertising by attracting as many users as it can and keeping them on the site for as long as it can. People complain about Facebook, but the sheer numbers show that they like the service. Offering journalism in such an environment is not necessarily a bad idea, but it comes without the news judgment we traditionally relied on for context and for understanding a story's importance.

As the media observer Jay Rosen said in a panel discussion that was broadcast on public television, it's a choice that the public itself has made. "There are advantages to consuming news through a social layer — which is what Facebook makes possible — in that you're connected to your friends and family through the news, and so it's going to be inherently more meaningful to you," Rosen said. "What's lost, of course, with that is editorial judgment and that extra emphasis that journalists once added to the flow of news so that they could say to us, 'You may not initially think so, but this is really important,' or 'This may not be the sort of thing that you normally pay attention to, but you really should.' And I think that's one of the things that's being lost through the new system. But we should also add that, in many ways, this change is being driven by users."[39]

In *The Shallows*, Nicholas Carr identifies Facebook as just another distraction — a contributor to the culture of the internet that is rewiring our brains and making it increasingly difficult to concentrate and engage. "Even when I'm not working," he writes, "I'm as likely as not to be foraging in the Web's data thickets — reading and writing emails, scanning headlines and blog posts, following Facebook updates, watching video streams, downloading music, or just tripping lightly from link to link to link."[40]

For many, though, Facebook has become a proxy for the web itself, not so much a distraction as it is what they do when they go online. It may be that the opposite of distracted reading is not immersion and concentration but, rather, community and conversation. I'm not sure where that insight leads. From the earliest days of online journalism, we've been talking about journalism as a conversation — about how journalism can be shaped and improved by journalists who take part in the virtual communities that the internet has fostered. Facebook is the ultimate virtual community, at least to this point.

Maybe the best way for traditional news organizations to offer the counterweight that Carr proposes is to embrace the human instinct for community that the internet has proved to be so adept at fostering. Just because we haven't done it all that well so far doesn't mean we shouldn't keep trying. It's easy to see right now what isn't working. That doesn't mean it will never work.

CHAPTER FIVE

GETTING BIG FAST

How the *Washington Post* Is Becoming the Amazon of News

AT THE VERY MOMENT Don Graham was signaling that the *Washington Post* was not for sale, an investment firm he had hired, Allen & Company, was talking to Jeff Bezos and other potential buyers.[1] But if Graham was being coy in his public pronouncements, he couldn't come close to the acting job turned in by his niece Katharine Weymouth. On August 4, 2013, the *New York Times* ran a profile of Weymouth on the front of its Sunday Styles section that made mention of her "athletic figure," her complicated family life, and her mixed record as publisher of the *Post*. It closed with a forward-looking quote from Weymouth that contained not a hint of the news that would be announced the next day: "I don't feel like my job is to be beloved. I certainly hope to be a great publisher, and if people want to love me, too, that's even better."[2]

The staff of the *Post* had no inkling of what was coming, either. On that Monday, August 5, staff members gathered in the *Post*'s auditorium for a 4:30 p.m. meeting. As rumor had it, Don Graham would announce that the paper's building had been sold. Those on hand soon learned that the news was of considerably more significance: the Graham family would be selling the *Post* to Jeff Bezos. *New Yorker* editor David Remnick, a *Post* alumnus who was on hand for the occasion, wrote that Don Graham was so overcome with emotion that he had to stop several times in order to compose himself. "The assembled," Remnick wrote, "were so stunned that when it came time for questions no one had any for a while; Graham had to urge them out of their silence." Bezos himself was absent. He issued a statement that Remnick described rather dismissively as conveying "all the correct and anodyne things."[3] Graham, echoing what he had been saying all along, told a *Post* reporter that the future of the paper did not depend on its being sold. Nevertheless, he said that continued Graham-family stewardship would have meant a subsistence existence for the *Post*, and he wanted more than that. "The *Post* could have survived under the company's ownership and been profitable for the foreseeable future," Graham said. "But we wanted to do more than survive. I'm not saying this guarantees success, but it gives us a much greater chance of success."[4]

A month later, Bezos, forty-nine years old at the time, arrived in Washington for two days of meetings to see what he was getting for his $250 million and to offer some preliminary ideas about where he hoped to take the *Post.* He rang a triangle — a *Post* tradition — to call the afternoon news meeting and sat quietly alongside Marty Baron. He met with legendary *Post* journalists such as Bob Woodward and Ben Bradlee. And he said he had no plans to make wholesale changes in the paper's leadership.[5] Two and a half years later, he had proved to be as good as his word. In the fall of 2014, he replaced Katharine Weymouth as publisher with Fred Ryan.[6] Baron and editorial page editor Fred Hiatt, though, remained in place. Hiatt's retention was noteworthy, as new owners often want to exert their influence on the opinion pages. But even though Bezos's politics were thought to be generally libertarian, the *Post*'s editorial stance — which could be described as moderately liberal with a taste for foreign intervention — did not change under Bezos's ownership. Perhaps even more surprisingly, Bezos left in place the *Post*'s chief technologist, Shailesh Prakash. One might have thought that Bezos would import someone from Amazon to take over a function so close to his own heart. It spoke well of Bezos's leadership qualities that he quickly concluded the *Post* already had the right person in place.

While he was in Washington, Bezos held a town hall–style meeting with *Post* employees. Even though he would not formally take possession of the paper for another month, he had thought a great deal about what the *Post* needed to do in order to move forward. To a large extent, the *Post* that developed over the next several years was the *Post* that Bezos envisioned in 2013. Among other things, he said, readers should be put ahead of advertisers — the sort of sentiment that newspaper owners tend to say more than they mean but that could fairly describe the *Post*'s aggressive courtship of a national digital audience. He promised to support the paper's deep investigative reporting efforts. And he identified a story that he particularly liked, "9 Questions about Syria That You Were Too Embarrassed to Ask," which combined substantive background information on that country's conflict, an informal tone, and even a link to a song by a Syrian pop star.[7] It was exactly the kind of serious story with a light, digital-friendly approach that has come to define a certain subset of *Post* journalism, especially in the online products it has developed.

Intriguingly, Bezos also outlined a couple of thoughts that seemed more in keeping with those of a digital troglodyte than with someone who had built one of the world's most successful technology companies. The first was his lament over the rise of aggregators such as the *Huffington Post*, which could rewrite "in seventeen minutes," as he put it, a story that had taken journalists months to report. The second was his belief in the primacy of the "bundle" — that is, the package of local, national, and international news, sports, culture, business, entertainment, the crossword puzzle, and everything else that made up the traditional print newspaper. Bezos was not advocating a return to print, of course, though he said it would continue to be an important medium for readers in the Washington area. But he did say that he thought selling a *Washington Post* bundle to subscribers via tablet was a far more promising proposition than asking people to pay for one story at a time on the web, as the late *New York Times* media columnist David Carr once suggested. Carr called it an "iTunes for news." Bezos called it a bad idea. "People will buy a package," Bezos said. "They will not pay for a story."[8] Nearly three years later, Bezos had not changed his mind, although he said that he wouldn't rule it out in the future. "I don't see evidence yet that consumers are amenable to those kinds of micropayments," he said, adding, "Habits and behaviors and patterns of consumers do change slowly over time, and maybe one day they will pay by the article."[9]

Bezos's embrace of the bundle brought a retort from one of the *Post*'s own journalists, Timothy B. Lee, who wrote that there was no way of bringing back the old aggregated newspaper, even in digital form, because Facebook, Twitter, and other social networks provided superior platforms for gaining access to the best journalism across the web. A new generation of news consumers, Lee said, had no interest in chaining themselves to a few outlets that were closed except to those who were paying subscribers. "Trying to recreate the 'bundle' experience in Web or tablet form means working against the grain of how readers, especially younger readers, consume the news today," Lee wrote. "In the long run, it's a recipe for an aging readership and slow growth."[10]

Generational change in how we consume news represents a challenge to the goal of persuading people to pay for digital subscriptions. As Lee observed, someone clicking on news stories via social media might access several dozen different sites on a regular basis. It is probably unrealistic to expect anyone to pay for more than one or two digital news subscriptions. The *Post* does point to some hopeful signs regarding the younger readers that Lee warned Bezos risked losing. Citing statistics from comScore, the *Post* reported that it had 56 million mobile users in March 2016, an increase of 61 percent over the preceding year. Even more encouraging, 45 percent of the *Post*'s mobile audience were millennials. Mobile usage is crucial. ComScore found in 2014 that not only were millennials — generally defined as people between the ages of eighteen and thirty-four — more likely to access the internet on their smartphones or tablets than were older generations, but a significant proportion of them used mobile exclusively.[11] That proportion is only going to grow over time.

Since the *Post* rarely reports how many digital subscribers it has signed up, let alone the demographic makeup of that group, it can't be determined how many of those young mobile readers are paying customers. But the vast majority of people who read *Post* journalism do so for free, clicking on links they encounter on social media or other forms of sharing; if anything, that would be even more the case with millennials.

According to David T. Z. Mindich, a journalism professor at St. Michael's College in Colchester, Vermont, who studies news consumption by people under forty, younger people, unsurprisingly, are more likely to rely on social media for their news than older readers. What was unclear, Mindich said, was whether younger news consumers were interested in journalism for informational purposes or simply so they could carry on a conversation with their friends. He also warned of another danger: though getting news from a variety of sources on social media might sound like a good way of exposing oneself to diverse viewpoints, a person might select those sources on the basis of compatibility with what that person already believes.[12] Observers had been warning against the danger of "filter bubbles" for years. But after the 2016 election, those warnings had gone mainstream, with liberal news consumers wondering how they could have been so wrong about the appeal of Donald Trump and the electoral strength of his supporters. Technology companies unveiled Facebook add-ons and browser extensions to expose users to different points of view so that they could get out of their bubbles.[13]

Mindich's concerns are reflected in the data. According to a study conducted by the Pew Research Center, millennials were more likely than those in other age groups to have learned about the 2016 presidential campaign through social media rather than through conventional news outlets. Among the most politically engaged millennials, 74 percent of Democrats and 50 percent of Republicans cited social media as the means by which they learned about the election.[14] The study did not reveal whether millennials' reliance on social media increased the likelihood that the political news they encountered was more weighted toward their partisan preferences than it would have been had they relied on more traditional sources. But since Facebook's algorithm is designed to show you content based on your past behavior, a biased newsfeed is pretty much guaranteed. On Twitter, users assemble their own feeds — which, again, provides an incentive to follow people and news organizations that you like rather than those you don't.

A good general-interest news organization like the *Washington Post,* the *New York Times,* or NPR offers mostly nonpartisan news and a mix of liberal and conservative opinion pieces. To older, traditional news consumers, the value of that bundle is beyond dispute. To millennials, it may seem like an artifact from an earlier age. It is difficult to imagine how the *Post* will be able to convert more than a tiny fraction of these younger browsers into bundle enthusiasts. That's not just a challenge to journalism; it's a challenge to the business of journalism. A partial solution may be to offer an attractive paid product and to charge a low enough price that it will attract users even if they know they're not going to spend a lot of time with it. That is one of the approaches the *Post* has taken.

Julia Beizer, who was the *Post*'s director of product when I interviewed her, told me the national digital edition — a colorful, low-cost magazine-like app — had succeeded not just with readers who spend thirty or sixty minutes a day with the bundle but also with skimmers. "People pay for what they think is useful, and in some cases that is just the top stories," she said.[15] Essentially, Bezos has taken a multifaceted approach, embracing the bundle that Timothy Lee disparaged as well as social media. And he is offering different versions of the bundle aimed at different types of news consumers.

Bezos is nothing if not methodical. In his meeting with the *Post*'s staff, he said that when Donald Graham's emissaries approached him to see if he had any interest in buying the paper, he reached his decision by thinking about "three gates" he had to pass through before he could consider it worthwhile. First, was the *Post* still an important institution? Second, was he optimistic about the paper's future? Third, could he personally make a difference in charting that future? The answer, he assured them, was yes to all three.[16] More than a year later, he returned to the "gates" analogy when he spoke at a conference in New York. He added: "I didn't know anything about the newspaper business, but I did know something about the internet. That, combined with the financial runway that I can provide, is the reason why I bought the *Post*."[17]

Bezos's reference to "gates" is a strong indication of the kind of analysis he brings to bear on solving problems, as he did in building up Amazon and as he has done at the *Post*. The business journalist Brad Stone, in his book about Amazon called *The Everything Store*, wrote that when Bezos was single he started taking classes in ballroom dancing, calculating that it would increase his exposure to eligible women. Later, when Bezos was trying to decide whether to walk away from a comfortable job and start the business that would become Amazon, he developed what he called a "regret-minimization framework" to help him with the process. A former colleague of Bezos's, Jeff Holden, told Stone that Bezos was "the most introspective guy I ever met. He was very methodical about everything in his life."[18]

To an extent not widely appreciated, Bezos's "gates" analogy was more than a geeky affectation — it was crucial to how he rebuilt the *Post*. The paper's ongoing importance wasn't enough. Neither was Bezos's optimism that it could regain its past glory. Rather, Bezos did not leap until he had satisfied himself that his own insights, and not just his money, could make a difference.

SO WHO IS JEFF BEZOS? He is the founder and chief executive of one of what are arguably the five most important technology companies (the others being Apple, Google, Facebook, and Microsoft). But the details of his life are not as well known as those of his celebrity peers such as Mark

Zuckerberg, Steve Jobs, and Bill Gates. His background, in some respects, is more conventional as well—he actually finished college (Princeton) and held a good job with a small financial firm, D. E. Shaw, before the entrepreneurial bug bit.[19]

For many years Amazon lost vast sums of money, thriving mainly through the benevolence of its true believers on Wall Street. Nor did Amazon look much like a technology company; selling stuff on the internet is more L. L. Bean than Google. But as Amazon diversified, its image as merely a retailer evolved. The Kindle changed the way we read books. Amazon Web Services, or AWS, provides cloud computing for organizations ranging from Netflix to the CIA. The Echo, a voice-activated device that plays music, compiles shopping lists, and automates various other tasks, proved so popular that Amazon couldn't keep it in stock.[20] As the company has evolved, its new ventures have proved to be highly lucrative as well. In 2015, the profitability of Amazon's core retail business was more in keeping with its brick-and-mortar peers than with other tech giants, as it reported a 3 percent operating margin on $71.8 billion in e-commerce sales. By contrast, AWS's operating margin was an eye-popping 24 percent, although revenue was a comparatively small $7.9 billion.[21]

The irony that the founder of a company that had burned through fearsome quantities of cash would add a newspaper to his holdings was not lost on Amazon-watchers. A characteristic jibe was published on Twitter by Ben Popper, editor of the *Verge*, shortly after the *Post* deal was announced: "Jeff Bezos has reputation for building great companies with little to no profit, perfect guy to own a newspaper."[22] Brad Stone told me that the parallels between Bezos's career at Amazon and his ownership of the *Post* were clear. "He's lost money more often than he's made money, and it's all part of his long-term plan," he said. "You've got someone with a real appetite for the pain of the news business right now."[23] And, of course, Bezos's focus on the long view paid off spectacularly for him and his investors at Amazon, whose market capitalization of $500 million in mid–2017 was up about 8,000 percent over the previous fifteen years. Hendrik Bessembinder, a finance professor at Arizona State University, called Amazon "one of the great wealth creators since 1926."[24]

But perhaps a better analogy is that just as Amazon morphed from a retailer into a technology company, so, too, has Bezos set his sights on transforming the *Washington Post.* To an extent that is unusual except at a very few news organizations, the *Post* has embraced sophisticated analytics, cutting-edge newsroom tools to make it easier for journalists to do their jobs, and digital publishing platforms tailored to different audiences. Some of that technology is already being licensed to other news organizations. And though it's unlikely that selling content-management systems to financially strapped newspapers will bring in as much money as AWS, they both represent creative attempts to build enterprises that help support the larger but less profitable parts of the business.

Stone's book is an object lesson in how difficult it can be to report on Bezos. Not only did Bezos decline to be interviewed for the project, but after *The Everything Store* was published, Bezos's wife, MacKenzie Bezos, wrote a withering one-star review of it on — yes — Amazon. Her major complaint was with Stone's depiction of Amazon's workplace culture, which comes across as abusive in the Darwinian manner typical of technology companies. If anything, though, Stone went easy on Amazon—especially in comparison with a 2015 *New York Times* exposé that featured tales of brutalized employees crying at their desks.[25] Stone also depicts Bezos as trying to tone down his excesses as he grew older. In one encounter, Bezos humiliated several of his top employees in what Stone calls "his customarily devastating way," started to leave — and then turned around and said, "But great work, everyone."[26]

What Stone describes as Bezos's efforts to improve his self-control have been evident at the *Washington Post.* His interactions with rank-and-file employees have not extended beyond a few appearances at the paper, but his top executives engage with him in regular conference calls and occasional retreats in Seattle. Of the executives I interviewed, not one suggested that Bezos was anything other than a supportive, caring boss. Yes, of course you would expect them to say that. But there are ways of getting across the idea that the Bad Jeff makes at least an occasional appearance. I heard none of that.

"He's just set the right tone. And that's what has helped all of us who deal with him, including my engineers, feel good about the work we do," said Shailesh Prakash, whose formal title is chief information officer and vice president of technology. "We believe we have an owner who respects the past but at the same time wants us to be innovative."[27] When I asked

Marty Baron about Bezos's reputation for being difficult, he replied, "I haven't encountered that at all. I think that he asks good questions. He likes data to support things rather than just feelings. But I have found him to be committed to our mission, has a good sense of it, has good ideas, and has brought not only the financial capital that we need but intellectual capital, which I think is at least as important. And my own experience doesn't reflect whatever has been written elsewhere, so it has been a positive experience as far as I'm concerned."[28]

If Bezos's occasionally vituperative style of leadership has not carried over to the *Post*, the story of how he built Amazon into a great company is nevertheless instructive and has obvious parallels with the way he wants Marty Baron, Shailesh Prakash, and company to run his newspaper. One of the most telling anecdotes offered by Brad Stone is that when Bezos was a sixth-grader in Houston, he developed a survey so that his classmates could evaluate their teachers. It was a serious exercise aimed at assessing teaching ability, and he plotted the results on a graph. Stone does not record how Bezos's teachers reacted to that particular enterprise. But he made such an impression that he was written about pseudonymously in a book titled *Turning On Bright Minds: A Parent Looks at Gifted Education in Texas.*[29] Years later, Amazon would become well known for its use of sophisticated metrics. And though many newspaper executives are relying increasingly on numbers to help them figure out how best to reach their readers, the *Post*'s measurements are particularly broad and deep.

Bezos founded Amazon in 1994, setting up shop not in Silicon Valley, as he would have preferred, but in Seattle. At the time, mail-order companies did not have to charge sales tax in a state where they had no physical facilities. By staying out of California, Bezos ensured that the state's enormous customer base could do its virtual shopping tax-free. As Brad Stone points out, that tax strategy was hardly unique to Amazon. Still, it reveals something about Bezos's attention to detail and single-minded focus.[30]

Some stories about Amazon are legend. Bezos built Amazon's first two desks himself in the brand-new company's headquarters — his garage — by using sixty-dollar doors from Home Depot. That exercise in frugality continued even as the company grew into a behemoth: years later, the company's corporate headquarters were filled with door desks. On another occasion Bezos turned down a suggestion that employees be given bus passes, reasoning that if they were tied to public transportation schedules, it would be harder to ask them to stay at work. And despite his reliance on algorithms and analytics, he was known for intervening personally in response to customer complaints. For instance, he decreed that emails promoting sexual aids should no longer be sent to Amazon customers who had browsed the site's Sexual Wellness section without buying anything — angrily overruling his managers, who argued that the emails brought in a significant amount of revenue. "It was a revealing — and confirming — moment," Stone wrote. "He was willing to slay a profitable aspect of his business rather than test Amazon's bond with its customers."[31]

Several Amazon moments stand out in particular for their relevance to the *Post.* There was his emphasis early on to "Get Big Fast," thus establishing Amazon as a formidable competitor in the marketplace before retail giants such as Barnes & Noble and Wal-Mart could respond. At the *Post,* too, the emphasis has been on building the digital audience as rapidly as possible. "He just wants us to grow. He wants us to get big," Marty Baron said during an appearance at Harvard in April 2016.[32]

Also intriguing is Bezos's embrace of disruption theory. He is said to be an admirer of Harvard Business School professor Clay Christensen's book *The Innovator's Dilemma,* the defining work on the subject. According to Christensen, established companies find it difficult, if not impossible, to respond to lower-cost competitors because they don't want to jeopardize their existing business. An example Christensen offers is Digital Equipment Corporation, whose minicomputers had disrupted the mainframe computer business. DEC, as the company was known, fell victim to its own reluctance to sacrifice minicomputer sales by refusing to respond to the threat posed by inexpensive personal computers.[33] Embracing disruption theory early in Amazon's rise, Bezos exploited Barnes & Noble's hesitation to go all-in with online book sales, a step that would have harmed its physical stores but that left the field clear for Amazon. Later on, Bezos issued instructions for developing what would become the Kindle: "Your job is to kill your own business. I want you to proceed as if your goal is to put everyone selling physical books out of a job."[34]

It's less clear whether Bezos can take advantage of disruption theory in advancing the prospects of the *Washington Post.* The newspaper business, after all, has been disrupted to a far greater extent than it's been the disruptor. A paper that Christensen coauthored with David Skok, the future top digital editor at the *Boston Globe,* and James Allworth argues that newspapers are being attacked from below by competitors such as Craigslist, which built a profitable enterprise by offering most classified ads for free, and by the *Huffington Post* and *BuzzFeed,* which began their existence aggregating other news sources (as Bezos himself ruefully noted) but later moved up the "value network" by adding high-quality original reporting. Nor is that a new model. As Christensen and his coauthors point out, *Time* magazine began its existence in the 1920s as an aggregator, summarizing "rip-and-read copy from the day's major publications," and then later grew to become a respected mainstream news source.[35]

Given that history, it's hard to imagine exactly how the *Washington Post,* whose mission is to produce expensive, labor-intensive original journalism, can transform itself into a fleet-footed disruptive force. But there are some signs that it is at least trying. Perhaps the most noteworthy example is the national digital edition, which, at $99 a year in 2016 (with frequent discount offers), was priced well below the *New York Times*'s digital products — and dramatically less than a subscription to the *Times*'s national print edition, which cost nearly $500 a year.[36] Superficially, the national digital edition seems like a textbook example of disruption from below, as the *Post* is competing with the *Times* not by rolling out a national print product but by coming out with an inexpensive digital alternative. But it would be an overstatement to suggest that the *Post* had specifically targeted the *Times*'s print edition. For one thing, the *Times*'s own digital products are as robust as the *Post*'s, and there are no signs that the *Times* is trying to preserve print at the expense of digital. For another, as the media business analyst Ken Doctor, the author of a book and a website both called *Newsonomics,* told me, loyal *Times* readers are not going to switch to the *Post* in order to save money. "I think the brand identification is what will protect them [the *Times*] to a large degree," he said. "I can see that they [the *Post*] can develop another market, but I don't think it's going to be mainly a takeaway game from the *New York Times.*"[37]

Perhaps Bezos does not see newspaper readership as zero-sum. By offering a new, inexpensive version of the *Post* to people who do not customarily pay for news, Bezos can expand the universe for the *Post*'s journalism. Or as Bezos himself once put it in explaining how he intended to make the *Post* financially viable, "We have to go from the business model where we used to make a relatively large amount of money per reader with a relatively small number of readers to a model where we make a relatively small amount of money per reader but on a very large number of readers."[38]

It is Bezos's embrace of long-term thinking at Amazon, though, that holds the most promise and significance for the *Post* — and for newspapers generally. "If you look at why Amazon is so different than almost any other company that started early on the internet, it's because Jeff approached it from the very beginning with that long-term vision," Bezos's friend Danny Hillis told Brad Stone. "It was a multidecade project. The notion that he can accomplish a huge amount with a larger time frame, if he is steady about it, is fundamentally his philosophy."[39]

IF IT WERE POSSIBLE to point to a single decision Jeff Bezos made that transformed the internal ambitions and external perceptions of the *Washington Post,* it would be his decision to turn the *Post* into a truly national newspaper. The move resolved a tension that had extended at least back to the Watergate era, when Katharine Graham attempted to take advantage of the paper's growing reputation by launching a national weekly edition. The edition, a compilation of *Post* stories from the preceding week, had a circulation of about 150,000 at its peak. By the time it was shuttered, in 2009, that number had slid to about 20,000.[40] (The *Post* announced in 2014 that it would attempt a new weekly print edition, to be distributed by regional partner newspapers.)[41]

Even though the *Post* was largely unavailable outside the Washington area during those years, much of its journalism was national in scope. A number of larger regional newspapers had national and international correspondents during this pre-internet era, but the *Post* was especially ambitious. Still, the *Post*'s reputation as a well-regarded paper that few people ever actually got to see outside the Washington area created problems for its reporters.

For instance, the journalist Michele Norris recalled the difficulties she had in trying to cover violent unrest in Los Angeles in 1992 following the acquittal of four police officers in the videotaped beating of Rodney King. "As a *Washington Post* reporter, it was harder for me," she said during a Nieman Foundation panel discussion in early 2016. "We had a harder time because people were thinking, 'Who's going to read this?' The *Washington Post* was not a national newspaper at that time. You could not find the *Washington Post* in Los Angeles. You had to go to a specific newsstand in Westwood. You would get it at two in the afternoon after it was flown cross-country."

By contrast, Norris's fellow panelist, Wesley Lowery, who had been covering the Black Lives Matter movement since the fatal police shooting of Michael Brown in 2014, said he had encountered no such obstacles. "When I got into Ferguson, Missouri, and I was talking to people on the street corners, no one was saying, 'I'm not going to talk to you because I want to talk to the *New York Times*,'" he said. "We're all national reporters. We're all starting from zero. I can build my credibility in this space. I can build a reputation in this space. There was a lot of opportunity there. We've taken advantage of a lot of that opportunity."[42]

Jeff Bezos was not the first to realize that digital distribution made it possible for the *Washington Post* to go national in a way that it couldn't previously. In 2004, when Steve Coll was managing editor, he headed a task force that recommended the *Post* leverage its website in order to reposition the paper as a national news organization. If Coll's idea had been adopted, it would have represented a significant shift: in terms of its circulation and its advertising base, the *Post* was fundamentally a regional paper, with one of the highest rates of local-market penetration in the country.[43] Don Graham was not pleased with Coll's report, which called for an investment of some $15 million, and he responded with uncharacteristic hostility. "Don got up and machine-gunned the room," a person who was there told the journalist David Kindred.[44] And instead of embracing a national vision, Graham moved even further in the direction of "for and about Washington," paving the way for nearly a decade of downsizing that ended only when Bezos bought the paper.[45]

Years afterward, Coll, who left the *Post* in 2005 and later became dean of Columbia University's Graduate School of Journalism, laid out the case for a national digital edition in a way that Bezos himself might have found persuasive. "The thumbnail history," Coll told me, "is that the *New York Times* embarked on a very explicit strategy to go national and international, pursuing a readership well beyond New York that was more of a magazine audience than a traditional regional newspaper audience." The *Times* expanded its national print edition, leaving the *Post*'s "very anemic" weekly in the dust. In 2002, the *Times* also pressured the *Post* to sell its half of the *International Herald Tribune*, a European newspaper that had been published by both news organizations, thus damaging the *Post*'s international reach just as the web was growing into a major news source. (The *IHT* had its roots in the *New York Herald Tribune*, a once-great paper that expired during the New York newspaper strike of the 1960s. After the *Post* sold its share, the paper was renamed the *International New York Times.*)[46]

Rather than retreat to the Washington area, Coll said, he and his task force "recommended a digital-first strategy for national and international news and audiences — kind of a version of what the *Guardian* eventually created." He added, "Don chose not to invest in that direction," a decision that Coll thought was "reasonable" given the *Post*'s locally based business model.[47] Indeed, the *Guardian* found itself in enormous financial difficulty in 2016 after many years of free online distribution in pursuit of a massive international audience for its high-quality journalism.[48] Graham, lacking Bezos's deep pockets, may not have been able to afford the patience that would have been needed to adopt Coll's ideas.

But where Graham saw only trouble in pursuing a larger audience, Bezos sensed opportunity. In late 2014, during a public interview conducted by Henry Blodget, cofounder and editor of *Business Insider*, Bezos explained why he changed the emphasis from local and regional to national and international. "Even though it had a national and global reputation, the product was local and that was by design," Bezos said. He added: "For a time, it was a good strategy, and as a business it was super successful for decades, but that is what we're changing. The *Post* has the good fortune of being the newspaper of the capital city of the United States of America, and that's a good starting point to be a national and even global publication."[49]

Among other things, the move toward a national focus and a national audience allowed Bezos to escape the conundrum in which the owners of other large regional newspapers found themselves. Although news organizations of all sizes have been severely disrupted by technological change, large regional newspapers have been especially harmed. There continues to be a demand for the mix of national and international news offered by the *New York Times*, the *Wall Street Journal*, and NPR. Local and hyperlocal journalism offered by small weekly and daily newspapers, local websites, and the like remains popular. But midsized dailies such as the *Boston*

Globe, the *Philadelphia Inquirer*, the *Miami Herald*, the *Chicago Tribune*, the *Los Angeles Times*, the *Orange County Register*, and others are neither large enough to appeal to the most serious consumers of national and global news nor small enough to carry the community-level news — obituaries, municipal trivia, and school lunch menus — that draws people to local journalism.

As we saw in chapter 1, the *Post* experimented unsuccessfully with community journalism in 2007 by offering a free website called *Loudoun Extra*. That ended a year later. Then, in June 2015, the *Post* closed some of its weekly community papers and websites in the Washington suburbs.[50] In a 2016 interview with the CBS News journalist Bob Schieffer and H. Andrew Schwartz of the Center for Strategic and International Studies, Marty Baron said that local and regional coverage remained central to the *Post*'s mission and that "the vast majority" of the paper's resources were devoted to various types of local coverage — news, sports, the arts. But he drew the line at hyperlocal community news, saying, "It's not something that we can do very well."[51]

Although even the *Post* earns most of its revenues from print, the shift to digital favors large national players over regional and local papers. As Matthew Hindman found in 2014, news sites receive only about 3 percent of all web traffic — and most of that goes to national news organizations, with barely half of 1 percent going to local news outlets.[52] In order to achieve the kind of growth that Bezos wants, moving away from the *Post*'s historically regional orientation was a necessity.

If pursuing a national strategy was a smart business move, retaining Marty Baron as the *Post*'s executive editor was, if anything, a smarter one. Baron, sixty-one when I interviewed him in March 2016, is widely recognized as the preeminent American newspaper editor. Before coming to the *Post*, Baron made stops as an editor at the *Los Angeles Times* and the *New York Times* and as the top editor of the *Miami Herald* and the *Boston Globe*, where he worked from 2001 to 2012. Baron's time at the *Globe* was, to invoke a cliché, one of triumph and turmoil. In 2003, the *Globe* won the most prestigious of the Pulitzer Prizes, the Public Service Award, for its coverage of the pedophile-priest crisis in the Catholic Church — the subject of the Academy Award–winning movie *Spotlight*. But it was also Baron's job to cut the newsroom. His choice — to eliminate the *Globe*'s international and national bureaus (except for a Washington bureau) in order to preserve the paper's regional coverage and investigative capacity — was surely the right one, but it was disheartening to longtime *Globe* readers and staff members.

Baron's office at the *Post*'s new headquarters was smaller than I had expected. We sat at a conference table next to a human-sized cardboard cutout of an Oscar statuette, which he said was waiting for him after he returned from the Academy Awards gala in Hollywood. He also showed me a small chocolate Oscar he'd brought home. Soft-spoken and businesslike, with graying reddish hair and a closely trimmed beard, Baron talked for an hour about life at the *Post* under Jeff Bezos.

"I was completely shocked, obviously," Baron said when I asked him about his reaction to the news that Bezos would buy the *Post*. "I told people when I came here that while the *Times* would probably like to sell the *Globe*, it was highly unlikely that Don Graham would be selling the *Washington Post*. So I was kind of stunned when I heard about it. But I thought that it could have some real advantages for us" — a reference to Bezos's preference for growth over cutting and his deep understanding of technology and consumer behavior. "I did not know if it would be a good thing for me personally," Baron added, "because obviously when a new owner comes in he has the absolute right to pick who he wants to run the organization that he has acquired. He said positive things at the beginning, but my sense was that it would be a year of figuring out the place and deciding what he wanted to do."

Even though Bezos bought a $23 million mansion in Washington in late 2016, he spends most of his time on the West Coast.[53] For the most part he manages his newspaper from afar, presiding over an hour-long conference call with the *Post*'s top executives every other week. "It starts on time, ends on time; it's very disciplined," Baron said. "He gets all of the material in advance. We don't use it to go through presentations. We use it to review any questions that he might have or to embark on any broader discussions. But typically all of the material is sent to him in advance in a narrative style, not PowerPoints. He doesn't like PowerPoints, thankfully. He typically has some questions, and those questions become a springboard to discussion of whatever we need to talk about." The *Post*'s leadership also travels to Seattle twice a year for a day of meetings. Baron said those meetings run from around noon to 6 p.m., followed by dinner.

Baron's observation about Bezos's dislike of PowerPoint presentations is an important one. Brad Stone writes about it in *The Everything Store*. At Amazon, PowerPoints were forbidden, and executives are required to write up their proposals as narratives, limited to six pages. "Bezos believes doing so fosters critical thinking," Stone writes, adding, "Each meeting begins with everyone silently reading the document, and discussion commences afterward."[54]

Beth Diaz, the *Post*'s vice president of audience development and analytics, discussed what it was like to get used to expressing her ideas as narratives. "I've probably written twenty-five memos in the last two years," she told me. "And I can tell you writing memos is an excruciating process. It is so much more time-consuming than doing a PowerPoint presentation or speaking. And it's not just about a memo. It's written in full prose. It forces you to crystallize your thinking. It's an excruciating process, but I am now completely sold on the value of it."[55]

I also asked Baron how the *Post* was able to amass as large a digital audience as the *New York Times* despite a staff that was about half the size. His answer was twofold: first, that the *Post* was not competing with the *Times* so much as it was competing for people's attention; and second, that "we are doing things that are much more attuned to the digital environment" by "treating the web as a distinct medium." Among the examples Baron cited: hiring young digital-native journalists who write with a distinctive voice and who are unconcerned as to whether their stories appear in print or are only posted online; embracing multimedia tools such as video, the publication of original documents, and annotation (debate transcripts, for instance, have been marked up with highlighted comments by *Post* journalists, adding context and occasional snark to the proceedings); and writing engaging headlines that are not constrained by the artificial confines of column width, as are print headlines. "I mean, look, radio is different from newspapers, television is different from radio," Baron said. "Here comes the web. We should be different, and mobile might be different, too."

Now, I would argue that the *Times*'s approach to digital, although different from the *Post*'s, is every bit as engaging and innovative. But in discussing the *Post*'s rapidly growing digital audience, there's an additional topic that can't be avoided: its reliance on a presentation of some types of material that is aimed at maximizing shares and eyeballs.

Baron doesn't like the term "clickbait," and I agree with him that that's not quite the right word. After all, "clickbait" suggests that the underlying story does not live up to the promise of the headline, and that's rarely the case with *Post* journalism. But the *Washington Post* experience can vary quite a bit depending on how you access that journalism. The print paper mixes heavy and light fare, the serious and the entertaining, in a way that isn't much different from what news consumers are used to. The website and the apps, though, often take a more viral approach.

That's especially true with the national digital edition — the magazine-like app for mobile and tablet that debuted on Amazon's Kindle Fire and later migrated to other platforms. For one thing, it omits local news so that its low cost won't lure Washington-area readers into switching from their more expensive print or digital subscription. For another, the story mix and the presentation often have a viral feel to them. For instance, as I perused the national app on my iPhone on a Wednesday afternoon in April 2016, I saw stories such as "O Cannabis! Canada Moves to Legalize Marijuana in 2017" (illustrated with a pot-festooned Canadian flag), "What Your First Name Says about Your Politics," and "Diet Coke Is Getting a New Look."

To be fair, these stories were well reported and were interspersed amid more serious news. If I'd been riding on the subway and looking for something to read, I'd have clicked on any of them. And there is nothing wrong with lightening things up as long as the core mission remains in place.

The longtime media critic (and *Post*-watcher) Jack Shafer, now with *Politico*, told me that he's an admirer of Baron's *Post*. "It's as good as it's ever been," he said. "In terms of accuracy, accountability, imagination, Marty Baron is a genius and an inspirational editor." As for what Shafer forthrightly called "clickbaitery," he said it was no different from newspaper editors of yore dropping in, say, a "Ripley's Believe It or Not" brief to fill a hole on a page. The idea, he said, is to make the *Post* a "habit," explaining, "You're sitting there, you're bored, or you're angry at your editor, and you just want a media moment. It turns out that there's a much larger market for that than we ever imagined."[56]

I also put the question about viral content to Julia Beizer — and, as I learned, she'd thought quite a bit about the subject. To begin with, she acknowledged that the news mix in the national app was different from what was on the *Post*'s other platforms, explaining that it was aimed at "a wider audience that wasn't necessarily familiar with the *Washington Post* brand." Thus the national app emphasizes more consumer news, more science and health coverage, and less political news. "On the national app," Beizer said, "we are much more approachable in headlines and much more approachable in visuals. It has a different editorial sensibility."[57]

She cited a story by Jim Tankersley from November 2015, headlined "Baby Boomers Are What's Wrong with America's Economy," which proved to be something of a viral sensation.[58] I wouldn't have necessarily thought of it as an example of viral content, but there is no question that the headline was click-friendly. To Beizer, it was also an example of exactly what the *Post* ought to be doing. "A well-reported piece about why baby boomers are what is wrong with this economy that cites a ton of research, that goes through all of the reasons why this particular generation is a drain on our economic resources, is not clickbait. It's *Washington Post* journalism, data-backed," she said. "It was written with a great voice. It was entertaining to read. And if that is what *Washington Post* journalism stands for in 2016, I'm 100 percent behind that. That to me is something I want to be a part of. If we say because we would like to stay on a perch of moral high ground to be the *Washington Post* and not reach as many people, not inform as many people, not do the kind of journalism we want to do, that to me is a loss to impress — who? The pundits of the media world?"

Marty Baron put it this way: "Being viral doesn't mean clickbait, and writing a headline and using a photo that would cause somebody to share something on a serious subject doesn't make it clickbait. We do write headlines that we think will lead to sharing, and in many ways they get to the point a lot better. They actually explain the story better than traditional newspaper headlines. I mean newspaper headlines are terrible, right? They all have to be constrained within column sizes, so if you have a one-column head it's all headline-ese. People don't speak in headline-ese. The web and our apps allow us to write in a way that people speak."

The *Post*'s digital growth has also been fueled simply by its sheer quantity of content (a word Baron doesn't like, by the way). To a degree unusual among newspapers, the *Post* publishes a lot of material online — about 1,200 pieces a day — and a good deal of that never finds its way into print.[59] (Disclosure: I was asked to write an unpaid blog post on the media and the presidential campaign for the *Post* blog *In Theory* in July 2016.)[60] Blogs such as *Morning Mix* and *World Views* aggregate national and international news reported by other media outlets, an answer to Bezos's complaint about the *Huffington Post.* Another online-only feature is *PostEverything,* opinionated essays by outside contributors. Some blogs, such as *Wonkblog* (which explains the background behind news and policy and has continued despite the departure of its founder, Ezra Klein, and some of his staff, who founded a similar venture called *Vox*) and Erik Wemple's media blog, are mostly online but occasionally break into print. *PowerPost* offers a deep dive into politics. And some blogs are actually independent ventures hosted by the *Post,* including *The Volokh Conspiracy,* which covers legal issues, and *Monkey Cage,* which delves into political science research. This sheer amount of stuff helps explain why the *Post*'s page views (988 million in March 2016, up 84 percent over the preceding year, according to comScore) are increasing at an even faster rate than its number of unique visitors (73 million, an increase of 40 percent).[61]

Wemple, a veteran print journalist (among other career stops, he was the editor and media columnist at the alt-weekly *Washington City Paper*), told me that he was untroubled about being a newspaper columnist whose work rarely appeared in the newspaper. "All of the messaging and the emphasis seems to be on digital," he said, adding that when he looked at the print paper, he often found it stale, as he saw stories that had appeared online a day or two earlier. "There's a clear focus on digital work here," he said. "That's what the feedback loop bears and that's what drives conversation."[62]

A subject that often arises when one is asking about Jeff Bezos and the *Washington Post* is whether the *Post* can cover Amazon independently and impartially. Of course, it's not unusual for a news organization to have an owner with outside interests that deserve coverage, as we have seen with John Henry and the Red Sox. Before Bezos bought the *Post,* the Washington Post Company's ownership of the for-profit Kaplan educational service created a potential conflict. Rupert Murdoch's multiple interests create conflicts for all of his news outlets, which in the United States include the Fox News Channel, the *Wall Street Journal,* and the *New York Post.* But Amazon represents a particular challenge given its size, influence, and cultural impact. Amazon, after all, is largely responsible for disrupting the book industry. Amazon Web Services does business with the CIA.

When Bezos met with *Post* staff members a month after he announced he would buy the paper, he told them that they should "feel free to cover Amazon anyway you want, feel free to cover Jeff Bezos any way you want."[63] By the spring of 2017, there were no reports that Bezos had tried to interfere with the *Post*'s news coverage. Indeed, within days of the announcement that he would buy the paper, the *Post* published an in-depth examination of Bezos and Amazon that could fairly be described as warts and all — he was described as "ruthless" and a "bully" in his dealings with competitors and a boss who was known for launching "tirades" that "humiliated colleagues." An infamous story was repeated about Amazon stationing an ambulance outside one of its Pennsylvania warehouses during a heat wave rather than installing air conditioning.[64] (Bezos's approach to dealing with labor at the *Post* has not been quite so brutal, but management has clashed with the Newspaper Guild under his ownership.)[65] Shel Kaphlan, Bezos's first employee, who left Amazon after his role within the company was marginalized, was quoted as saying, "I saw him just completely destroy people on several occasions." Kaphlan added that he felt "nauseous" at the prospect of Bezos owning the *Post* and the possibility that he would convert it "into a corporate libertarian mouthpiece."[66] If there is an example of newspaper reporters' sucking up to the new boss, well, this was surely its opposite.

As is his custom, Bezos refused to cooperate with the team of reporters who worked on that story. But the national investigative reporter Kimberly Kindy, who was among those journalists, told me there were no repercussions from Bezos after publication. "I don't think that we have shied away from covering him. And he certainly has invited us to," she said.[67] Kindy's *Post* career has thrived under Bezos's ownership. Among other things, she was deeply involved in a massive effort to document fatal shootings of civilians by police officers — a project that won the 2016 Pulitzer Prize for National Reporting.[68]

Yet it was the *New York Times*, and not the *Washington Post*, that produced a lengthy, highly critical investigative story about Amazon's workplace culture — a story that created a sensation when it was published in the summer of 2015.[69] For anyone who had read Brad Stone's book, there was little new information. Indeed, it struck me that the *Times*, unlike Stone, missed some crucial context in its implication that Amazon was uniquely awful rather than merely awful in the manner that's typical of hard-charging technology companies. As the technology writer Mathew Ingram put it in criticizing the *Times*'s reporting, "To take just one example, Apple co-founder Steve Jobs' treatment of his staff makes anything that Amazon has done (or likely ever will do) seem like a day at the beach."[70]

The former White House spokesman Jay Carney, who'd become Amazon's senior vice president for global corporate affairs, fired back by writing a blog post in which he accused the *Times* of relying on a handful of disgruntled ex-employees.[71] Carney also took to the airwaves, including CNN, to defend Amazon.[72] Bezos himself wrote in a memo to his employees, "The article doesn't describe the Amazon I know or the caring Amazonians I work with every day."[73] Months later, Bezos defended his company when asked about the *Times* story, saying at a conference organized by the technology website *Recode*, "I'm very proud of the culture we have at Amazon. I think of it as a gold standard culture for innovation and pioneering work."[74]

Regardless of the merits of the *Times*'s story, it may be too much to expect that the *Post*, of all media outlets, would take the lead on in-depth enterprise reporting about the dark side of Amazon. "To expect a newspaper to be a fifth column against itself and its owners is naive and probably without precedent," Jack Shafer said.[75] Erik Wemple, on the other hand, said he hoped the *Post* could engage in such reporting if it was warranted. "It would be incredibly awkward to commission a big investigative story. And I hope we do endure that awkwardness," Wemple said. "Bezos's dream of a paper of record necessitates tough coverage of Amazon." He added, "The difficulty is always one of self-censorship. That's a serious concern of any news organization that has a mogul running it."[76]

Baron, for his part, said he had no intention of letting Bezos's ownership of the *Post* interfere with the way his journalists covered Amazon. "Jeff said at his first town hall here, 'You should cover me and cover Amazon the way you would cover any other company and any other chief executive, and I'm fine with that,'" Baron said. "On multiple occasions since then he has repeated that. He said the same thing to me personally. And I said, 'Good, because that's what I'm planning to do.' And I have never heard from him about a single story about Amazon."

In his early days at the *Boston Globe*, Baron kept an exceedingly low profile. As the news business shrank, Baron slowly began to emerge as a voice for embracing change while at the same time maintaining high journalistic standards. In 2012, when he was still at the *Globe*, he gave a speech in which he urged journalists to fight against the "fear" that had overcome them—fear of being accused of bias, of losing customers, or offending advertisers: "Fear, in short, that our weakened financial condition will be made weaker because we did something strong and right, because we simply told the truth and told it straight."[77]

In 2015, Baron spoke at the University of California at Riverside, recounting how quickly media technology had changed during the second half of the internet era (two reminders: Facebook was founded in 2004, and the iPhone was introduced in 2007) and telling his audience: "We are moving from one habitat to another, from one world to another. We are leaving a home where we felt settled. Now we encounter behaviors that are unfamiliar. Our new neighbors are younger, more agile. They suffer none of our anxieties. They often speak a different language. They regard with disinterest, or disdain, where we came from, what we did before. We're the immigrants. They're the natives. They know this new place of ours well. We're just learning it. Welcome to the neighborhood!"[78]

Baron's public persona has only become more prominent since the release of the movie *Spotlight.* After the stunning victory of Donald Trump in the 2016 presidential campaign, marked by unprecedented attacks by Trump on the media, and especially on Jeff Bezos and the *Post*, Baron made use of his public platform to call for tough, independent coverage of the incoming president. "If we fail to pursue the truth and to tell it unflinchingly—because we're fearful that we'll be unpopular, or because powerful interests (including the White House and the Congress) will assail us, or because we worry about financial repercussions to advertising or subscriptions—the public will not forgive us," Baron said in accepting an award named for the late iconoclastic journalist Christopher Hitchens. "Nor, in my view, should they."[79]

Some months earlier, sitting in his office on a Wednesday afternoon, I had asked Baron about his emerging role as a voice of conscience in the news business. It was a moment that I found surprisingly poignant. Nearly fifteen years earlier I had interviewed him at the *Globe* for the first time. In those days he was virtually unknown outside the newspaper business. Now he was the most famous editor in the country by virtue of *Spotlight*, as well as a respected advocate for excellence at a time when many newspapers were just a shadow of what they had once been. "We could use more leadership in the industry," he said in response to my question. A few moments later he added: "I think that people are searching for how to survive and succeed in the current environment while not abandoning our core principles. To the extent that I have helped shape the thinking in our profession about how one might do that, I feel pleased by that."

CHAPTER SIX

THE END OF FREE

The *Boston Globe* Tells Readers to Pay Up

FOR SOMEONE who's developed a reputation as a bit of a recluse, John Henry can exude a certain offbeat charisma when the occasion calls for it. I had experienced the Henry aura several times before I ever interviewed him. In October 2011, shortly after the Red Sox' epic collapse that year, Henry showed up unannounced on a sports radio talk show to defend himself against what he called a "smear campaign" — the program's hosts had claimed that Henry and other team officials spread rumors about just-departed manager Terry Francona's personal life. "Blaming me personally for being the person who said those things . . . that's why I came here. You're misleading the public," he said during some ninety riveting minutes on the air.[1]

In early 2014, Henry held several hundred members of the Greater Boston Chamber of Commerce in thrall as he explained how he hoped to revive the *Globe* the same way Red Sox executives had steered the team to three World Series victories over the previous decade, including in 2013. "I see my role at the *Globe* as roughly identical to what was needed when we purchased the Red Sox," he said. "We knew if we were going to compete with the Yankees we had to substantially increase revenues. I knew that if the *Boston Globe* was to become sustainable over the long term we had to stabilize and we will increase revenues."[2]

On a Monday afternoon a little more than two years after that speech, I visited Henry at the *Boston Globe*. The front office had a decidedly dressed-down ambience. A tieless Mike Sheehan, then the *Globe*'s chief executive officer, greeted me and spent several minutes laying out some initiatives he was working on. After that I was introduced to Henry, who was wearing jeans, brown loafers, a colorful checked shirt over a turquoise T-shirt, and an open outdoor-style vest, also turquoise.

Henry, sixty-six years old at the time, was even more soft-spoken than usual. Tall, thin, and bespectacled, he was coughing a fair amount, and he told me he had been fighting a sore throat for a couple of weeks. He had made it clear that this was to be an off-the-record meet-and-greet. Any comments for publication, he said, would be by email. But almost as soon as we began our conversation, Henry started talking substantively about what was going on at the *Globe* and in the newspaper business as a whole, a subject of which he had become a keen student. I asked if I could take notes. Sure, he said. And for the next two and a half hours we talked, mostly on the record, about why he had purchased the *Globe* and whether he thought the paper could ultimately achieve financial sustainability.

As was the case on the radio and in front of the Chamber of Commerce, Henry proved in many ways to be the *Globe*'s best spokesman, quietly passionate, somewhat pessimistic about the news business overall, but determined to find a way to save the journalistic and civic institution he had purchased. "What really matters is where we go from here," he said. "We need to be the best we can be, be essential to our readers."[3]

Henry said that he was reading *Starving to Death on $200 Million,* James Ledbetter's inside account of the rise and fall of the *Industry Standard,* a high-profile magazine that covered the internet economy in the late 1990s and early 2000s. "You look at the *Globe*—we have about $300 million a year in income and we can't make money," he said. "The cost of making money is high."

Unlike Jeff Bezos, who has reimagined the *Washington Post* as a national digital news source, or Aaron Kushner, who bet everything on the idea that he could attract readers, advertisers, and revenues with a vastly improved print edition, John Henry does not appear to have an overarching vision. Perhaps that is just as well given the uncertain prospects for large regional newspapers such as the *Globe.* "No one's come up with a magic bullet for this," he said.

Indeed, at the beginning of our interview he told me about an exceptionally mundane problem that had been galling him. Google News had begun adding the label "Subscription" next to *Globe* stories, even though the sort of people whose Google searches led them to those articles rarely encountered the paper's digital paywall, which at that time allowed five free stories a month. The move caused traffic to plummet, Henry said, and it took months to straighten out. The problem, he added, was Google's operating principle that all content should be free, which punished news organizations that charge for online access — even those with a relatively generous metered paywall such as the *Globe*. (By mid-2017, the *Globe* was offering only two free stories every forty-five days.)[4]

Henry has become an evangelist on the subject of free news. Much like the newspaper analyst Alan Mutter, who has called the decision to give away news online the business's "Original Sin,"[5] Henry firmly believes that newspapers must charge for their digital content. The *Globe* charges a dollar a day for digital subscriptions and has had some success with that price even though it is considerably more than most papers are charging. "There seems to be this feeling that people won't pay for news," Henry said. "Television used to be completely free, but people decided there is certain content worth paying for. The music business made a deal with the devil — Apple. The music ecosystem for content creation collapsed. TV didn't because people in the industry protected their content. For some reason news organizations decided they should give it away."

For much of the past decade, newspapers have slowly been moving toward paid digital, with the *Globe* ahead of the curve even before Henry bought the paper. It may turn out that Henry, with a deep, lifelong immersion in the world of finance, will prove particularly well suited to figuring out the details.

OWNING A MAJOR LEAGUE BASEBALL TEAM or, for that matter, a metropolitan daily newspaper is not for anyone other than the truly wealthy. By one measure, John William Henry II was worth $2.2 billion in 2016, making him the twelfth-richest person in Massachusetts.[6] Henry rose from humble origins. Born in Quincy, Illinois, and raised in Forrest City, Arkansas, and Southern California, he applied his passion for numbers to the world of finance, parlaying his abilities into a vast fortune. The story is told in Seth Mnookin's book about the 2004 Red Sox, *Feeding the Monster*, the team that finally broke the Curse of the Bambino.[7]

As Mnookin writes, Henry took up commodities trading after discovering that he liked it better than managing his family's Arkansas soybean farm, to which he had returned following the death of his father. Henry's homecoming followed stints at the blackjack tables in Las Vegas and playing bass in a rock band — called, auspiciously enough, the Elysian Fields, a term rooted in mythology but also the name of the spot in Hoboken, New Jersey, where the first recorded baseball game was played in 1846.[8]

Even though Henry had not finished college, he found that he had a talent for trading. He soon discovered, though, that talent was no substitute for knowledge. Acting on a hunch, he invested in soybeans and watched the price nearly double. He was saved from disaster when his girlfriend at the time panicked and convinced him to get out. The price crashed. Having avoided financial ruin, he set about applying the lessons he had learned in his college philosophy classes. He also studied more than a century's worth of commodities prices. The idea was to identify broad market trends rather than merely to predict where prices would go. "It's the whole notion of 'what is,' not 'what should be,'" Henry told Mnookin.[9]

The method Henry developed was spectacularly successful. In 1981, he opened John W. Henry & Company, selling shares of managed futures funds. Within seven years he was able to turn over the day-to-day management of the company to his employees. It was at that point that he began thinking about his lifelong dream of owning a baseball team. Henry had loved baseball since he was a boy, listening to St. Louis Cardinals games on the radio even as he was too shy to ask if he could join in when his friends would organize games at the Henrys' farm.[10]

After flirting with buying the Kansas City Royals, he got involved in Minor League Baseball in Arizona and Florida. He dropped out of the sweepstakes to start a major league expansion team in Colorado, angered at a process he thought had become overly politicized. He bought a 1 percent share in the New York Yankees. And finally, in 1998, he acquired the Florida Marlins from Wayne Huizenga, who had dismantled his World Series–winning team after claiming he had lost $30 million.[11]

Huizenga's complaint that he couldn't make money with the Marlins was not without merit. Henry himself believed the Marlins couldn't succeed without a new stadium and that taxpayer money would be needed to finance it. But Henry's plan to raise $300 million of the $400 million cost from a tax on luxury cruises came to naught. Various other tax schemes and locations were given an airing until, finally, the state senate killed the measure without a vote.[12]

Ironically, in May 2001, on the day that Henry's dreams of a new stadium died, he was sitting at the ballpark with the executive editor of the *Miami*

Herald, Marty Baron, who pops up as either a major or minor player in virtually every story in this book: Baron had edited the *Los Angeles Times*'s Orange County edition, which competed with the *Orange County Register,* and was the editor of the *Globe* when Aaron Kushner tried to buy the paper before moving on to the *Register.* Of course, Baron was the executive editor of the *Washington Post* when Jeff Bezos acquired it from the Graham family and has been instrumental in the *Post*'s reemergence as a national newspaper.

As Henry tells the story, it was Baron who gave Henry the news that the stadium deal had collapsed. "And Baron doesn't even like baseball," Henry said. Henry added he was so stunned at the news that he responded, "Well, I'm out of here," and got up and left. Baron confirmed the details when I asked him about it. "He got on the phone and then disappeared, leaving me to watch the game alone," he said. "At about three in the morning, he sent me a note apologizing for having abandoned me."[13]

Before long, Baron and Henry would be reunited in Boston — Baron as the editor of the *Globe,* Henry as the principal owner of the Red Sox.

DAN SHAUGHNESSY WAS IN A FROTH. It was days before Christmas in 2001, but the *Boston Globe* sports columnist was not exactly ho-ho-ho-ing. The Red Sox had just been sold to a group headed by John Henry for $700 million, the highest price ever paid for a Major League Baseball team. And Shaughnessy didn't like it one bit. "Shame on John Harrington," he wrote, referring to the team's chief executive. "The cowardly little accountant had a chance to do something great and important here." He added: "The record will show that when it came time to step up, Harrington caved to commissioner Bud Selig and the Lords of the Sport. He chose to serve the Boys in the Club rather than loyal, long-suffering, top-dollar-paying citizens of Red Sox Nation."[14]

As Shaughnessy's rant suggests, the Red Sox are as iconic a Boston institution as the Old North Church, and considerably more popular. Their fate matters. Since 1933, they had been run by the Yawkeys or their designees — first Tom, then his widow, Jean Yawkey, and finally, after her death in 1992,[15] the Yawkey Trust, headed by Harrington. The Yawkeys' record was hardly spotless; Tom Yawkey was overtly racist, and as a result the Red Sox were the last team in the major leagues to add a black player to their roster.[16] The Yawkeys also never spent quite enough to win it all, especially during the later years of their ownership. But they had refurbished Fenway Park, developed stars such as Ted Williams and Carl Yastrzemski, and were viewed as a benign and kindly presence, at least among their overwhelmingly white fans.

What had enraged Shaughnessy was the widely held belief that the baseball commissioner, Bud Selig, had steered the team away from Joe O'Donnell and Steve Karp, respected local businessmen, and toward John Henry and his "band of carpetbaggers." Speculation was rampant that Selig wanted to see the Red Sox run as a low-budget team in keeping with his goal of holding down player salaries throughout the major leagues, whereas O'Donnell and Karp had both the money and the passion to bring home a World Series. Henry had impressed no one as a spendthrift during his brief stint with the Marlins, and there were fears that he would bring his penny-pinching ways to Boston. Henry and his lead partner, the television producer Tom Werner, said all the right things about moving to the Boston area and winning a championship. But they had a lot to prove.[17]

And prove it they did, winning it all in 2004, 2007, and 2013, the third victory an unexpected comeback from a last-place finish the year before that helped unite a community shaken by the Boston Marathon bombings. From the moment that David Ortiz took the field a few days after the attacks and defiantly told the fans, "This is our fucking city," the Red Sox became a symbol of Boston's resilience.[18] Moreover, far from being the cheapskates Shaughnessy had feared, Henry and his fellow investors spent lavishly on the team and on upgrades to Fenway Park. Thus it's not surprising that once it became clear that the New York Times Company was losing interest in the *Globe*, Henry's name started coming up in discussions about a possible buyer.

Rumors that the *Globe* might be for sale began circulating as far back as 2006, when a group headed by the retired General Electric chief executive Jack Welch, who was a Boston-area native, and the local advertising executive Jack Connors were reported to be nosing around. At the time, the *Globe* was said to be valued at somewhere between $550 million and $600 million, vastly more than the price Henry would pay seven years later. But the Times Company wasn't selling — at least not yet.[19] The following year, Ben Taylor told me that he might be interested in returning to ownership in some capacity if the *Globe* were put on the market. But he added that he thought such a development was unlikely. "I can't imagine a scenario where that would be an opportunity," he said, "but you never know, I guess. Stranger things have happened."[20]

Ben Taylor and his cousin Stephen Taylor, also a former *Globe* executive, became involved in a bid to buy the paper in 2009 when the Times Company finally put the paper on the market. So did a Beverly Hills, California–based outfit known as Platinum Equity. With the Taylors thought to be undercapitalized and with Platinum having gutted the first newspaper it bought, the *San Diego Union-Tribune*, *Globe* employees were nervous about their future.[21] Although it was not a matter of public knowledge at the time, there was a third possibility. After the Times Company put up the *Globe* for sale, Brian McGrory, a popular columnist who was then serving a stint as the paper's metro editor, decided to call around town to see if any public-spirited business executives might be interested. Among those he contacted was John Henry. "I asked him at that time why he wouldn't flip the paradigm," McGrory told me. "It used to be that newspapers would own sports franchises. Why not have a sports franchise owner own a newspaper? Because without a healthy *Boston Globe*, which causes community discussion about a sports team — I made the argument, right or wrong; I have no idea if it was right — the value of a sports team might be diminished. And I did it because I thought he would be a very thoughtful, steady owner."[22]

Nothing came of it. The Times Company pulled the paper off the market that fall and showed little interest in selling it during the next few years, as Aaron Kushner would learn to his disappointment. But when the Times Company put the *Globe* up for sale again in 2013, Henry reached out to McGrory, who by then had succeeded Marty Baron as editor. "We had a long, long lunch during which he said he was not interested in buying the *Globe* but that he would like to partner with NESN and Boston.com" — that is, New England Sports Network, in which the Red Sox held a majority ownership share, and the *Globe*'s free website. "We must have sat for three hours discussing the possibilities. And then, next thing I know, he surfaced as a bidder for the *Globe*."

Still, Henry would have to overcome a series of obstacles, including other potential buyers and his own self-doubt. Jack Connors, who had partnered with Jack Welch in 2006, was back in the picture, as was a local developer, John Fish. Steve and Ben Taylor were making another run, this time in league with Jack Griffin, a former chief executive of Time Inc. (Griffin would later resurface as a business partner of Aaron Kushner's. Still later, he would sue Kushner.) Several out-of-town possibilities were looking at the *Globe* as well, including Douglas Manchester, a San Diego developer who had bought the *Union-Tribune* from Platinum Equity in 2011. Under Manchester's ownership, the *Union-Tribune* — which he unforgivably renamed *U-T San Diego* — was run "like a brochure for his various interests," in the words of the late *New York Times* media columnist David Carr. Manchester was known as "Papa Doug," and according to an account in *Boston* magazine, he urged McGrory to call him that when they met during the pre-sale period. McGrory declined.[23]

"It felt like every kook and crook was walking through here, kicking the tires on whether to buy us, and it was really goddamn scary," McGrory told me when I asked him about his encounter with Papa Doug. "There were a couple of good potential outcomes, but I'll be honest, I was scared to death. I feared for the future of this organization at that time. Doug Manchester was certainly one of the things that I feared. There were others, too: Digital First Media for a while seemed very, very serious about this. That scared the hell out of me. Aaron Kushner — who I'd never met, seems like a fine guy — scared the hell out of me."

John Henry, meanwhile, was pondering his options. His original idea was to bid for the *Globe* through his Fenway Sports Group, which owned the Red Sox, NESN, a soccer team in Liverpool, and other interests.[24] Henry also considered putting together a proposal to run the *Globe* as a nonprofit organization. But McGrory discouraged him from pursuing the nonprofit idea, and Henry eventually changed his mind. "I view it as waving the white flag," Henry told me. "If you don't see an endgame, you can at least get a tax deduction for giving it away." Finally, Henry decided to make a personal offer, without partners, to avoid conflicts of interest and so that he could run the *Globe* as he saw fit. "I made the decision that prospects were so dark that I could not in good conscience bring them along," he explained to me. "I realized that there were such tough decisions that had to be made that in order to make them I had to be insulated from partners."

There were some bumps along the way. One low point came in late spring or early summer of 2013. Henry had dropped out of the bidding. That day's Red Sox game had been rained out. Henry and Tom Werner were in the upstairs bar at Post 390, in downtown Boston, when they spotted McGrory and several friends. Werner approached McGrory and asked him to join them. "I stopped by," McGrory said, "they asked me to sit, and John said very directly something to the effect of 'I'm out. I'm not buying the *Globe*.' I said something to the effect of 'What the hell happened?'" What had set Henry off, McGrory recalled, was that he thought the Times Company wasn't providing him with accurate information about the *Globe*'s finances. But Henry's friend Werner was convinced that it was too soon to rule Henry out. "As I said goodbye," McGrory said, "Tom said something like 'You haven't heard the last of John. He's going to buy the *Globe*.'"[25]

What changed Henry's mind and put him back on track was a weekend in Nantucket with his wife, Linda Pizzuti Henry. She was originally opposed to buying the paper. Among other things, the Henrys were raising two young children, and owning and running the *Globe* struck her as a commitment too far. But as Henry recalled, during a walk in Nantucket his wife was "just miserable that I had pulled out a week or two earlier."[26]

Interestingly, Pizzuti Henry doesn't remember it quite that way. She told me it was her husband who was miserable that weekend. "That day walking in Nantucket — a Sunday, I believe — he called his personal lawyer, and we decided to move forward on our own," she said. "He really wanted to be a part of putting the *Globe* on a sustainable path." Regardless of who was more miserable than whom, Pizzuti Henry would become a visible presence at the *Globe*, more so than her husband, assuming the title of managing director and involving herself in matters such as sitting in on editorial board meetings, taking charge of Boston.com, and creating, along with local universities, a *Globe*-branded annual series of events related to the area's innovation economy called HUBweek. "I am so proud to work at the *Globe*," she said. "I love being there, I am inspired by the people that I get to work with. It is a distinct feeling to know that the work that you do really matters, and has a big impact. We convene on issues that matter. The business challenges are real and frustrating, but we are making progress."[27] A *Boston* magazine profile described Pizzuti Henry as "the public face of Boston's premier power couple, the one who moderates panels and emcees charity events."[28] And given that she is nearly thirty years younger than her husband, it is not unreasonable to imagine that she will be the paper's publisher someday.

The deal was announced on Saturday, August 3, a day after Peter Gammons — a former *Globe* baseball writer who had worked for Henry at NESN — broke the news on his blog.[29] The terms were staggeringly favorable to Henry. In return for $70 million, he would receive the *Globe* and its real estate as well as the *Worcester Telegram & Gazette*, two papers for which the Times Company had paid a total of about $1.4 billion. Henry would also acquire Boston.com, the Times Company's 49 percent stake in *Boston Metro*, a free tabloid aimed at commuters, and GlobeDirect, a direct-mail marketing company. He wouldn't even have to assume the *Globe*'s pension liability, estimated at $110 million.[30]

Some of the other prospective buyers had offered more. But Times Company executives were said to be swayed by two factors: Henry was willing to pay cash, making for an uncomplicated, straightforward transaction; and company officials were reluctant to take the public relations hit that would have come from selling to owners who would turn around and make drastic cuts.[31] In a way, it was like the Red Sox deal all over again. Just as Major League Baseball maneuvered to bring Henry into the fold in 2001, so too did the Times Company steer the *Globe* to Henry, leaving money on the table in order to ensure that the paper would be in safe hands. Henry was both civic-minded and wealthy. For a newsroom — and a region — worried about the likes of Papa Doug Manchester coming to town, Henry's emergence was very good news indeed.

"This is a thriving, dynamic region that needs a strong, sustainable *Boston Globe* playing an integral role in the community's long-term future," Henry said in a statement on the day that the sale was made public. "In coming days there will be announcements concerning those joining me in this community commitment and effort."[32]

THE NEWSPAPER that John Henry acquired was considerably smaller than it had been during its peak years. As recently as the early 1990s, the *Globe*'s paid circulation exceeded 800,000 on Sundays and 500,000 on weekdays.[33] By the time Henry arrived on the scene, the paper's paid print circulation had fallen to about 297,000 on Sundays and 167,000 on weekdays.[34] There were about 46,000 digital-only paid subscribers as well.[35]

In parallel with the *Globe*'s declining circulation, the newsroom had also shrunk. A dozen years earlier, the paper had employed more than 500 full-time journalists. In 2012, as the Times Company prepared to put the *Globe* up for sale, it reported having 339 full-time journalists.[36] Cutting continued, and by November 2013, shortly after the sale to Henry was finalized, the *Globe*'s news and opinion operations employed about 285 full-timers.[37]

Despite its threats to close the *Globe* in 2009, the Times Company had proved to be a relatively good steward. A corporate chain owner intent on maximizing profits surely would have cut into the newsroom much more deeply. Except for its Washington coverage and an occasional foray overseas, the *Globe* had long since given up most of its international and national ambitions. Still, Marty Baron and Brian McGrory had maintained the paper's quality in covering regional and local news. With a staff far larger than that of any other news organization in Greater Boston, the paper remained a major force in investigative and accountability journalism, shining a light on government and other institutions. The question was whether Henry would end up presiding over further decline, or if he could reverse industrywide trends that were battering circulation and advertising.

The first indication of what Henry hoped to accomplish came in October 2013, just days after the sale was finalized. In a 2,900-word essay published on the Sunday op-ed page headlined "Why I Bought the *Globe*," Henry laid out his life's journey and explained how it had led him into the newspaper business — from writing and publishing his own newspaper at the age of sixteen, to working as a volunteer for Eugene McCarthy's presidential campaign in 1968, to becoming involved in Boston's civic life through his role with the Red Sox. "I invested in the *Globe* because I believe deeply in the future of this great community, and the *Globe* should play a vital role in determining that future," he wrote. "I invested in the *Globe* because it is one of the best and most important news organizations in the world. We saw this vividly in the days and weeks after the tragic Boston Marathon bombings, and we also see it in many other ways every day."[38]

Stirring words, but hardly surprising. As for how Henry planned to restore the *Globe* to financial sustainability, he invoked what would become the hallmark of his ownership: reversing two decades of newspapers' giving away content online. "As I studied the problems that beset the newspaper industry, I discovered a maddening irony: The Boston Globe, through the paper and its website, had more readers than at any time in its history. But journalism's business model had become fundamentally flawed. Readers were flocking from the papers to the internet, consuming expensive journalism for free." He promised to "push the kind of boldness and investment that will make the Globe a laboratory for major newspapers across the country." And he espoused what he called "the Globe Standard," which he defined as a commitment to excellence encompassing the paper's news reporting, opinion writing, and even the usefulness of the links built into the paper's online content.[39]

Around the same time, John and Linda Henry dropped in on the *Globe*'s pressroom one night to take a look around and meet some of their new employees. One of the pressmen, Tim McMahon, told *Boston* magazine that the visit reminded him of the days when Bill Taylor used to come by. McMahon added that no representatives of the Times Company had ever stopped in to introduce themselves. Several weeks later, the Henrys returned to the pressroom so that they could pose for pictures with the World Series trophies they had brought along.[40]

It was a feel-good moment in a series of feel-good moments, culminating in Henry's speech to the Chamber of Commerce. Later that day, though, the glow faded a bit when the *Globe* announced that Christopher Mayer was stepping down as publisher. A popular *Globe* veteran, Mayer had been instrumental in separating the *Globe*'s website from Boston.com and pursuing a strategy of selling paid digital subscriptions—precisely the path that Henry himself wanted to accelerate. Several weeks later, Henry named himself as publisher and brought in Michael Sheehan, an advertising executive who was already advising Henry, as the chief executive officer.[41]

Mayer had nothing but good things to say when I asked him about Henry. "If John wanted to be more involved rather than less, then that would be the right time for me to transition out," he said.[42] The choice of Sheehan was an interesting one. He had recently retired as the head of Hill Holliday, a high-profile Boston ad agency. His predecessor at Hill Holliday was Jack Connors, one of the would-be purchasers of the *Globe*. (As evidence of what a small town Boston can be, Mayer, after leaving the *Globe*, went to work as the executive vice president and chief innovation officer at Suffolk Construction, headed by yet another former *Globe* aspirant, John Fish. Fish later became the leading advocate of a failed attempt to bring the Olympics to Boston in 2024—and the *Globe* was criticized by some anti-Olympics activists for its editorial stance in favor of the bid.) Sheehan had earned plaudits for creating and managing the One Fund, which raised more than $70 million for victims of the Boston Marathon bombings.[43] And he was a friend of Brian McGrory's dating back to their teenage years in Weymouth, a suburb south of Boston. "We grew up together, played CYO basketball together," Sheehan told me.[44]

If Mayer's departure was lamented in some quarters, at least everyone understood that Henry had a right to assemble his own team. The same could not be said of the way that he disposed of the *Worcester Telegram & Gazette*, a venerable daily paper that served New England's second-largest city. The problem was in what Henry said — or, if you will, what people thought they heard him say — during a visit to the *Telegram*'s newsroom in late November 2013. According to an account in the *Telegram*, Henry told the assembled staff that he wanted to sell the paper, but only under the right circumstances. "I think you need a local owner," Henry said. "A local owner can sit down with advertisers, readers, and community leaders and ask for their support." He added, according to the article, "This is not a forced sale. If we don't find the right owner, you're stuck with me."[45]

Six months later, Henry sold the *Telegram* to Halifax Media Group of Daytona Beach, Florida, amid complaints from former editor Harry Whitin, who had headed a group seeking to purchase the paper, that Henry "had absolutely no interest in finding a local buyer."[46] The following January, Halifax was sold to GateHouse Media of Pittsford, New York, a national chain that owned more than a hundred daily and weekly newspapers in Eastern Massachusetts and that was notorious for its cost-cutting and emphasis on the bottom line.[47]

So what happened? Mark Henderson, who was a top digital editor at the *Telegram*, told me that he was among those who heard Henry promise not to sell unless a local owner could be found — a pledge Henderson said Henry also made in a separate, smaller meeting of the paper's executives. "I sat across the table from him when he talked about that," Henderson said. (Disclosure: After leaving the *Telegram*, Henderson founded a for-profit online news service called the *Worcester Sun* and asked me to serve as an unpaid adviser.) But Chris Mayer, who was with Henry at the *Telegram* that day, told me that he couldn't recall hearing Henry make any such pledge. "I was there," he said, "but that didn't pop for me as an oh-my-goodness moment. The reporting is the reporting, but I just don't recall."[48]

When I asked Henry about it, he replied that he did not remember making any such promise. "I went there that day and met with the newsroom," he said. "And they said, 'Just don't sell to GateHouse.' And I said, 'OK.'" Henry struck me as genuinely pained that the paper had ended up in GateHouse's hands anyway. And he seemed even more pained by an online article published by *CommonWealth* magazine that described him as "The Man Who Lied to Worcester."[49]

The full story of what happened may never be known. It could be that Henry got caught up in the moment and made a promise he hadn't intended to make. It could be that he was misunderstood. In any case, offloading the *Telegram* allowed him to concentrate on the *Globe.*

THE NEWS WAS STRAIGHTFORWARD: the *Boston Globe* was launching a Friday political section, Capital, in print and online. It was the messaging, though, that really mattered. On a late-spring evening in 2014, about a hundred invited guests mingled in the lobby of the historic Paramount Theatre, elegantly restored by Emerson College, helping themselves to free food and an open bar.

John Henry joined the minglers, working the room like one of the politicians his reporters might write about. And if you didn't quite get the messaging, Mike Sheehan and Brian McGrory were there to explain. "You can't cut your way to success. You can only grow your way to success," Sheehan said. Added McGrory, "We are investing in our political coverage at a time when virtually every other paper is retreating."

The print version of Capital's debut issue was thick and attractive, comprising twelve pages — among them three full-page ads and a smaller bank ad on the front page. The stories included features on the implications of a presidential race likely to be without a Massachusetts candidate for the first time in years, an intriguing if confusing "social networks dashboard" tracking the "biggest influencers" on Twitter, and a poll on that year's governor's race.[50]

Ever since taking the helm of the *Globe,* Henry has shown a willingness to experiment. Some of those experiments haven't worked out, as we saw with *Crux.* Some have, such as Score, a Monday print section that runs during football season and is aimed at the region's rabid Patriots fans. (Joe Sullivan, the *Globe*'s sports editor, told me that Score was launched at Henry's behest; it debuted in November 2013, just weeks after the sale of the paper to Henry was finalized.)[51] And some, like Capital, are a mixed bag. Although the section appeared to be successful through the 2014 state election campaign, by 2016 it had withered to little more than a Friday column by James Pindell, the paper's multimedia political reporter. Despite that, McGrory believes Capital was a success: it offered high-quality coverage and brought in ad revenue during the 2014 Massachusetts campaign, as intended, and could well be revived in 2018 if a hot state election season attracts enough advertising to warrant it. "Capital worked while Capital worked," he said. "The key to Capital was only keeping it while it was bringing in revenue."

The changes and improvements under Henry have been many. The *Globe* replaced its unloved g section, a daily tabloid insert for arts and entertainment, with broadsheet-size themed sections for each day of the week. Business, travel, and real estate coverage has been upgraded — all areas that are attractive to advertisers. The Sunday arts section is outstanding, though cuts in arts coverage in the Monday, Tuesday, and Wednesdays editions have drawn criticism from the city's large and active arts community.[52]

McGrory's retort: "Trust me when I say arts has taken absolutely no more and I'm pretty certain less of a hit than other really vital sections of the *Globe*. How can you look at our Sunday section, and our Friday section, and our Thursday section, and say arts has taken a big hit?" At the same time, McGrory acknowledged that the *Globe* was trying to come up with ways to offer more high-impact arts coverage while dropping some of the secondary and tertiary reviews of events that few readers care about. "Do we really need reviews of performances that don't get a whole lot of attention, that are one-and-dones, where the only thing we're reviewing is what happened?" he asked. "We're not giving our readers advice on whether they should go or not. It's already over. In the name of making sure that we're properly covering world-class institutions, like the BSO, the MFA, the ICA [that is, the Boston Symphony Orchestra, the Museum of Fine Arts, and the Institute of Contemporary Art], I'll make that trade-off any day."

Henry's most crucial contribution has been his ongoing commitment to investigative journalism and enterprise reporting. The *Globe* has basked in the glow of *Spotlight*. But unlike the situation at many other papers, the

Globe continues to have a robust investigative team and to break the kinds of regional and local stories that really matter. "Our core mission is to be able to shine a light on the powers that be," Henry told me. "It's not the Spotlight Team that pays the bills, but that's our core mission."

Investigative reporting at the national level is not in danger. In early 2017, the *Washington Post* and the *New York Times* were competing fiercely to break stories about the Trump administration's ties to the Russian government. Nonprofit news organizations with a national focus such as ProPublica and the Center for Public Integrity were thriving as well. What is truly endangered is accountability journalism at the local level. Under Henry, the *Globe* has continued to produce it on a regular basis.

As a reader, I have the sense that the *Globe* would be as willing to devote the resources to the pedophile-priest story in 2017 as it was some fifteen years earlier. Indeed, in 2016, the paper published a series of articles on sexual abuse at private schools. It has also done important, difficult work on topics like the deinstitutionalization of the mentally ill, the hazards created by surgeons who oversee two patients simultaneously, the city's corrupt taxi industry, and severe deficiencies in off-campus housing for the area's vast student population.

The paper also publishes deeply reported features on a wide variety of topics, often with vibrant digital treatments, ranging from a young Maine boy being raised in poverty by his grandparents, to a quest to save a right whale injured by rope in which it had become entangled, to a series about a boy with a rare form of cancer who survived because his parents and their doctor fought the medical establishment and pushed for a new type of treatment. The opinion pages have been especially innovative, publishing a fictional but prescient front page months before the 2016 election about what a Trump presidency would look like, as well as a special section in favor of gun control whose online version included animated data visualizations and an interactive feature making it easy for users to tweet at key members of Congress. The paper won four Pulitzer Prizes for news reporting, photography, and opinion writing between 2014 and 2016, and easily could have won several more.[53]

Ellen Clegg is a longtime *Globe* staffer who was named editorial page editor after Peter Canellos — among several editors thought to be a candidate for the top job that went to McGrory — took an early-retirement buyout in

September 2014. (Canellos subsequently was hired by *Politico* and in late 2016 was named an editor-at-large.)[54] The opinion pages are the one part of a newspaper's journalism where it is expected that ownership will assert itself. Clegg told me that it was with the encouragement of the Henrys that the paper published its mock front page about Trump and its interactive feature on gun violence. "John has been one of the motivating forces behind our most powerful editorial presentations," she said. "He has pushed to have more high-impact writers on the op-ed page, and to be more creative and forward thinking on reader engagement."[55]

Linda Henry, Clegg added, sits in on the editorial board's Monday meetings and is at the *Globe* most other days as well. "She's a digital thinker and challenges us to find novel ways to meet our audience," Clegg said. "We work closely with our analytics team so that we know when our audience is hungry for opinion content. Turns out, our peak audience is reading opinion from 6 a.m. to 9 a.m. So we created a dawn patrol during the campaign season, which continues to this day. We write and publish from home — and then commute in." The change, Clegg said, resulted in a doubling of online page views in 2016. "Linda Henry is super smart, engaged, passionate about the future of the city, and connected to innovative thinkers in the startup community," Clegg said. "She's also a good listener. She grew up here. She gets it."

But as McGrory's remarks about the newsroom "taking a hit" suggest, John Henry's willingness to spend money in order to make money has diminished since the unveiling of Capital. There was a major downsizing in October 2015.[56] The Saturday paper was redesigned and thinned out.[57] By early 2017, the full-time staff of about 285 that Henry inherited was down to about 240, according to several sources I consulted. Boston.com, its mission diminished as the *Globe* deemphasized free content, had perhaps fewer than twenty employees. The hope was that the move to more efficient space would result in enough savings that the *Globe* could break even. But that was still in the future — and things can go wrong. "We will not be profitable in 2017," Henry told me. "*Globe* revenues have always been extraordinary, but not nearly as extraordinary as expenses." He added: "We have to get to a sustainable future. I see that as my primary role: assuring the community that the *Boston Globe* news organization is sustainable while producing high quality journalism."[58]

TO COUNTER THE ONGOING DECLINE of newspaper advertising, the *Globe* under Henry — and during the final years of Times Company ownership — has taken a number of steps to persuade readers to pick up an increasing share of the cost, both in print and online. When Chris Mayer was running the business side, the *Globe* adopted a policy of charging as much as the market would bear for the print product. The result was that even though some customers stopped subscribing, overall revenues stabilized.[59]

As of early 2017, the print edition remained expensive: $2 on weekdays and $4.50 on Sundays, more than what peer newspapers, such as the *Philadelphia Inquirer,* the *Miami Herald,* and the *Portland Oregonian,* were charging.[60] Katie Kingsbury, the *Globe*'s managing editor for digital, wrote in the *Nieman Journalism Lab* that print should be viewed as a specialty item for those willing to pay for it. "In the United States," she said, "print is no longer the media for the masses but a bespoke product to be managed — which might be the best thing that ever happened to it."[61]

Yet the *Globe*'s ongoing commitment to print did not prevent what was probably the worst failure of the Henry era: the disastrous rollout of, and hasty retreat from, a change in print distribution vendors starting in the final days of 2015.

Top *Globe* officials were unhappy with both the price and the performance of Publishers Circulation Fulfillment, or PCF, which delivered not just the *Globe* but virtually every other paper in the Boston area, including the *New York Times,* the *Wall Street Journal,* and the *Boston Herald.* Not only was the *Globe* "getting gouged," Henry told me, but "the number-one reason for cancellation was delivery issues." The paper signed an agreement with another vendor, ACI Media Group, which was not up to the challenge. Papers went undelivered in many neighborhoods in and around Boston. At one point the head of ACI, Jack Klunder, said it might take four to six months before the earlier level of service could be restored.[62]

The situation became such a crisis that *Globe* employees were asked during the first weekend in January to help assemble and deliver the Sunday paper. For the *Globe,* it was a huge and embarrassing story. Along with reporters from other media organizations, I showed up at the *Globe*'s Newton distribution center late that Saturday night and interviewed the paper's journalists as they went about their duties. "We're fighting for our survival here, and I like doing what I'm doing. Not just because I get paid, but because I love journalism," the technology columnist, Hiawatha Bray, said. Todd Wallack, an investigative reporter, added: "People deserve their paper. I agree with all our readers. They have a right to expect the paper to be there every morning."[63]

Within days, the *Globe* began transitioning back to PCF. Henry published an apology in the *Globe* that contained such classic lines as "Our region is full of old houses, curvy roads, and hidden cul-de-sacs" and "People want their paper every day in a particular place at a particular time. It might be 6 inches to the right of the first step."[64] This was at a time when many subscribers weren't receiving a paper at all. Still, Henry and Mike Sheehan recognized that they had a disaster on their hands, and the old system was more or less restored in a matter of weeks — though stray complaints trickled in for some time after that, and many journalists continued to help deliver the paper until the situation was resolved.

Surprisingly, the fiasco did not appear to affect print circulation all that much. According to the publishers' statements that newspaper owners are required by the US Postal Service to print each year, the *Globe*'s Sunday paid print circulation fell from about 266,000 to 243,000 between the fall of 2015 and 2016. Weekday print circulation declined from 158,000 to 143,000. Given that paid print circulation has fallen at virtually all newspapers every year over the course of several decades, it would be hard to say that what happened at the *Globe* was any worse than what would have been expected if the home-delivery mess had never occurred.[65]

Indeed, from the second quarter of 2016 through the beginning of 2017, print circulation was down just 1.8 percent, according to Pete Doucette, the *Globe*'s chief consumer revenue officer. He called that "a very low rate of decline, compared to prior years and many major metros." What's more, he added, new print subscriber sign-ups in 2016 increased by about 8,000, or 13.8 percent, compared with 2015.[66] "So we've lost basically zero," Doucette told me when I asked him about the long-range effect of the home-delivery problems. "It was an event, it had an impact, but I think we've recovered well from that, and our trajectory over the last nine months has been very strong."[67] Sheehan was more philosophical about what had happened. "I kind of got involved toward the tail end of it," he said. "I think certainly, what I learned is how to deal with a crisis and act fast. It was a matter of days before we had all the decisions made to fix it. But that was a good experience. I think, long term, you've got to be careful with people's expectations." One effect, he added, was that more time was being taken to plan the relocation of the printing operation to Taunton than might have been the case previously.[68] Unfortunately, within months the Taunton operation had turned into another disaster, as I will explain below.

The *Globe*'s progress with paid digital subscriptions has been more encouraging. Like virtually every newspaper, the *Globe* got off to a late start, giving away the paper online for many years before establishing a paywall. The engine of the paper's online efforts was Boston.com, launched in 1995 as a hub with a number of local media partners. At a moment when it was not yet clear that larger forces were going to decimate the digital advertising market for newspapers, free news looked like the future.

Michelle Johnson, a top editor with Boston.com in its early days, told me that, in retrospect, the biggest mistake newspapers might have made with their digital strategy was to offer their content for free. Trouble was, no one knew it at the time. "Back in the day, if somebody had said 'you have to charge for this,' I would have thrown my body on the tracks and said 'no way.' That's not the culture," said Johnson, now a multimedia journalism professor at Boston University. "But in hindsight, if we had pushed to figure out a business model from the start, maybe something could have been different.[69]

At first, Boston.com had an entirely separate staff from the *Globe*, as well as its own headquarters in the Back Bay, across from the Boston Public Library. The site was not part of editor Matt Storin's portfolio. Gradually, though, the content and culture of Boston.com changed. The other media partners drifted away as it became easier for them to set up their own websites. Storin's successor, Marty Baron, assumed a supervisory role. Boston.com was widely seen as a success, mixing *Globe* content with breaking news, community blogs, slideshows, and the like. Baron jokingly referred to "the Red Sox diaspora," people who would drop in on the site from around the country to see how their team was doing. With the *Globe*'s staff shrinking, Boston.com was eventually moved to the paper's headquarters.[70]

But as a business model for free news failed to emerge, Chris Mayer began to think about Boston.com's future. What he, Baron, and others came up with was a two-track strategy: a paid site, BostonGlobe.com, alongside

Boston.com, which would continue to be free. BostonGlobe.com would have a metered paywall, and some *Globe* journalism would continue to be published on its free sister site. But the emphasis would be on selling paid digital subscriptions. The new BostonGlobe.com was unveiled in September 2011. There was no mobile app. Instead, the site was written in HTML5, which adjusted itself to whatever device a reader was using — technology known as "responsive design." As a bonus, by not offering an app the *Globe* was able to avoid the 30 percent fee Apple charged for inclusion in its online store.[71]

BostonGlobe.com has done well from the start. Boston.com, on the other hand, was cast adrift without a mission or a focus. In the spring of 2014, the site was separated from the *Globe* entirely and relaunched as a mobile-first product without any *Globe* content. The new Boston.com debuted without an editor, and when one finally came aboard that fall, he stayed for only a few weeks. The goal seemed to be to provide free, ad-supported viral content aimed at millennials who presumably could not be enticed into buying a subscription to the *Globe*. There were embarrassments and apologies. At one point, a staff member was caught jokingly selling a T-shirt online that mocked a lawyer whose feud with a Chinese-restaurant owner she had been reporting on.[72] At another point, an apology was ordered up after a second staff member made fun of a death threat against then–US House Speaker John Boehner, as well as Boehner's alleged drinking habits.[73]

Those missteps were big news at the time. And it was never clear what a free *Globe*-owned news site should look like if it didn't have any *Globe* content. Of considerably more significance, though, were the financial undercurrents threatening free-news sites. When Boston.com relaunched in 2011 and again in 2014, there was still a sense that there might be a place for ad-supported free news. Within a few years that idea was all but dead except for a few mega-sites such as *BuzzFeed* and the *Huffington Post*.

By early 2017, Boston.com mainly offered wire copy and brief summaries of *Globe* stories along with come-ons to sign up for BostonGlobe.com. Vestiges of earlier ideas hung on: RadioBDC, an underpromoted online radio station that played vintage 1980s-era rock music, and a morning show in partnership with a local radio station. Linda Henry, who had taken charge of Boston.com, told me that she could envision an ongoing, if reduced, role for the site. "While we firmly believe that newspapers should charge for their journalism, there are some community aspects, news, and marketplaces that do not need to be behind a paywall," she said, citing sports scores, weather, commuting information, and breaking news, as well as advertising initiatives in real estate and car sales.[74]

The *Globe* has done much better with its paid website. The strategy has been similar to that pursued by the *Washington Post*, only on a smaller scale: attract as large an audience as possible through social media, newsletters, and the like, give people a chance to sample the *Globe*'s journalism by offering a few free articles each month, and try to persuade a percentage of those visitors to become paying customers. According to comScore, BostonGlobe.com attracted 9.6 million unique visitors in October 2016, nearly double the number of visits to Boston.com.[75] In early 2017, the *Globe* reported having signed up about 75,000 digital-only subscribers, an increase of 15 percent, or about 10,000, over the year before. That number was higher than any newspaper in the country could claim except the *New York Times*, the *Wall Street Journal*, and the *Washington Post*.

And then the Trump effect kicked in. Like many other newspapers and magazines, the *Globe* experienced a rapid increase in paying customers: the number of digital subscribers reached 84,000 by late May.[76] The paper published a feature that documented the highlights and lowlights of the Trump transition, including the president-elect's tweets, and was linked to *Globe* coverage, thus driving more traffic and increasing the likelihood that visitors would hit the paywall and be asked to subscribe.[77] The *Globe* also launched a promotional campaign playing off concerns over "fake news" by using the Twitter hashtag #FactsMatter and publishing a mission statement under the headline "Why We Do What We Do."[78] Pete Doucette told me that his goal was to reach 100,000 paid digital subscribers by the end of 2017 or early 2018. As of May, it seemed possible that he might have to readjust his numbers upward.

A digital subscription to the *Globe* was not cheap. Typically a newspaper charges less than $20 a month for online access. At John Henry's insistence, the *Globe* increased its price to about $30 a month — that is, $1 a day. The pricing structure is complicated, especially for customers who sign up for some combination of print and digital. But digital-only subscribers are moved up to the full price after a year.[79] In early 2017, Doucette told me, some 60 percent of the *Globe*'s digital subscribers were paying the full rate.

For the *Globe,* that's pure revenue: even though the print paper brings in more money because of the advertising it publishes, it's also expensive to produce. In contrast, the cost of adding a digital subscriber is essentially zero.[80]

Chris Mayer, who crafted much of the *Globe*'s digital strategy before Henry bought the paper, explained that in an era of cratering ad revenue, his hope was to cover the basic operations of the newsroom with subscription revenue (which he likened to "annuities") and bring in ad money ("equities") to pay for extras. In rough terms, he said, a newsroom of 300 people might cost $70 million a year — a cost that would be fully covered if 350,000 print and digital subscribers could yield $200 each per year. "Then the advertising becomes all gravy," he said.[81]

So what is the *Globe*'s ultimate goal for digital subscriptions? "If we got to 100,000 things would be feeling an awful lot better," Brian McGrory said. "And if we got to 200,000, I think we'd be well on our way to establishing a truly sustainable future." When I asked Henry the same question, he replied, "I don't see a compelling reason why we should not have 500,000 subscribers at some point. Perhaps more than 300,000 of them will be solely digital and more than 100,000 will be weekend print."[82] He also pushed back when I suggested to him that $30 a month was "a very aggressive price." "I do not believe 99 cents a day is close to being an 'aggressive price' for the *Boston Globe* or for any serious daily newspaper delivered digitally," he said. "I see it as a tremendous bargain for readers in return for trusted journalism." He added: "That has significant, real value in comparison to a daily $3.99 cup of Starbucks. The more New Englanders who believe 99 cents a day is a reasonable cost for journalism in our region, the better our journalism will be."

I don't disagree. And yet our two leading newspapers, the *New York Times* and the *Washington Post,* are charging less — the *Post* substantially less, especially for Amazon Prime customers and Kindle Fire users. Both papers offer world-class coverage of national and international news. Given that reality, the ceiling for the number of people willing to pay more for the *Globe*'s regional and local news may be lower than Henry imagines.

As is the case with many newspapers, the failure of digital advertising to offset the decline in print advertising has led the *Globe* to pursue new types of ad revenue. Online ads may never come close to producing the sort of financial bonanza that print newspapers enjoyed during their heyday. But Mike Sheehan hoped that native advertising — sponsorships by local businesses such as banks and universities that supply their own editorial content — would prove to be much more valuable than programmatic ads served up by Google. By early 2017, both the *Globe*'s website and Boston.com featured a number of native ads. All of them were labeled with language such as "from our partners" or "sponsored by," so it seemed unlikely that any other than the most unsophisticated news consumer would be fooled into thinking that he or she was looking at *Globe* journalism.

Sheehan described the strategy as one of helping local businesses tell their story. "It's going to be with events, it's going to be with our sponsorships, it's going to be with sponsored content," he said. "That's how you get the higher-ticket long-term agreements that you can then sell around." But, Sheehan added, the *Globe*'s effort in that area was "probably at 15 to 20 percent of where it needs to be" as of early 2017.[83]

Another issue the *Globe* needed to address was the quality of its digital presence. By 2017, its responsive website was more than five years old, and its once-innovative technology was showing its age. The problem was that though BostonGlobe.com offered a better user experience than most regional newspapers, it lagged far behind the *Times* and the *Post*, especially on mobile devices. Compared with those papers, the *Globe*'s site loaded more slowly and required a strong, steady internet connection of the sort not always available on the region's commuter rail lines and subway systems. For a while the *Globe* offered a mobile app with a limited number of stories; but it was buggy, and it was eventually withdrawn. Another unloved app displayed the paper as it appeared in print, which was particularly hard to navigate on a phone.

Katie Kingsbury told me in late 2016 that several improvements were in the works. At some point, she said, BostonGlobe.com would be redesigned, possibly along the lines of the sports section, which got a colorful overhaul under her predecessor, David Skok. She also said she was seeking a third-party solution to offering a new mobile app, possibly by licensing the *Washington Post*'s technology. "Over the last three weeks I've downloaded twenty-six different news apps, and I've been flipping through them and doing my own personal research project on trying to use them every day," she said, adding that about a half-dozen were under consideration.[84]

When I asked Henry about the possibility that the *Globe* would license the *Post*'s technology, he responded with surprising vehemence about the problems created by each newspaper attempting to come up with its own digital platforms. "Why should every newspaper create its own technology and maintain it? It makes no sense," he said. "There should be a spreadsheet or word-processor equivalent for newspapers that could eliminate huge annual costs for the industry. Off-the-shelf templates would do more for our industry than anything else other than charging adequately for journalism."[85]

What Henry said made a great deal of sense. Individual newspaper owners do not have to figure out how to print their papers, what size they ought to be, and where to put stories, photographs, and ads. The basics of print newspaper production were standardized many decades ago. Yet when it comes to digital, every newspaper, it seems, goes about building its website and apps from scratch at great expense in terms of both money and pain inflicted on its readers. It is nothing short of lunacy for a newspaper to risk driving readers away not because they don't like the journalism but because it's too hard to access on a phone. That's especially true given that some newspapers have gotten it right.

JOHN HENRY'S BOLDEST MOVE as a news publisher was to launch *Stat*, a standalone, mobile-first website covering health, medicine, and life sciences that debuted in November 2015. Unlike *Crux*, *Stat* is not part of the *Globe*. Rather, it is a separate entity that, like the *Globe*, exists under the umbrella of Boston Globe Media Partners, the limited-liability corporation Henry put together to hold his various media properties.

When I asked Henry about the *Globe*'s online-only ventures in early 2016, he made it clear that he was getting ready to pull the plug on *Crux* and *BetaBoston*. But he talked about *Stat* as a project he saw as central to the *Globe*'s mission. "*Stat* is something we have to do, I think," he said. "The *San Jose Mercury News* should have owned coverage of Silicon Valley but failed miserably. This is the world epicenter for life sciences. We have to own this."

Stat is lavishly funded. Its editor, Rick Berke, had previously held top editing jobs at the *New York Times* and *Politico*. The journalism produced by its staff—thirty-five full-time journalists plus another ten or so freelancers, developers, and engineers—is excellent. *Stat* was a leading source of information about the Zika virus, offering daily round-ups called "Zika in 30 Seconds." The site was also the first to interview President Trump's physician, Dr. Harold Bornstein, who turned out to be as combative as he was controversial, telling *Stat*'s Ike Swetlitz that he'd decided he didn't want a story after all. "I'm going to make sure you don't ever work again if you do this," Bornstein was quoted as saying.[86] In early March 2017, *Stat* unveiled a partnership with ProPublica, *Vox*, and Kaiser Health News to fact-check what members of Congress were saying about efforts to repeal and replace the Affordable Care Act.[87]

Berke told me the day before *Stat* launched that he hoped the site would help bolster the *Globe*'s bottom line. "I see great potential in what we're doing for the *Globe*," he said. "If we can have a sustainable business model here and pull in revenues, that could ultimately help the whole Globe Media organization across the board."[88]

Despite Berke's optimism, *Stat* was not universally hailed inside the *Globe*. Unlike the *Globe*'s newsroom employees, *Stat*'s journalists were non-union. Worse, the site debuted just three weeks after about forty journalists had been laid off or taken voluntary buyouts at the *Globe*, as had another dozen or so at Boston.com.[89] Soon, *Stat* stories began appearing in the *Globe*'s business section and, occasionally, on the front page. Sources I spoke with said they understood that Henry had the right to make cuts at the *Globe* in order to stem losses as well as to launch new ventures. Nevertheless, the timing was awkward.

More than a year after the launch, the site was as vibrant as ever, but it was difficult to see a path to sustainability in the short term. Its long-term prospects might be better. *Stat* was attracting 1.4 million to 1.7 million unique visitors a month.[90] Ads on the site were few, although *Stat*'s email newsletters were bringing in revenue through sponsorships by pharmaceutical companies and organizations like the Alzheimer's Association. In late 2016, *Stat* announced a paid edition with premium content called *Stat Plus* — but at just $300 a year, it seemed that *Stat* was leaving money on the table.[91] For instance, *Politico* charges anywhere from $6,000 to more than $20,000 a year for its various "Pro" editions, which are aimed at policymakers, lobbyists, and the like.[92]

When I reconnected with Berke in early 2017, he declined to disclose the number of paying customers *Stat* had signed up, although he said he was "encouraged." As for the low price, he replied that *Stat Plus* was just the first foray into paid subscriptions. "We think we've been ambitious to launch a subscription model just one year in," he said, adding, "We do think there is a market for even deeper subscription coverage in the worlds of health and science, but we want to be careful not to try to do too much too soon. My motto on this project was 'ambitious, but judicious.'"[93]

The paid digital offering was not *Stat*'s only new venture. In the spring of 2017, *Stat* unveiled a quarterly Sunday print supplement featuring some of its best stories that appeared inside the Sunday *Globe*. The goal, Berke and Linda Henry told the *Nieman Journalism Lab*, was to place the supplement in other Sunday newspapers as well. "It'd be cheaper to get our section than to hire a full-time reporter because we can draw on all our reporters around the country and have it all ready to go," Berke said. "All you have to do if you're a local paper is to print it, which is not cheap, but it's cheaper than having your own reporter."[94]

THE BEGINNING OF 2017 was a time of transition for the *Boston Globe*. On January 1, Mike Sheehan left as chief executive officer, succeeded by Doug Franklin, a top executive with the Cox newspaper chain. In a memo to the staff, John Henry praised Sheehan for his work in untangling the *Globe*'s business affairs from the New York Times Company and for putting the paper on a path to moving out of its obsolete plant on Morrissey Boulevard in Dorchester. "These initiatives are as complex as they are risky," Henry wrote. "Any one of them would be a once-in-a-lifetime challenge for an executive. But the leadership team, working under Mike, has tackled each of them."[95]

Several weeks after he stepped down, Sheehan reflected on his tenure. He told me he had always intended to leave after his three-year contract was up, explaining that he had business interests he wanted to return to that would have begun to shrivel if he'd stayed at the *Globe* any longer. Sheehan was especially proud of his work in getting the paper out of its aging, half-empty plant — and not just for financial reasons. "A company move is a once-in-a-lifetime opportunity to change the culture of an organization," he said. "There is nothing else like it. I would say it's almost impossible to change the culture of an organization to the positive by staying at Morrissey Boulevard. There is something about walking into that building—you feel like you put on a twenty-five-pound vest."[96]

In recent years the *Globe* had built up a substantial business printing other newspapers, including the *Boston Herald,* the *New York Times, USA Today,* and about thirty weekly papers. I asked Sheehan how the *Globe*'s commitment to a new printing plant squared with its future as a mostly or, someday, exclusively digital news source. "I would say that print will pay the tuition for digital," he replied. "But you need to pay the tuition or you're not going to get there. You're not going to get to that stage. That's why Taunton was so important."

Sheehan also came closer than John Henry ever had of saying that the *Globe* was on the verge of becoming sustainable. Sheehan estimated that the *Globe* would save $22 million a year by moving the printing operations to Taunton, along with another $8 million to $10 million a year from closing the inefficient, expensive-to-operate Dorchester plant. Once those steps were complete, he said, "I think it should be pretty close to break-even, if not profitable." To put those savings in some perspective, $30 million is about 10 percent of the *Globe*'s annual revenues.

Doug Franklin declined my request for an interview, explaining he was too new to the job. But in March, he announced some ambitious goals for the coming years: to sign up 200,000 paid digital subscribers, to double digital ad revenues through "audience-based advertising, such as sponsored content," and to "pursue leveraging our brand as a convener of events and activities." He added that "our mission will change very little; how we do it will change dramatically."[97]

But the Franklin era proved to be shockingly brief. In mid–July 2017, Franklin suddenly announced he was leaving, writing in a memo to the staff, "While John Henry and I share similar passion and vision for the *Globe,* we have our differences [over] how to strategically achieve our financial sustainability." Henry said in a memo of his own that Franklin would effectively be replaced by Vinay Mehra, an executive with *Politico,* although he would have the title of president and chief financial officer rather than the CEO's position. Henry added that he and his wife intended to become more involved in running the *Globe,* writing, "I will be a more active publisher and Linda will take on more responsibility as we push for financial sustainability in an environment that is extraordinarily challenging for news organizations dedicated to communities where facts and context matter."[98]

A *Globe* story reporting on Franklin's departure noted that the transition to the Taunton printing plant had been rocky, although it said that "the printing problems pre-date Franklin."[99] As spring turned to summer, though, home-delivery customers began receiving regular emails apologizing for late delivery. The logistics of the transition also required the staff to meet earlier and earlier deadlines, resulting in print editions that often left out the final results of Red Sox games even when they were played on the East Coast. In September, the printing problems reached a crisis stage, with one of the *Globe*'s clients, the *Herald*, publishing a toughly worded statement to its readers complaining that its print edition was "poorly reproduced [and] frequently late or not delivered." The *Globe* itself published a front-page story reporting that the problems might not be resolved for months.[100] Rumors began to circulate that the *Globe*'s newsroom would be downsized once again to cover the cost John Henry was incurring. With memories still fresh from the home-delivery fiasco of a year and a half earlier, the *Globe*'s continued inability to deliver an up-to-date paper to its customers' doorsteps every morning was an ominous sign.

When I asked Henry what had led to Franklin's departure, he did not answer directly, although he absolved him of responsibility for the Taunton problems. "I've been told by a number of people who have gone through it, that printing the size that we do (for ourselves and others), you expect to encounter issues," he said. "We have." He added that readership was nevertheless moving in the right direction, with about 2,000 new digital subscribers per month more than offsetting an average loss of 800 print subscribers.[101]

Although it's not hard to find skeptics about the Henrys' qualifications for rebuilding the *Globe*, no one else has come up with a compelling formula for saving regional daily newspapers. John and Linda Henry are the ones who have financial skin in the game as well as a local reputation to uphold. As long as they listen to the right people, they're as likely to figure it out as anyone else. A *Globe* employee who asked not to be identified put it this way following Franklin's departure: "John and Linda are great stewards of the *Globe*, but also admirably impatient to usher in the future here. It's a good sign that John says he will become a more active publisher and that Linda will have an enhanced role."[102]

The new year was a time of transition for Brian McGrory, as he prepared to reorganize the paper's coverage in response to a reinvention effort that had just concluded. When the Times Company put the *Globe* on the market a few months after he'd been named editor, he would joke that he might become the shortest-serving editor in *Globe* history. By 2017, though, he seemed as firmly ensconced as Marty Baron, Matt Storin, and Tom Winship had been. Perhaps reflecting his long years as a columnist, the *Globe* projected a bit more voice and attitude under McGrory than it had under Baron. And despite a depleted staff, the paper regularly produced a half-dozen or so must-reads every day. "Happily I ended up, in my mind, with a tremendous editor," Henry told me. "Brilliant, sensitive, passionate about Boston. I'm his biggest fan. My only regret is that he doesn't write from time to time. He's a tremendous writer."

Walter Robinson, a legendary investigative reporter who led the paper's coverage of the pedophile-priest story, put it this way: "If you'd had a vote, he would have been elected editor overwhelmingly, and Chris Mayer sensed that." Added Mayer: "I think Brian's doing a great job. He was fabulous in the transition, he was fabulous during the whole process."[103]

In April 2016, McGrory announced an effort to rethink how the *Globe* went about covering its region with a smaller staff and with an increasing share of its readers switching to digital. Outside consultants were brought in, and staff members formed teams to look at everything from the beat structure to how the newsroom could work more closely with the business side without compromising its independence. "To help shape the discussion," McGrory wrote in a message to the staff, "consider this question: If a wealthy individual was to give us funding to launch a news organization designed to take on the *Boston Globe*, what would it look like?"[104]

In another memo sent to the staff in early January 2017, McGrory laid out some of the results of all that brainstorming. The most important takeaway was that the *Globe* would no longer attempt to be a "paper of record," publishing obligatory stories about the minutiae of city and state government, the courts, and the like. Rather, it would seek to become an "organization of interest," developing enterprise stories out of those traditional areas of coverage that made more of a difference to readers' lives. It was an ambitious goal; when McGrory and I talked, he acknowledged the challenge of producing such time-consuming stories while simultaneously keeping tabs on the everyday business of governmental agencies — which is how, after all, high-impact stories are often discovered. Other parts of the memo included accelerating the paper's digital-first approach, anchored by an "express desk"; setting up temporary hubs to provide saturation coverage of big stories; and establishing a "print desk" to handle the print edition so that most of the newsroom could focus on journalism without regard for its eventual destination.[105]

"It was really pretty basic," McGrory told me. "After the significant layoff that we had in October of 2015, it became very clear to me that I didn't want to keep doing this. I didn't want to keep cutting what we had. It felt like we were the same news organization we were five years earlier; we just kept lopping it off, and it was in some ways like playing a dangerous game of roulette. So I started launching an initiative that would look at starting from scratch, what the *Globe* would need to be in 2016, 2017, 2018, and how we could go about doing that."

When John Henry took charge of the *Globe* in late 2013, all was hope and optimism. A little more than three years later, reality had set in. He often said that his goal was neither to make money nor to lose money. Like nearly every other owner of a daily newspaper, Henry was losing money.

At the same time, though, there was widespread recognition inside the *Globe* that things could have been worse. Not a single person I spoke with, either on or off the record, expressed the wish that someone else had bought the paper or that the New York Times Company had kept it. Both John and Linda Henry were seen as public-spirited, devoted to the *Globe*, and willing to make investments well beyond what a corporate chain owner would spend.

"I would say that John and Linda have been good owners and have really stabilized the place after several tumultuous years of *New York Times* ownership," said the metro columnist Adrian Walker. "In general I think we're not in a bad place." One shortcoming Walker, who's African American, did point to was that the leadership of the paper was almost monolithically white. "I think management diversity is a real issue," Walker said. There is no question that the lack of diversity is a problem in a city that has grown well beyond its old reputation as an Irish American and, frankly, racist outpost. It's something the Henrys should address in the years to come.[106]

Also giving the Henrys a passing grade was Frank Phillips, the *Globe*'s longtime statehouse bureau chief. "He came in saying you've got to spend money to make money," Phillips said. "Suddenly he came up against the realities of today's journalism world. I think it was pretty brutal for him to be losing money. He started to have to make cuts. But I think generally speaking, the ownership has been a hell of a lot better than New York."[107]

Ellen Clegg, the editorial page editor, said the Henrys deserved to be compared to the Taylor family in terms of their stewardship of the *Globe*. "They had a soaring vision for Boston and for the *Globe* as a chronicle of civic life and a force for innovation and change," she said of the Taylors. "It strikes me that the Henrys have a similar vision — for a new century."[108]

When John Henry bought the *Globe*, he may have been thinking about the paper's legacy. Now it is his legacy as well. In the long run, the unexciting decisions he has made about how to move forward will have more to do with the *Globe*'s survival than an attention-getting project like *Stat*, Capital, or *Crux*. If closing the Dorchester plant saves the $30 million a year that he and Mike Sheehan predicted, that's $30 million that doesn't have to be cut elsewhere. If 200,000 or 300,000 people can be persuaded to pay $1 a day for digital access, not only will Henry have returned the *Globe* to sustainability, but he'll be able to start expanding the paper's journalistic mission — pointing the way for large regional papers around the country.

Walter Robinson and I sat in the *Globe* cafeteria on a Thursday afternoon in October 2015. In a few weeks, *Spotlight* would make its debut, and we were interrupted several times by people who wanted to talk about it. Robinson praised both Henrys. It was Linda Henry and Mike Sheehan, he said, who had the marketing sense to take advantage of *Spotlight* by republishing a book the *Globe* had produced years earlier and to make a web documentary about the Spotlight Team — something he believed would not have happened when the Times Company was in charge. "She's good at getting people to do stuff, she's good at getting people to think differently," he said. "She runs a mean meeting."[109]

As for the ultimate outcome of the Henrys' ownership, Robinson took the long view. "I strongly believe that he strongly believes first and foremost in the quality of the newspaper," he said. "I believe that Henry has concluded that he will be judged in life by people who count very little on how the Red Sox do and an awful lot more on how he does with this newspaper."

CHAPTER SEVEN

ORANGE CRUSH

From California Dreaming to an Epic Nightmare

FROM THE MOMENT that Aaron Kushner arrived in Southern California, no one was more outspoken or skeptical of his plans for the *Orange County Register* than Gustavo Arellano, the editor of the alternative *OC Weekly*. Skinny and bespectacled, funny and profane, Arellano wrote several articles and numerous blog posts about Kushner, at first expressing reservations, later openly mocking him as Kushner's overambitious hiring and spending spree failed in exactly the way that one might have supposed it would. Arellano compared Kushner to the Al Franken character Stuart Smalley, an annoying self-help television host who believes that your desires will become reality if only you express them frequently and sincerely ("I'm good enough, I'm smart enough, and doggone it, people like me!").[1]

"It's all about affirmations," Arellano told me in March 2015 on the day after Kushner had stepped down from running the *Register*. "It's all about spinning everything to something that's going to reflect positively, period. Even if not necessarily on himself. I don't think it's about aggrandizing himself. I don't see him as a megalomaniac. I do think he's an egoist. A megalomaniac is all about me, me, me, me, me. He was always about 'follow my vision for this paper.'"[2]

If Arellano (who quit the *Weekly* amid budget cuts in late 2017) was not a fan of Kushner, the reverse was also true. Once when I asked Kushner about a particular article that had appeared in the *Weekly*, he replied with notable sarcasm. "As you can imagine I'm a huge fan of *OC Weekly*," he said. "I think they did fabulous journalism, always." Kushner's main partner in the Orange County venture, Eric Spitz, was considerably more blunt. "I think Gustavo is a scumbag," Spitz told me. "I think he doesn't understand the line or that there is a line between propriety and impropriety." Still, neither Kushner nor Spitz cited any specific factual problems with Arellano's work, with Spitz going so far as to say that "the accuracy of his reporting was fine."[3]

Although Arellano's principal critique of Kushner was that his out-of-control spending made no logical or financial sense, he also offered a meta-analysis. The thirty-four cities of Orange County, traditionally the white, ultraconservative home of Disneyland, Robert Schuller's Crystal Cathedral, and rock-ribbed Republicanism, had changed utterly. Though the *Register*, founded more than a century ago, had gone through both good and bad stretches over its history, its fundamental problem in Arellano's view was that it failed to adjust to the region's growth and increasing diversity. With an estimated 2015 population of nearly 3.2 million residents, the county was larger than all but a few states.[4] Its people come from a dizzying array of ethnic groups, especially Mexican (like Arellano) and Vietnamese. In his 2008 autobiography, Arellano described the *Register* as a paper that "no one respects" because it was "a major metropolitan daily that still thinks covering the birth of puppies is headline news."[5] Kushner, according to Arellano, made no effort to break free of that outmoded paradigm.

"If Kushner had been really brilliant," Arellano told me, "he would have realized, 'OK, I'm buying this paper covering this amazing county in the sense that it's really a metaphor now for the changing of America. Let's do it. Let's get at it.' But I think he was so much in his bubble that he never saw the full Orange County. He just ingratiated himself with the lords of Orange County, who are very much of that old school. So, of course, he was doomed to fail."

Arellano is a living example of the new Orange County that he said Kushner did not grasp. The son of a Mexican mother born in Arizona and a Mexican father who entered the United States as an undocumented immigrant at the age of eighteen, Arellano attended public schools in Anaheim, where the students were overwhelmingly Mexican; most of the teachers were white and many were openly racist. He was an intelligent but indifferent student until an unusually astute white teacher, upset that he and a friend had deliberately failed her math class, urged him to work harder and give college a try. He took her up on it, starting at Orange County Community College and then moving on to Chapman University. He began freelancing for the *OC Weekly* while he was still a student and joined the staff after completing graduate school at UCLA.[6]

Arellano is best known for a controversial humor column he writes for the *Weekly* called "¡Ask a Mexican!," a satirical look at Mexican American life that wallows in the stereotypes he seeks to puncture. In one column, he recounts in his autobiography with some glee, he wrote that "Mexicans and Irish were 'drunk, degenerate, fornicating Catholics' and also that Mexican men treat women the same as chickens: 'as purveyors of breasts, eggs, and little else.'"[7] At the time that we met, Arellano was working as a consultant for an animated sitcom then in development called *Borderland*. He was also a sought-after speaker; I drove out to the foothills of Claremont to hear him address a gathering of about fifty counselors from the Puenta Project, which is based at community colleges and works with Latino kids to help them get into four-year schools. "Your job is to create the next me," he said, urging the counselors to tell young people, "It's OK to be angry. It's absolutely OK to be angry. But what are you going to do with your anger?"[8]

In other words, it's difficult to imagine two people more different from each other than Gustavo Arellano and Aaron Kushner. They talked for the first time in late 2012, after Kushner had been running the *Orange County Register* for a few months. It was early in the Kushner regime, hiring and spending were the rule of the day, and Arellano pulled his punches just a bit. Arellano told me that his approach in that initial encounter was "to be as unskeptical as possible." Kushner wouldn't let Arellano visit the *Register*, saying he didn't think it was "particularly appropriate" for a *Weekly* journalist to be on the premises, but he was expansive in a telephone interview.[9]

"'Why newspapers?' is an easy one," he told Arellano. "They matter — a lot. As to why now? Why not? Sooner is better than later, and I've been working on developing a model of all the pieces to be able to publish a newspaper, to have something like the *Orange County Register* grow again and thrive." Kushner added: "I've always felt that newspapers were important and valuable. I don't know that there was a specific time — that 'OK, great, let's go buy a newspaper' — that made me want to buy the paper. Certainly for a bit I've been working full-time on newspapers. The reason that newspapers *do* matter is that manifestation is what binds communities together."

Kushner also told Arellano that he had never visited Orange County until the spring of 2012, when he decided to look into buying the *Register*. This would have been anywhere from one to three months after his courtship of the *Portland Press Herald* had ended, which suggests the intensity with which he wanted to enter the newspaper business. And then he said something that didn't sit right with Arellano. Asked where he was living in Orange County, Kushner replied that the information was "private." He was similarly evasive when he was asked about hotels and restaurants he had patronized, telling Arellano, "I can't say."

Arellano was gobsmacked. "As a local reporter," he told me, "you want to let people know if he's living in Newport Beach — OK, that makes sense, he's a rich guy. Or if he's living maybe near the coast down at Laguna Beach — OK, he wants the beach closer. Just to give us an idea of what this guy is. And then he said something like, 'That's not cogent to the conversation.' And from that moment, I'm like, OK, this guy is full of shit. Everything that's going to come out of his mouth is shit."

ORANGE COUNTY WAS CREATED by a newspaperman. Although there had been talk about the region's breaking away from Los Angeles County for many years, it wasn't until 1889, when a pugnacious figure named Dan M. Baker took up the cause, that it became reality. Baker was the owner of a mediocre paper called the *Santa Ana Standard.* As described by the historian Jim Sleeper, Baker did not make reporting the news his main priority; he let other papers do that, contenting himself with producing overwrought prose that apparently passed for what was considered stylish in that time and place.[10]

Contrary to what you might imagine, Orange County did not take its name from the fruit, which only much later became a major crop in Southern California. Nor was it named for Orange County, Virginia, as some have claimed. Instead, the name was adopted by boosters who hoped to induce people into moving to the region by invoking, as Sleeper put it, "a semi-tropical paradise."[11]

Following several false starts, the final, successful drive to create Orange County began with the efforts of a state assemblyman from the region, Eugene Edwards. Oddly enough, both he and Dan Baker not only had grown up in Indiana, but knew each other when they were living in the frontier town of Chariton, Iowa. Edwards at that time was a young lawyer on the make, and Baker was the publisher of a newspaper he had founded called the *Chariton Leader.* By 1889, their separate journeys had taken both of them to Santa Ana. Edwards was a Democratic member of the state assembly. Baker, in addition to publishing the *Standard,* was also chairman of the local Democratic committee. He and Edwards worked together in the service of "The Great Division," as the hoped-for separation from Los Angeles County was known.[12]

The story of how Orange County came into existence is a convoluted one; a few details will suffice. The *Los Angeles Times*, apoplectic at the prospect of Los Angeles County's being carved up, claimed that members of the state assembly had been bribed into agreeing to put the measure on the ballot. The *Times* wasn't the only newspaper whose proprietors were unhappy. Orange County's first paper, the *Anaheim Gazette*, launched in 1870,[13] long a supporter of division, turned against it when it became clear that Edwards had drawn the map in such a way that Anaheim was unlikely to become the county seat. Baker, a vicious racist (at various times he called Mexicans "savages" who should be "exterminated," referred to Chinese as "uncivilized leeches," and once responded to charges that he was a white supremacist by saying, "Allegation, hell. It's *true*!"), wrote a tedious "playlet" mocking the accent of the *Gazette*'s German owner. Politicians from Santa Ana and Orange fought over which community would become the county seat. Santa Ana won.[14]

"It would be Dan Baker's justifiable boast," Sleeper wrote, "that his paper had 'labored for county division since 1883 and lived to see the grand measure adopted. It has taken a hand in every fight or quarrel of a public character that has been in the Valley since that time.' Indeed, it had fomented half of them, but helping to create the County of Orange was Dan's crowning achievement."[15]

The *Orange County Register* — originally known as the *Santa Ana Register* — was founded in 1905 by about a dozen local community leaders. The region was still a backwater: in 1900, there were fewer than 20,000 residents in the county, with 60 percent living on farms, compared with 50 percent nationally.[16] The paper was first run by two men named Fred Unholz and Frank Ormer. A year later they sold a majority share to J. P. Baumgartner, who was the publisher and editor until 1927, when the *Register* was purchased by J. Frank Burke. But the *Register* did not truly find its voice until 1935, when it was bought by Raymond Cyrus Hoiles, who positioned the *Register* as a quirky tribune of extreme libertarianism.[17]

Unlike the *Washington Post* and the *Boston Globe*, the *Orange County Register* has never been the subject of a serious book. What little can be gleaned about the Hoiles era comes from the occasional newspaper or magazine article. In 1980, though, the *Register* produced a commemorative book on the occasion of the paper's seventy-fifth anniversary that included a surprisingly brief section on the *Register* itself. D. R. Segal, an editor who worked for several of Hoiles's newspapers, described his boss as "a small, irascible bundle of pure energy, a hard-talking soft touch. He had a deadly hobby which he called 'close reasoning.' I'd never thought of a lot of things until R. C. Hoiles. I had never realized, for example, that I was a socialist; that I was not a close-reasoner; that Immanuel Kant was one of the best 'close-reasoners' in history; that people who had empty whiskey bottles in their trash generally didn't pay their paper bill; that our enemy is the state; and that the state had no authority to do anything that I didn't have a right to do myself."[18]

Outside observers were more withering in their assessments of Hoiles and his newspaper. Gustavo Arellano wrote that, under Hoiles, the *Register* was "a guilty pleasure for fans of antiquated bigotry."[19] An especially brutal profile of Hoiles was published by *Time* magazine in 1963, when the publisher was eighty-four years old and his Freedom Newspapers empire spread across five states. "Hoiles's foes say he is to the right of Herod; he is, they say, an anarchist who carries laissez-faire economics to its illogical extreme," wrote *Time* in an article headlined "Making Money by Making Enemies." The story went on to note that Hoiles had denounced Herbert Hoover for being too left-wing, had referred to all taxes as "the theft of wages," and had called for most government services — even the armed forces — to be maintained through voluntary contributions. When teachers tried to argue with his virulent opposition to public education, he reportedly replied, "How can an inmate of a house of prostitution discuss chastity?"[20]

Hoiles was as eccentric in his personal affect as he was in his political views. Marty Smith, the editor of *Orange Coast Magazine,* who joined the *Register* in the mid-1980s, heard stories about how the old man would clip a rose from his garden every morning and pin it to his suit, thus ensuring that aphids would crawl over his shoulders the rest of the day. Or about how he demonstrated his opposition to speed limits by zooming around the *Register* parking lot, with employees hurtling to avoid getting run over.[21]

Following Hoiles's death, in 1970, the *Register* became a much better paper. Starting in the 1980s under Chris Anderson, a young editor recruited from the *Seattle Times*, the *Register* thwarted an attempt by the *Los Angeles Times* to move in on its turf. Shucking off its image as "the Crazy Uncle Harold of Southern California Newspapers," as *Los Angeles* magazine put it, the *Register* charged into battle with aggressive reporting, a sharp appearance enhanced by state-of-the-art color reproduction, and an underdog mentality that pushed the *Register*'s underpaid journalists to compete hard even though an estimated two-thirds of them had their résumés on file at the *Times*. In 1983, the *Register*'s circulation reached 271,000, an increase of 35 percent over 1979. By contrast, the circulation of the *Times*'s Orange County edition in 1983 was 161,000, a decline of 6,000 in just one year. "The change in the *Register* has been the most exciting thing I've seen in my career," Ed Trotter, chairman of the communications department at Cal State Fullerton, told *Los Angeles* magazine in 1984.[22] Among the editors dispatched by the *Times* to oversee Orange County coverage during these years, as I've noted previously, was none other than Marty Baron, the future editor of the *Boston Globe* and executive editor of the *Washington Post*.[23] Baron served from 1993 to '96 before leaving to take a job at the *New York Times*.[24]

In 1952, the paper's name had been changed from the *Santa Ana Register* to simply the *Register*; in 1985, it was changed again, to the *Orange County Register*, which better reflected the sense of regional identity the paper was attempting to foster. And the changes went far beyond the cosmetic: the paper won its first Pulitzer (for its photographs of the Los Angeles Olympics) in 1985, followed by additional Pulitzers in 1989 (for coverage of the military establishment in Southern California) and 1996 (for an investigative project looking into unethical practices at a fertility clinic).[25]

Kimberly Kindy, a national investigative reporter for the *Washington Post*, worked at the *Register* from 1996 to 2006. She remembers it as both an exciting time in her career and as a formative experience. "It was great," she told me. "We were fiercely competitive with the *LA Times*, and we beat them to a bloody pulp. They had to retreat, and it was fantastic to be able to do that. God, it was just great to be there in the heyday. It was fun, and being surrounded by brilliant people — I just felt like an incredibly lucky person."[26]

Within the Hoiles family, though, all was not well. In 1980, Harry Hoiles, a son of R. C. Hoiles, ran into opposition from other family members when he sought to become chief executive officer of Freedom Newspapers. He responded by demanding the breakup of the company, taking his family to court so he could receive his one-third share; he died in 1990.[27] A little more than a decade later, the falling-out among family members led to a decision that proved to be their undoing. In 2003, they bought out Hoiles's descendants who wanted to cash in by selling a 40 percent share of Freedom to two private equity firms for $460 million; the transaction saddled the company with debt that it could not pay off. In 2009, Freedom, owing $770 million, filed for Chapter 11 bankruptcy protection, and control of the company was assumed by its lenders.[28]

Meanwhile, the changes hollowing out newspapers everywhere were taking a toll at the *Register* as well. After 2005, with print circulation shrinking, the *Register* began chasing after online clicks and eyeballs. Christopher Smith, who worked at the *Register* during those years, wrote that coverage of weighty topics such as higher education, religion, and the region's ethnic communities was out; stories about video games, fast food, and other consumer-friendly topics were in. Especially disheartening was what *Register* staff members referred to as the "T&A beat," a cleavage-heavy approach that Smith called "a nonstop cavalcade of speculation on which celebrities had had plastic surgery, with tsk-tsking about how good the work was or wasn't."[29]

The lenders who had taken over Freedom Communications brought the company out of bankruptcy in 2010 and started looking for a buyer—a process that extended into 2012. The rumors of who might acquire it were ghastly. One possibility was MediaNews Group, whose chief executive, Dean Singleton, was well known for cutting costs to the bone. Another was none other than "Papa Doug" Manchester, the San Diego developer whose later interest in buying the *Boston Globe* would send a chill through the *Globe*'s newsroom.[30]

So when a young, self-confident entrepreneur from the Boston area was announced as the new chief executive and principal owner of Freedom Communications, *Register* employees breathed a sigh of relief.

AARON KUSHNER MET HIS STAFF for the first time late in the afternoon on July 26, 2012, shortly after he and his 2100 Trust had acquired the paper. Kushner spoke from the middle of the newsroom, standing on a platform, wearing a blue suit with no tie. Kushner outlined a vision for expansion following years of cuts under previous owners. He told about 200 employees that he intended to hire more reporters and editors and that their job would be to focus on quality rather than chase after digital page views. The emphasis would be on the printed word. "We are the *Orange County Register*," Kushner said. "I want you to get your sense of swagger back."[31]

It seemed implausible, but Kushner came across as someone who knew what he was doing and who presumably had the means to turn his vision into reality. Moreover, although the financial numbers behind his acquisition were not revealed until many months later (and then only by mistake), it didn't seem likely that he had paid too much for the company given the diminished state of the newspaper business. Kushner was reportedly planning to sell off the six smaller papers that Freedom owned, bringing in more revenue that he could invest in the *Register*.[32] In other words, there was a certain reasonableness to what he was saying. And it was a welcome contrast to the standard formula by which a corporate chain owner would borrow money to buy the paper and then pay off the debt with more cuts.

"What he says is well-practiced, well-rehearsed, well-believed, but it comes from his belief system — it's not marketing chatter," Ken Brusic, who had been the *Register*'s editor since 2002, told Gustavo Arellano. "He didn't come into this cold — he did his research." Kushner's mandate to Brusic was to start hiring — and he did, bringing in not just new staffers but also popular old-timers who had left. "There is a sense of possibility now, and that's the most important thing," Brusic said. Yet Brusic made it clear to Arellano just how fragile he regarded the paper's newfound prosperity, saying, "We'd be fools not to have fears" about whether Kushner could succeed. "I worry about everything," he said. "If we can't succeed, it can't succeed anywhere else."[33]

A former *Register* reporter, speaking anonymously, put it this way to Arellano when she was asked about Kushner's plans: "I think he's deluded. Good intentions, but crazy. That doesn't mean I won't apply for my job back, though."[34]

Kushner's new paper had been shrinking drastically over the past decade, although no more drastically than most other daily papers. The paid circulation at its 1991 peak was about 372,000 on weekdays and 430,000 on Sundays. By 2012, paid print was down to 160,000 on weekdays and

294,000 on Sundays. The size of the newsroom staff had declined from 380 during the 1990s to about 180 at the time that Kushner acquired it.[35] It was an ugly trajectory. And here was someone who was saying it didn't have to be that way.

Even though Kushner may have been "deluded" and "crazy," his plans to emphasize print and reverse years of cuts were met with — well, optimism wouldn't be quite the right word for it, but with a notable lack of derision and mockery. Both inside and outside the *Register*, most observers withheld their criticism. Some of Kushner's pronouncements contained at least a kernel of logic — that a print-first approach might work given that print ads were more valuable than their digital counterparts; that the online edition, rather than being free, should cost just as much as the print edition; and that cutting staff, pages, and coverage only served to drive readers away, which in turn would lead inevitably to yet another round of cuts.

In the second half of 2012, the *Register* expanded its business and sports sections, increased its local enterprise reporting and entertainment coverage, converted the *Register*'s twenty-four community weeklies from tabloids to broadsheets (with additional staff members), and was planning to expand its niche magazine holdings. The quality of the paper used in the printing process was upgraded as well.[36]

The era of good feelings engendered by Kushner peaked in early 2013, by which time he had added about ninety journalists to the staff and the horizon was nothing but sunny California blue skies. It was then that Christopher Smith, the former staff member, sat down with Kushner for an interview with *Orange Coast Magazine.* After the Boston and Maine setbacks, Orange County was obviously Kushner's third choice in his personal newspaper-ownership sweepstakes. (Or fourth if you count his attempt to buy the Media General chain, the prize he lost to Warren Buffett.) But he expressed confidence that he'd bought the right paper in the right location. "No market, no institution is perfect, obviously," he said. "But on balance it was very quickly clear that the *Register* and Orange County were fabulous for what we want to do." He added, "I don't believe that 'newspapers are dying' is fated as such."[37]

The key to Kushner's plan, Smith wrote, was to move away from the newspaper business's traditional dependence on advertising and balance that by charging a high price for a growing, improving product: a dollar a day. As I noted earlier, the *Boston Globe* had already begun moving in this direction, and by 2016–17 it was more or less received wisdom throughout the newspaper business as it became clear that advertising would not bounce back to its previous levels. At one time, advertising at a typical newspaper was responsible for 80 percent of revenues, with paid circulation accounting for the other 20 percent. Today, at many newspapers the ratio is closer to 50–50, and in the future it is likely to tilt even more toward subscriber revenue and away from ad dollars. Kushner deserves credit for realizing that subscriber revenue was crucial at a time when the dream of advertiser-supported free-news sites had not quite yet given up the ghost. Kushner told Smith that $7 a week was "less than a movie ticket, and I think we're more entertaining."

At the time, Kushner had not yet set a price for digital. Not long after, though, he decided that online access would cost exactly the same as a print subscription. "Our content's incredibly valuable, and our focus is on subscribers," Kushner told Ryan Chittum of the *Columbia Journalism Review.* "For the people who were in essence cannibalizing our business, they can make the decision: Either our content is valuable enough that they want to pay a dollar a day, or they don't, and we haven't done our job to convince them." Chittum appeared to be impressed but wary, writing, "It's an audacious and expensive bet, and its outcome may reveal whether American newspapers can survive, much less flourish."[38]

Among those who were intrigued by the Orange County experiment was the newspaper analyst Ken Doctor. In early 2013, Doctor called Kushner's approach "addition by addition," explaining, "Addition of costs in the short run, aimed at the addition of both revenues and profits in the longer term. If there were a Pulitzer for getting the most done in six months, Aaron Kushner should win it." Doctor called Kushner's approach "a strategy of would-be virtuous circles" — an "upward spiral" based on "building back of what had been a much-diminished metro newspaper."[39] Among the initiatives Doctor cited favorably were the Golden Envelope program, by which subscribers designated their favorite nonprofit organizations to receive free advertising in the *Register* — which, as we have already seen, was marred by attempts to pressure those financially strapped nonprofits into buying paid advertising they couldn't afford. But Doctor had no way of knowing that at the time, and so he saw it as a promising exercise in community-building.

Even with more pages, expanded coverage, and ninety additional journalists (twenty-four of whom were low-paid interns), Doctor thought there was a chance that Kushner could make a go of it. "Long story short," Doctor wrote, "it's *possible* the Register could take in about as much new money in circulation revenue as it is putting into its expanded news products. It still wouldn't be enough to make up for ad revenue decline, but that's a problem common among metros."[40]

The expansion continued. By the spring of 2013, the *Register* had added a total of nearly 150 journalists to bolster its investigative reporting efforts, to staff up its Washington bureau, and to work at its community weeklies, among other things.[41] His next move was to add newspapers. In August 2013, he launched a new daily, the *Long Beach Register*, putting him in direct competition with Digital First's *Long Beach Press-Telegram*. That October, he and his partners bought the *Riverside Press-Enterprise*, a respected daily, from the A. H. Belo chain for $27.25 million. (Unlike the purchase price of the *Orange County Register* itself, the cost of the *Press-Enterprise* was known because Belo was a publicly traded corporation.) At its peak, editorial staffing across all Kushner's papers ballooned to more than 400.[42]

And then began the great unraveling.

An early sign that all might not be right with the new ownership came in February 2013. It had nothing to do with financial problems but, rather, with a somewhat odd stance Kushner took regarding negative political advertising. An ad taken out by an activist organization claimed that Anaheim's city council members had violated the state's open-meeting law. The nonprofit website *Voice of OC* reported that the *Register* then changed its ad policy to forbid criticizing politicians by name after two of those council members complained to Eric Spitz. Kushner said the change was made because the *Register*'s policy regarding political ads was "inconsistent." But Marc Cooper, a journalism professor at the University of Southern California's Annenberg School for Communication and Journalism, called the no-names policy "cowardly and hypocritical."[43]

Much more serious trouble began in late 2013 and early 2014. In January, seventy-one editorial employees were let go at the *Register* and the

Press-Enterprise — a significant reversal of the buildup that had defined the preceding year and a half. Among those leaving: the *Register*'s editor, Ken Brusic, who retired — or resigned in protest, according to some accounts — and was replaced by Rob Curley, a divisive, much-traveled veteran of digital journalism who'd been brought in to remake the paper's community weeklies. The bad news was followed by the bizarre. Within days, the remaining *Register* employees were told that the company wanted to buy life insurance so that the company would receive a payoff whenever any of them died. As Michael Hiltzik reported in the *Los Angeles Times*, it was not unheard of for a company to take out life insurance on a few key executives — but to buy it for rank-and-file workers was, he wrote, "ghoulish" as well as highly unusual. In a follow-up, Kushner complained about the "ghoulish" characterization and called Hiltzik's story "a reminder of the kind of newspaper and journalism of which we want no part."[44]

Despite the downsizing, Kushner forged ahead with perhaps his most ill-advised idea: the mid-April launch of the *Los Angeles Register*, with a staff of forty journalists, supplemented by the newsrooms of Kushner's other papers. "We are going to bring our fabulous brand of local journalism and political perspective to a very large market," Kushner said.[45] He also sought to position the *Register* as a conservative alternative to what he believed was the liberal orientation of the *Times*: "We are very much pro-business, right of center. The *LA Times* sits on the other side."[46] Ken Doctor guessed that Kushner's main goals were to spread his rising costs out over more papers (he noted that the *LA Register*'s staff had been imported from Orange County) and to put himself in a position to buy the *LA Times*, whose corporate owner — then known as Tribune Company — had been in turmoil for years.[47]

By June 2014, it was obvious to everyone that nothing was working out as planned. After Kushner announced that employees would be required to take mandatory two-week furloughs over the summer, he sat down for a contentious interview with Larry Mantle of Southern California Public Radio. Among other things, Kushner disputed Mantle's claim that the *Long Beach Register* would be killed off, with its coverage folded into the still-new *LA Register* — even though that's precisely what was happening. "It's not that we weren't successful," Kushner said. "We were and are being successful in Long Beach. The *Long Beach Register* has grown up and is now the fully developed *Los Angeles Register.*" Most of the interview consisted of Mantle pressing Kushner for details and Kushner responding with his usual boilerplate that all was well. A sample: "We have over doubled the size of our newsroom and, yes, unfortunately some of that wonderful talent will have to find their success elsewhere." Toward the end of the interview, Mantle put this to Kushner: "I have to say, if I worked for you, hearing your description and the lack of specifics, I'd be very nervous about the future." Kushner's answer: "Any other questions?"[48]

The next day a bombshell exploded. Someone had sent Gustavo Arellano a PowerPoint presentation that Kushner made to investors in December 2013, which Arellano promptly shared with readers of the *OC Weekly.* A year and a half earlier, when the PowerPoint had been created, all was outwardly rosy with Kushner's burgeoning newspaper empire. Inwardly, though, there was turmoil. A. H. Belo was threatening to renege on the *Press-Enterprise* deal over Kushner's inability to meet all of its terms. The lenders who sold Freedom Communications to 2100 Trust had filed a lawsuit, claiming that the new owners owed them money. The solution, Kushner decided, was to seek out investors who were willing to sink $12 million into Freedom. And he was already planning more drastic steps, such as selling off the *Register*'s massive Santa Ana headquarters. "What's most fascinating about Freedom's PowerPoint presentation," Arellano wrote, "is its optimistic description of how Kushner planned to dig himself out of debt even as it showed a dark future ahead."[49]

Several days later Ryan Chittum, whose earlier *Columbia Journalism Review* article had called Kushner's plans "an audacious and expensive bet," was back with an analysis on where that bet had gone wrong. A former *Wall Street Journal* reporter who knew his way around a balance sheet, Chittum wrote that Kushner's slideshow revealed that the 2100 Trust had purchased Freedom for $50 million and assumed the company's pension obligations as well. The deal was paid for with $45 million in loans, "presumably of the very high interest variety." Kushner's next step was to sell off most of Freedom's other newspapers, raising $42 million, and then spending $33 million to bolster the pension plan. "That implies that they dipped into Freedom's cashflow to do so," Chittum wrote. "So, Freedom aggressively paid down long-term obligations while it was, at the same time, dramatically increasing operating expenses by adding a total of 400 jobs and print production costs. Without a capital cushion, something had to give."[50]

Rather than consolidate, though, Kushner had doubled down on his financial risk-taking. The *Press-Enterprise* was purchased with what Chittum called "super-high-risk debt." Kushner tried to sell investors on the idea that Freedom was a good bet because it was headed in the right direction. Indeed, the PowerPoint claimed that circulation revenue would be up 16 percent in 2013 and advertising would be up 17 percent. But as Chittum noted, those were estimates, not hard numbers. And paid print circulation was actually down for the September 2013 reporting period compared with the 2012 figures — about 267,000 on Sundays, a drop of 28,000, and 150,500 on weekdays, a decline of 9,500. Kushner had raised subscription rates, so there was no direct correlation between falling circulation and falling revenues. But given that fewer people were subscribing to the paper in late 2013 than when he had bought it, his claim of a massive rise in circulation revenue seemed unlikely even with the higher rates.[51]

The picture that emerged from Kushner's PowerPoint presentation was that neither he nor investors had anywhere near enough money for the patience and experimentation that would have been required to turn around a shrinking newspaper beset by forces that no one in the business had been able to overcome. Essentially Kushner had one big idea — dramatically improve and expand the paper, and customers would flock to it in such numbers that revenues would quickly offset the cost of creating that improved product. And if the customers failed to materialize, there was no Plan B.

By the end of June, it was clear to everyone that Kushner had not succeeded and was unlikely to turn things around. Ken Doctor reported that Kushner was seeking to reduce his newsroom body count by as many as a hundred people.[52] The *OC Weekly* ran a cover illustration of a smiling, naked (as in "the emperor has no clothes") Kushner swinging on a wrecking ball that was headed toward *Register* headquarters as people — presumably *Register* employees — fled for their lives. In the accompanying article, Arellano described a meeting Kushner had called to outline what was next. The optimism of 2012 and early 2013 was gone, but Kushner's self-confidence was unabated. "Everyone says our strategy has failed," Kushner told his staff. "Perhaps they should be saying that our strategy has not succeeded?"

Soon after the meeting, Arellano wrote, dozens of staff members took early-retirement buyouts, reducing the size of the newsroom to what it had been when Kushner acquired the paper in 2012.[53]

The details of the dire straits in which Kushner found himself piled up. Kushner had lost $24 million in 2013 and was projected to lose another $8 million in 2014. The *Los Angeles Times*, which handled home delivery for the *Orange County Register*, walked away because of nonpayment. An ink company representative arrived at the *Register* one evening with a message: no check, no barrels. Kushner also found himself in a dispute with the Associated Press — he reportedly refused to pay extra for running AP content in the Los Angeles and Long Beach papers, arguing that they were part of the Orange County paper. Kushner, as was his custom, denied the allegations either in full or in part. And when Arellano accidentally sent Kushner a draft of a particularly brutal story about the *Register* he was working on while they were exchanging emails, Kushner told him that he "got the sense that you enjoy tearing things down much more than building things up." Moving forward, Kushner predicted profits and said the *Register*'s staff and the size of the paper were still 50 percent larger than when he arrived.[54]

I could go on, but we already know how this story turns out. By the fall of 2013, employees were being asked to help deliver the paper. The dispute with the *Los Angeles Times* had turned into a crisis, with the *Times* suing Freedom Communications for $3.5 million in unpaid bills. Other legal woes arrived on Kushner's doorstep, one in the form of a $3.6 million lawsuit filed by the publishing executive Jack Griffin, who claimed Kushner hadn't paid him for work he had performed. Griffin had helped Kushner with his unrequited quest to buy the *Boston Globe* and was a partner in the abortive *Portland Press Herald* deal. In Orange County, Kushner's business partners began to ease him out the door, as the casino executive Richard Mirman was brought in to serve as interim publisher. With Mirman and the new, digitally focused editor, Rob Curley, in charge, the paywall was quietly abolished. And the *Los Angeles Register* was closed after only five months.[55]

There is no evidence that the *LA Register* ever had any impact. Michael Hiltzik of the *LA Times* told me it was nearly impossible to find a copy anywhere in Los Angeles. Incredibly, in the midst of all this chaos Kushner told the *New York Times*, in Stuart Smalley fashion: "We just had a nicely profitable month. We're going to have a nicely profitable quarter."[56]

BY THE TIME I ARRIVED at the *Register* the following March, Aaron Kushner was one day away from stepping down. Curley declined to be interviewed on the record and offered no insights into Kushner. Curley was an early innovator in digital journalism, earning national accolades for his work at the *Lawrence Journal-World* of Kansas and the *Naples Daily World* of Florida. In 2006, *Fast Company* magazine published a gushy profile, calling Curley a "hyper-local hero" who "appears to have figured out what most newspapers haven't: how to do the Internet right."[57] But Curley proved to be a controversial, difficult figure when he moved on to the *Washington Post* and, later, at the *Las Vegas Sun* — and, as I learned in the course of my reporting, at the *Register* as well, which was perhaps inevitable given that he had succeeded the popular Ken Brusic in early 2014.

Curley once wrote a post for his blog saying that Brusic was one of his "heroes" and that Brusic had recruited him to succeed him as the *Register*'s editor.[58] Both Aaron Kushner and Eric Spitz confirmed in my interviews with them that Brusic had indeed recruited Curley. Brusic did not respond to several requests for an interview. In any case, I have no reason to believe that Curley had anything to do with Brusic's departure. It is more likely that Brusic decided to retire once it became clear that Kushner was going to have to dismantle what he had only recently built up.

On the afternoon of Tuesday, March 10, 2015, Kushner, Spitz, and Mirman spoke to the staff about some big changes at the top. Kushner and Spitz were leaving their executive positions — Kushner as chairman and chief executive officer of Freedom Communications, Spitz as president. Mirman, who'd put on Kushner's publisher's hat the previous fall, would be in overall charge of Freedom as well. "It has been a privilege and honor to serve as a leader of this institution," Kushner said, according to an account by Gustavo Arellano. "Thank you for hard work, your patience, and commitment to the *Register*."[59]

Next up was Spitz, whose tribute to Kushner came across to many as weirdly inappropriate. After describing Kushner as "a dreamer of great dreams," Spitz said, "I'd like to suggest to the rest of you that we take the balance of this week and think about what we are thankful to Aaron for. We all take it as an assignment — we're all writers . . . write Aaron a note. Tell him what you're thankful for . . . Thank you, Aaron."

Finally, Mirman broke the tension. "The room's so quiet," he said. "I hear you guys breathing." Mirman spoke for several minutes, according to Arellano, and promised the staff more specifics in the weeks to come.

Spitz's remarks on behalf of Kushner struck a number of observers as tone-deaf. But when I asked Spitz if he had any regrets about what he said that day, he insisted that he did not. "I would do it again the same way," Spitz told me. "The most important thing for me was for Aaron to retain his dignity. That was what was going on in my mind. I wanted people to realize that he had done something very difficult. He had done a lot of good things. The rebirth we had, if only for a fleeting moment, was worthy of their respect." Spitz added that his own resignation was strictly for appearance's sake — he soon reemerged as chairman of Freedom, and he later worked with Mirman in an attempt to buy the papers.

Spitz's praise for Kushner aside, it was the employees who paid the price for his huge gamble. The day that the *Los Angeles Register* closed, I learned, managers were tapping staffers on the shoulder and telling them to report to human resources. From there, they were escorted to the parking lot — shades of Renaissance Greeting Cards in 2005. Many of those who kept their jobs were faced with lengthy commutes from Los Angeles to Santa Ana, as they had rented apartments in LA with long-term leases.

Of course, the journalists who got the worst of it were not those who found themselves with a longer commute, but those who took jobs with the *Register* believing — or at least hoping — that Kushner's ideas would work out. Kimberly Kindy, the *Washington Post* journalist who'd previously worked at the *Register*, offered a harsh assessment of the Kushner era. "What I saw was from the outside, but it involved all my friends," she told me. "I saw people take buyouts, get laid off. And then a wealthy businessman comes in, and then a massive amount of recruiting and rehiring of many of the people who left. People who moved to another state and took a job moving back to California for a second opportunity at the *Orange County Register.* So it's been heartbreaking to see people get their hopes up, return, and then have to leave again. I feel like it's unforgivable to come in and do a cash infusion knowing that the spigot is going to turn off pretty fast if a miracle doesn't happen. And that felt cruel and unethical to me. Learning that there was no viable business plan behind it — ever. It was heartbreaking to watch that."[60]

Two days after Kushner's and Spitz's resignations, Richard Mirman talked about what had happened, and what was next, on public radio station KCRW of Santa Monica, closing the Aaron Kushner chapter once and for all. "Aaron was and is an entrepreneur," Mirman said. "And he came in like most entrepreneurs into industries that sort of are struggling and believe they have a model. Aaron went for it and tried to grow it. The challenge was that the revenues didn't materialize to the extent that Aaron and Eric had hoped, but the costs certainly did. So now we're in a phase of making some adjustments, learning from things that worked and adjusting some things that didn't work."[61]

Asked by the host, Warren Olney, if he was preparing the *Register* and the *Press-Enterprise* for sale, Mirman replied, "That's not part of my goal. My goal is to stabilize the business and get it back on a trajectory of growth." Asked about Kushner's emphasis on print, Mirman said that was already changing. "There was a very strong commitment to paper potentially at the expense of the digital," he said. "We've turned that back on. I think you're starting to see and will continue to see a lot more innovation that comes out of our digital product than ever before."

IN ASSESSING what Aaron Kushner tried to do in Southern California, it's important to keep in mind that he pursued two strategies, one sensible, the other profoundly risky. The sensible strategy was to end free distribution of his papers' journalism, to improve the print product, and to charge readers the same amount of money whether they were print or digital subscribers. No, it wasn't a strategy that was especially forward-looking given the long-term decline of print, but at least it was defensible. The risky strategy was to spend large amounts of money he didn't have on a dramatically larger staff in the hope that a better product would instantly bring in so much more new revenue that it would cover his costs. As I wrote earlier, Kushner himself essentially admitted as much, saying he wished he'd taken ten years to build up his papers rather than ten months.

So why did he do it? Kushner blamed the pension obligations he took on when his group bought Freedom Communications. He blamed the failure of his bid to add the *San Diego Union-Tribune* to his holdings, saying that would have brought rationality to the Southern California newspaper market. (The *Union-Tribune* was purchased in May 2015 by Tribune Publishing, owner of the *Los Angeles Times*. At the time, Tribune's chief executive officer was none other than Kushner's former partner Jack Griffin.)[62] But still: Why did he make the fundamental mistake of hiring many dozens of journalists that he couldn't afford? "You have to take your shots," he replied. "If you only have one, you'd better make it a good one." He added: "I think in the newspaper business you have to make mistakes. The biggest risk we felt going in — and I still feel the biggest risk — is not trying new things."

Why did he decide to buy the *Riverside Press-Enterprise* and to launch new dailies in Long Beach and, especially, Los Angeles, which debuted even as budget cuts were beginning to take hold? His answer: The *Los Angeles Register* was a success. "It was both growing quickly and approaching operating profitability," he said. "With under forty people we were able to produce a newspaper that by most measures was as good as the *LA Times*."

What did he have to say to the journalists who had taken a gamble on his vision only to find themselves out of work in a matter of months? "We were very explicit that we were going to try something that no one had ever tried before," he replied. "We were going to put it all on the line to try and fight our way through to a different and healthier growing newspaper. I was very explicit with the people that I recruited, with the other executives on the team, that this was going to be a really challenging experiment."

Later, in a follow-up interview, Kushner said he believed that newspaper owners were starting to emphasize quality as a way to make their papers more attractive — and he believed that had begun with the improvements he had made to the *Register*. "Prior to that there were only really two veins of thought," he said. "One was that newspapers are in a permanent and irretrievable death spiral, and it's happening really fast and no one can stop it. The other vein of thought was that the absolutely only hope — and where everyone should spend 100 percent of their time — is on digital. As you look today at some of the leaders in the industry, even the ones who are primarily focused on digital, there is a steady and consistent secondary stream, and in some cases a primary stream, that focuses on the quality of the journalism. I wouldn't say I'm personally responsible for that, but we were the leading proponents of quality and that the core work really matters, not just from an academic perspective but from a business perspective. And I think that the legacy of that outlasted my leadership of the *Register*."

At the time that I interviewed Kushner and, a few days later, Eric Spitz, it was clear that the two did not get along. Kushner, in his elliptical manner, criticized his "former partner" for writing and speaking critically about other newspaper executives. Spitz, much more direct, told me, "My personal feeling about Aaron is that he's a nice guy, a smart guy. I think he's one of the worst people managers that I've ever met in my life."

Spitz remained a firm believer in what I've referred to as the sensible half of the strategy that he and Kushner pursued. Indeed, he referred me to a *Wall Street Journal* commentary he wrote in which he asserted: "The newspaper industry has erected two idols that must be smashed. The first is the notion that digital information must be free. The second is that the newspaper business can only be saved by digital solutions. Both are false."[63] And he touted a YouTube video of a talk he had given at the Reverend Rick Warren's Saddleback Church, located in Orange County, in which he offered an analogy to describe what he considered the mistake newspapers made in giving away their journalism online. "I like to point to McDonald's," he told the assembled crowd. "McDonald's does a great job. You walk in the store, they'll give you ketchup, they'll give you napkins, they'll give you Wi-Fi in the stores and a beautiful television with cable TV on it. But they'll never give you a cheeseburger."[64]

As Spitz told it, he deferred to Kushner during the early days of their Southern California adventure but began to assert himself — behind the scenes — as it became clear that Kushner was hiring and spending his way to ruin. Additional papers were bought and launched, Spitz said, not because it was a good idea, but because of the need to spread out the new hires and to find new sources of revenue. I asked him about Kushner's contention that the *Los Angeles Register* had been close to profitability when it was shut down. "It is a farce to believe that it was anywhere close to a success. It was a silly idea," Spitz replied, though he agreed with Kushner that the journalistic quality was good. (Kushner told me by email that he didn't have a paid-circulation number for the *LA Register*.[65] Spitz said he wasn't sure, but estimated it at somewhere between 11,000 and 15,000.) The money owed to the *Los Angeles Times* and the Associated Press? Kushner, Spitz said, "thought it was a reasonable medium-term plan to finance the business on the backs of the vendors. We had so much vendor debt that it was crazy. That's what ended up stopping us. That's when the train stopped moving."

According to Spitz's narrative, it was he who brought in Richard Mirman to replace Kushner as publisher (Kushner said at the time[66] and, many months later, repeated to me that it was his own idea), and it was he who engineered Kushner's and his own resignations from their management jobs in March 2015. Spitz said he resigned as president so that Kushner would not be the only executive to step down, helping him to save face. In reality, Spitz stayed on until the paper was sold months later.

It would be an exaggeration to suggest that Spitz — a graduate of MIT's Sloan School of Management and the former chief financial officer of the Narragansett beer company — is bullish on the newspaper business. But even after his experience with Freedom Communications, he believed that he and Kushner might have succeeded if they had taken a more modest approach as they pursued their strategy of emphasizing print and ending free distribution.

"It's important to me that the story be told correctly," he said. "And it is also important to me that what we were trying to do is understood. I still think our strategy is correct. And correct doesn't mean it's going to be a super successful strategy. But it's the only strategy left. The newspaper solution is not going to be a digital one." Despite the precipitous drop in newspaper advertising, Spitz observed that nearly all newspapers still make most of their revenues from their print editions. Consumers find print to be the most satisfying form of advertising, he said, and digital the least. No one, he added, clicks on banner ads (by one measure, the rate in 2015 was fewer than two clicks per 1,000 impressions).[67] And ad-blocking software, he noted, was proving to be a popular way of avoiding commercial intrusions.

Spitz reserved his real venom, though, for the idea that newspapers should give away their content online. I pushed back, pointing out that customers can't be blamed for believing that content should be included in the hundreds of dollars a month they spend on internet access and digital devices or that journalism on television and radio has traditionally been free. Spitz would have none of it, saying that the economics of newspapers has never supported free content. "The biggest strategic mistake in the history of American business was the moment when the industry as an industry determined that it was OK to take its core product and price it at zero," Spitz said. "In addition to losing the revenue, you are training an entire generation of people that your product has no value. It is a race to the bottom."

IF AARON KUSHNER HAD had Jeff Bezos's or John Henry's deep pockets, he could have operated his Southern California papers at a loss in perpetuity if that's what he wanted to do. With sufficient capital, Kushner also would have had the flexibility to readjust, scale back, and try something else. He should not be criticized for an experiment, even a grand one. Rather, as Kimberly Kindy said, he should be taken to task for experimenting with large amounts of other people's money and other people's lives knowing — as only he and a few others knew — that he would have to start dismantling the whole thing if his unicorns-and-rainbows projections fell short.

But could a less ambitious version of Kushner's plan have worked, as Spitz and Kushner himself have suggested? It's possible. The paper he and his fellow investors acquired had been decimated by years of cuts. An improved print paper might very well have proved popular with Orange County readers. And if he had adopted a metered paywall rather than closing off digital access to all except paying subscribers, the *Register* could have pursued digital advertising and used online content to entice visitors into becoming customers, as the *Washington Post,* the *Boston Globe,* and many other newspapers are doing.

"If all he did was hire twenty-five new reporters, that would have won him the goodwill of the newsroom. That would have won him positive publicity," Gustavo Arellano told me. "It would have won him maybe not all the NPR, *USA Today,* and *New York Times* stories. But at the very least, it would have won him the newsroom. And the sad part is, the *Register* had been beaten down so much that they literally fell for a confidence man. That's what he is, ultimately. A confidence man."

Gabriel Kahn, a former *Wall Street Journal* journalist who's now a professor at the University of Southern California's Annenberg School for Communication and Journalism, offered a similar assessment. Not long after Kushner had acquired the *Register,* he delivered a talk at Annenberg. Kushner's analysis of what had gone wrong under the previous ownership, Kahn told me, was smart and on point. "I thought the initial strategy had some potential," Kahn said. "There were elements of it that seemed to make sense to me — putting some more resources into the print product. Trying to make that more attractive. I think there's a sensible way to close down some of the free digital access. Having an iron gate slammed down in front of people is not the way to do it."[68]

What Kahn found astonishing was that Kushner kept expanding his empire even as it was becoming obvious that his ideas weren't working. Buying the *Press-Enterprise* seemed like a good move to Kahn because it was a money-making paper in a contiguous market. Launching the *Long Beach Register*, though, struck him as "foolhardy." The *Los Angeles Register*? "Beyond delusional." Months later, I asked Kahn what he thought of Kushner's contention that the *LA Register* had come close to succeeding. His response echoed Spitz's. "Let's look at history," Kahn told me by email. "How many times has a new entrant into a newspaper market ever made ends meet, ever? It's a trail of tears."[69]

And yet I would argue that Kushner does have one important quality in common with Jeff Bezos and John Henry: he is genuinely civic-minded, and he believes in journalism as a way of knitting together the fabric of a community. You can only shake your head over his out-of-control spending and how unlikely it was that he would ever get ahead of that curve. But he wanted to do something great. As his confidential plan to purchase the *Boston Globe* put it: "This is about who brings us together as a community. This is about what our community looks like without the paper. This is about what our community could look like with the paper filling even half of its potential."[70]

In the fall of 2015, Freedom Communications declared bankruptcy for the second time in less than a decade. The *Register* reported that the declaration "would end Kushner's ownership stake in Freedom." Mirman, as chief executive officer and publisher, and Spitz, who had been named chairman at some point after his stage-managed "resignation," would retain their ownership stakes and would lead a group that intended to purchase the company. "I am confident our bid will be successful," Mirman wrote in a memo to employees, "and the company will emerge with a solid financial foundation and well-positioned for future success."[71]

It was not to be, as the local group was outbid. The courts rejected an offer from Tribune Publishing on antitrust grounds. Given that the company already owned the *Los Angeles Times* and the *San Diego Union-Tribune*, the Department of Justice argued and a federal judge agreed that allowing Tribune to own the *Register* and the *Press-Enterprise*, the two largest daily newspapers in between, would give it an illegal monopoly. Instead, Freedom was acquired by Digital First Media, which owned a group of smaller papers in the region, for just a bit under $50 million. Digital First celebrated its victory with a purge. Seventy employees from across the company were let go — including Rob Curley, who was later named editor of the *Spokane Spokesman-Review.*[72]

In September 2016, the new owners announced that the *Register* would move from Santa Ana to Anaheim. The move would allow the building's owner, Mike Harrah, to redevelop the site. Freedom had sold the building to Harrah in 2014 as its finances were spinning out of control.[73] Later, Spitz told me, Harrah was part of his and Mirman's bid to buy Freedom out of bankruptcy.

Sadly, the *Orange County Register* and the *Riverside Press-Enterprise* had become exactly what Aaron Kushner disdained: corporate, chain-owned dailies, focused on the bottom line, cutting expenses in the hope of staying ahead of losses, and — in all likelihood — waiting for the next sucker to come along believing he or she had come up with a better way of running a newspaper.

CHAPTER EIGHT

MONEY ISN'T EVERYTHING

Why Wealthy Ownership Doesn't Guarantee Success

FOR ALL THE LARGER FORCES that have battered the newspaper business over the past quarter-century, the good papers have remained good because of the character and intentions of the people who own them. It has ever been thus. The *New York Times* is the *New York Times* because Adolph Ochs and his descendants were dedicated to great journalism. The *Washington Post* changed history because Katharine Graham stood up to Richard Nixon. What makes Jeff Bezos's ownership of the *Post* and John Henry's of the *Boston Globe* interesting and important is that they understand their newspapers' civic and journalistic mission. So did Aaron Kushner, flawed though his vision for the *Orange County Register* may have been.

Bezos and Henry are not the only wealthy individuals who have purchased newspapers in recent years. From Omaha to Philadelphia, from Chicago to Las Vegas, billionaires have scooped up papers in the hope of making money, feeding their ego, or serving a political agenda. Not one of them, though, has put journalistic excellence first. The unfortunate result is that all have fallen short in developing a financially sustainable model while serving the information needs of the communities.

Corporate chain ownership remains very much a part of the newspaper scene as well. With their relentless focus on the bottom line in an era of declining revenues, many of the papers these corporations own have been downsized so drastically that they can offer only a fraction of the coverage they did years earlier. What happens when the local daily paper no longer fulfills its vital role? At the close of this chapter I'll take a look at Burlington, Vermont, where several small news organizations have risen to the occasion by filling some of those gaps.

First, though, let us consider Warren Buffett, the kindly billionaire who has emerged as a significant owner of midsized newspapers. Buffett is by no means the worst owner a newspaper could have. But anyone who hoped he would establish himself as an innovative force in recalibrating the economics of journalism has to be disappointed.

WHEN BUFFETT'S BERKSHIRE HATHAWAY investment company purchased sixty-three newspapers from the Media General chain in 2012 for $142 million, the news was greeted with the hope that the legendary octogenarian might be just the person to show the way forward. Buffett bolstered his new holdings by extending loans to those papers totaling $445 million. It was a generous gesture with which Aaron Kushner and his investors, who also wanted the papers, could not compete. A year earlier Buffett had bought his hometown paper, the *Omaha World-Herald*, along with six other papers for $200 million. He already owned the *Buffalo News*. And in those pre-Bezos days, he held a substantial number of shares in the Washington Post Company. "Does Warren E. Buffett want to be a media mogul?" asked the *New York Times*.[1]

Certainly Buffett had the right pedigree. Not only was he a brilliant financial thinker, but he had long loved newspapers and had been a close adviser to the Graham family at the *Washington Post* for many years. He even had a hand in winning a Pulitzer Prize: in 1973, when he was the owner of the *Omaha Sun*, he helped his reporters investigate a local charity by finding documents, providing financial analysis, and even assisting with the writing.[2] Katharine Graham praised Buffett fulsomely in her autobiography, saying that he became a trusted confidant after he invested in the Washington Post Company. "By the spring of 1974," she wrote, "Warren was sending me a constant flow of helpful memos with advice, and occasionally alerting me to problems of which I was unaware."[3]

Yet Buffett, astute financier that he is, expressed skepticism about prospects for the newspaper business after it entered its long decline. In 2009, for instance, he said he had no interest in purchasing papers, because their financial outlook was so grim. "For most newspapers in the United States, we would not buy them at any price," he said. "They have the possibility of going to just unending losses."[4] And though he later reversed himself, his acquisition strategy gravitated toward papers of the type that still do reasonably well: those in medium-sized markets where the local paper is the principal source of regional and community news and where competition from the internet is less a factor than it is in large cities. Buffett's papers carry little debt and are profitable. In the spring of 2016, though, he admitted that the picture was continuing to darken for the newspaper business and that he was no closer to finding a way out than anyone else.

"We haven't cracked the code yet," he told *USA Today.* "Circulation continues to decline at a significant pace, advertising at an even faster pace. The easy cutting has taken place. There's no indication that anyone besides the national papers has found a way." He added that even though all of his papers were making money (at that time he was up to thirty-two dailies and forty-seven weeklies), that might not be the case in future years. "If you have a problem in five years, you have a problem now," he said.[5] Buffett doubled down on those remarks in early 2017, telling CNBC that the *New York Times,* the *Wall Street Journal,* and possibly the *Washington Post* were the only newspapers he believed had an "assured future," explaining, "They have developed an online presence that people will pay for."[6]

Less than two months later, the hammer came down at BH Media, the company Buffett had set up to manage his newspapers. BH Media announced the termination of 289 positions throughout the chain, including the elimination of 108 vacant jobs. The BH Media president and chief executive officer, Terry Kroeger, told the *Omaha World-Herald* that Buffett had been informed of the reductions but that "his opinion was not sought or offered," in keeping with Buffett's hands-off investment philosophy. Kroeger blamed the papers' declining revenue on changes in retail advertising, and especially on the move to online shopping — an irony given how the most successful of the new breed of newspaper owners, Jeff Bezos, made his money.[7] Buffett's *World-Herald* did not suffer any cuts at that time. But then, in May, BH Media reduced the size of the Omaha paper and eliminated three jobs, according to a memo to the staff from the executive editor, Melissa Matczak.[8]

For a self-confessed newspaper fan whose net worth was roughly the same as that of Bezos (more than $60 billion apiece in mid-2016),[9] Buffett's role in helping to figure out the future of journalism might be considered disappointingly modest. Perhaps it would be too much to expect someone in his mid-eighties to dedicate himself to figuring out the future of the newspapers he had acquired. But he was ideally positioned to bring in the sorts of minds who might apply themselves to the task of saving smaller papers in much the same way that Bezos and Henry were attempting to reinvent their much larger properties. Surely Buffett understands as much as anyone that readers and advertisers will put up with an ever-diminishing paper for only so long before an irreversible downward spiral sets in.

IF WE MIGHT WISH that Warren Buffett would take a more active role rather than play the avuncular Daddy Warbucks presiding benignly over the long, slow death of his newspapers, then surely the opposite is the case with Sam Zell. In 2008, Zell, a pugnacious Chicago real estate magnate, purchased what was then known as Tribune Company for $8.2 billion. Although Tribune was a diversified media company (among other holdings, it owned the Chicago Cubs at the time of Zell's acquisition), it was best known as the home of some of the country's most storied newspapers: the *Chicago Tribune,* founded by Colonel Robert McCormick, a notorious right-wing eccentric; the *Los Angeles Times,* transformed into one of the great American newspapers in the 1960s and '70s by Otis Chandler, scion of the families that had run the paper since shortly after its founding in 1881; and Connecticut's *Hartford Courant,* begun in 1764 and considered to be the oldest continuously published newspaper in the country.[10]

Zell was not the only billionaire owner to wreak havoc at the newspapers he acquired, nor is he likely to be the last. For instance, in 2015, the casino mogul Sheldon Adelson secretly purchased the *Las Vegas Review-Journal,* possibly for the purpose of tormenting a judge he had tangled with. The evidence: Two small Connecticut newspapers owned by an Adelson associate who was brought in to manage the *Review-Journal* published a long, plagiarism-filled, apparently pseudonymous article that was critical of the judge. To say the least, it seems unlikely that readers of those Connecticut papers, the *Bristol Press* and the *New Britain Herald,* had any interest in the arcana of the Nevada state court system.[11]

Adelson's purchase of the Las Vegas paper stands out just for its plain weirdness. Zell deserves special mention, though, because of the sheer size and influence of his newspapers. Tribune had suffered through years of unstable ownership before Zell arrived. He promptly went about making things much worse. A particularly memorable moment took place in early 2008, when he told journalists at one of his newspapers, the *Orlando Sentinel,* that they should be in the business of giving their readers what they wanted. A female photographer responded sarcastically that readers preferred "puppy dogs" to real news, which brought this retort from Zell: "You're giving me the classic . . . journalistic arrogance of deciding that puppies don't count." And more to the point: "Fuck you."[12]

Zell reportedly called the photographer at least twice to apologize,[13] but it's not known whether he ever apologized for the mess he made of his newspapers. The late David Carr of the *New York Times* wrote a monumental takedown of Zell's ownership in 2010, noting that Zell had managed to purchase the company with just $315 million of his own money, financing the rest by borrowing and by raiding the employee stock ownership plan. Carr portrayed Tribune as a dystopian hellhole of sexual harassment, incompetent management, and vulgarity that Zell drove into bankruptcy less than a year after he bought it. Some 4,200 people lost their jobs. "They were like fourteen-year-old boys — no boundaries at all — but with money and power," an employee named Liz Richards told Carr.[14]

Tribune emerged from bankruptcy in late 2012, but the following years were no less tumultuous. In 2014, the post-Zell company was split in two, with the profitable television stations being placed under the umbrella of Tribune Media and the newspapers going with Tribune Publishing.[15] Despite talk of spinning off some of the papers, the executives running Tribune Publishing kept them together. Indeed, Austin Beutner, the well-regarded publisher of the *Los Angeles Times* in 2014–15, was fired amid reports that he was pushing for the *Times* and the Tribune-owned *San Diego Union-Tribune* to be sold to local owners. In a speaking appearance at Harvard University in early 2016, Beutner said he still hoped local ownership might be the future for those two papers, adding he thought they should be combined with the *Orange County Register.* A Southern California newspaper group, he said, could have "a more rational conversation with advertisers" than a national chain.[16] As we saw earlier, though, government antitrust regulators and the courts had other ideas about the Southern California market.

Beutner's wishes aside, the executives running Tribune Publishing showed no sign that they wanted to break up their holdings — or, for that matter, to sell them to anyone else. The maneuvering for control of Tribune Publishing grew especially confusing and contentious in 2016. Michael Ferro, a Chicago investor who emerged as chairman, pushed out the company's chief executive, Jack Griffin, the erstwhile Aaron Kushner partner who later sued him. Ferro also had to fight off a lawsuit against Tribune

Publishing charging that the company had ignored its fiduciary duty to shareholders by spurning a takeover bid by the newspaper chain Gannett.[17]

Then came one of the more bizarre moments in the annals of the newspaper business. In June 2016, the company issued a press release announcing that it was changing its name to tronc, Inc., with a lowercase *t*. The name was bad enough, but the strategy was couched in the sort of corporate gobbledygook that inspires — depending on your inclination — tears or laughter. Tronc (which stands for "tribune online content") would be "a content curation and monetization company focused on creating and distributing premium, verified content across all channels."[18] So much for "Honey, get me rewrite." For a while, Gannett continued its fight to acquire the company. In the fall, though, Gannett finally walked away — although others entered the picture, and turmoil over the future of tronc continued well into 2017.[19]

Sam Zell may be gone, but his legacy will linger for years at the newspapers he once ran. If Warren Buffett has shown that small, debt-free newspapers can be profitable, Zell demonstrated that bad ownership can push precarious newspapers that much closer to the edge and endanger their long-term viability.

IT IS HARD TO IMAGINE two major metropolitan newspapers more similar than the *Boston Globe* and the *Philadelphia Inquirer*. They sell almost exactly the same number of copies (the *Globe*'s paid print circulation was 138,000 on weekdays and 252,000 on Sundays in early 2016; the *Inquirer*'s was 138,000 on weekdays and 277,000 on Sundays).[20] They serve regions of roughly equivalent size (according to 2015 census estimates there were nearly 4.8 million people living in the Boston metropolitan area and slightly more than 6 million in metro Philadelphia).[21] And they share similar histories. Both papers won their first Pulitzer Prizes relatively late, the *Globe* in 1966 for reporting on an ethically dubious judicial nomination, the *Inquirer* in 1975 for a deep dive into the Internal Revenue Service.[22] And both papers thrived under legendary editors, with Tom Winship running the *Globe* from 1964 to 1985 and Gene Roberts directing the *Inquirer* from 1972 to 1990.[23] The two papers have won multiple Pulitzers over the years and were considered among the best regional newspapers long after their marquee editors had retired.

There was, however, one significant difference. The *Globe* benefited from responsible ownership after the newspaper business started to decline. By contrast, the ownership situation at the *Inquirer* and its sister paper, the tabloid *Daily News*, was confused and, at times, chaotic. Joel Mathis, who covered the media scene for *Philadelphia* magazine for a number of years, put it this way: "Everything that could go bad has gone bad. And multiple times."[24]

At the dawn of the new century, the *Inquirer* was part of the Knight Ridder chain, a quality-conscious group of newspapers that included the *Miami Herald* and the *San Jose Mercury News.* Knight Ridder's excellence extended to its national reporting. In the run-up to the war in Iraq, the chain's Washington bureau produced work that was notably skeptical about the Bush administration's claims that Saddam Hussein possessed weapons of mass destruction — journalism that might have changed US policy if it had been published, say, in the *New York Times* or the *Washington Post.*[25]

Within Knight Ridder, though, all was not well, as the chain's business executives sought to squeeze their newspapers in order to drive up profits. In April 2001, the editor of the *San Jose Mercury News,* Jay Harris, briefly attained celebrity status by quitting rather than imposing budget cuts ordered by Knight Ridder that were likely to result in layoffs. "I neither believe nor will accept that the current trend can't be changed, that the proper balance can't be restored, that the unwise is somehow unavoidable," Harris said in a speech before the American Society of Newspaper Editors.[26] Later that year Marty Baron left Knight Ridder's *Miami Herald* after just eighteen months as executive editor in order to accept an offer to become editor of the *Globe.* Although Baron did not publicly criticize his former employer, the *Herald,* like the *Mercury News,* was cutting back on international coverage — something the *Globe* did not do until years later.[27] Among media observers, the consensus was that Baron had gotten out while the getting was good.

Knight Ridder ceased operations in 2006, selling its thirty-two newspapers to the much smaller McClatchy group for $4.5 billion. That proved to be little more than a pit stop for the Philadelphia papers, as McClatchy immediately announced that twelve of its newly acquired papers would be spun off, including the *Inquirer* and the *Daily News.* Although all twelve were reportedly profitable, they were located in less affluent cities where the prospects for growth were dismal.[28] Within weeks, the Philadelphia papers were acquired for $562 million ($412 million of it in the form of debt) by a local group calling itself Philadelphia Media Holdings and headed by Brian Tierney, a Philadelphia public relations executive, who became the publisher.[29]

By most accounts, Tierney was not a bad owner — just an underfunded one. One of his best decisions was to hire Bill Marimow as his editor. Marimow, a Pulitzer Prize winner who'd worked for Gene Roberts, had a stellar track record that included stints at NPR and as editor of the *Baltimore Sun.* Tierney also invested millions of dollars in both print and digital. Still, he found himself unable to turn around the papers' finances, and by mid-2007 he was already cutting back, telling the *Columbia Journalism Review* that "in the end, we've got to do what we've got to do, and keep moving ahead. The dogs bark, the caravan rolls on."[30]

Michael Schaffer, the editor of *Washingtonian* magazine, covered Philadelphia city politics for the *Inquirer* from 2003 to 2007. Tierney, he said, seemed to believe that the personal touch was all it would take to restore his battered papers. "His whole shtick was 'the old guys let the place go to shit,'" Schaffer told me. "This was such a classic Philadelphia thing, where hack-to-hack personal transactionalism will make everything OK. To me there were a lot of reasons why department stores were buying less ads than they used to. Maybe it was Knight Ridder being lazy, but most of it had to do with rational things. A lot of people reduced their ad buys in newspapers in the first decade of the twenty-first century. It wasn't because of personal warmth or a lack of personal warmth."[31]

C. W. Anderson, an associate professor of media culture at the College of Staten Island, studied the Philadelphia newspapers for his 2013 book, *Rebuilding the News: Metropolitan Journalism in the Digital Age.* He told me that Tierney's biggest problem was that he paid too much and couldn't find a way to get out from under the debt he had taken on. Without that burden, he said, Tierney might have found a path forward. "He was not at the point where he was harvesting the papers for their organs," Anderson said. In fact, Anderson believed that Tierney's ideas for transitioning from print to digital were promising. "He moved the entire Philly.com staff out of the *Inquirer* building and gave them slick corporate offices downtown," Anderson said. "It was a very different sort of feel and culture and mission than the *Inquirer* and the *Daily News* had. To me that's not stupid. That's not a bad idea. It just didn't work."[32]

In February 2009, Tierney took his papers into bankruptcy, setting off a long period of chaos. Tierney had hoped to emerge as the head of a new, restructured newspaper company, but it was not to be.[33] Hedge funds took over, and Bill Marimow was demoted to the reporting ranks; a short time later he left for Arizona State University. Despite it all, the *Inquirer* began work on a story that won the 2012 Pulitzer for Public Service, on violence in Philadelphia's public schools. Marimow approved it and his replacement, Stan Wischnowski, saw it through. In his book *Pulitzer's Gold*, Roy J. Harris Jr. wrote that "even as the story progressed, the *Inquirer* newsroom felt more and more like it was being torn apart in a battle for control by rival teams of owners."[34]

The ownership woes seemed to be winding down in early 2012 when a group of local investors purchased the papers. Marimow was brought back as editor.[35] But the new owners fought one another for control. Marimow was actually removed again in October 2013 for, among other things, refusing to carry out several firings ordered by the publisher. Marimow was reinstated a month later by the judge who was presiding over a lawsuit involving the warring co-owners.[36] Resolution came in the spring of 2014 when two of the pro-Marimow investors — Lewis Katz and H. F. "Gerry" Lenfest — won an auction to acquire the properties for $88 million, a fraction of what the Tierney group had paid just eight years earlier. Then, incredibly, Katz and six other passengers were killed just a few weeks later when the small plane in which they were flying crashed in Massachusetts.[37]

That left Lenfest in charge. A philanthropist who had made his fortune in the cable television business, Lenfest was in his eighties at the time of Katz's death and was, at best, a reluctant owner. Joel Mathis believes Lenfest and Katz never even wanted the papers. As part-owners already, he said, they were likely trying to drive up the auction price in order to get a better deal. "Gerry Lenfest has said multiple times since then that he did not expect to win that auction," Mathis told me. "He did not expect to have to write a check that day. He thought he was going to be getting a check that day."[38]

It wasn't long before Lenfest started looking for a way out. In the fall of

2015, *Billy Penn,* a start-up online-only news site, broke a story that Lenfest was exploring the possibility of turning over the *Inquirer,* the *Daily News,* and Philly.com to a nonprofit institution, most likely Temple University.[39] Within weeks, the papers announced a round of downsizing and layoffs, with the three newsrooms being merged into one.[40] By the time the cutting was over, the newsroom was down to about 250 staff members for the three entities, compared with 400 in 2007 and more than 600 in the golden era of the 1990s.[41]

Then, in January 2016, Lenfest made an announcement that garnered national attention. It wasn't quite what *Billy Penn* had reported, but it was close. Lenfest donated the Philadelphia Media Network, or PMN, as the three media properties were then known, to a branch of the nonprofit Philadelphia Foundation set up for the purpose of running the papers called the Institute for Journalism in New Media. He also endowed the institute with $20 million of his fortune. The media properties would remain for-profit, though they would be reorganized as a "public-benefit corporation," easing the standard corporate requirement that it maximize earnings. The nonprofit institute that would run the papers would be governed by a board of civic leaders and journalism experts. "Of all the things I've done, this is the most important. Because of the journalism," Lenfest said.[42] A year later, the organization he established was renamed the Lenfest Institute for Journalism.[43]

The Philadelphia media outlets weren't the first for-profit media holdings to be owned by a nonprofit organization, although there were aspects of the "public-benefit corporation" arrangement — too obscure to get into here — that made Philadelphia unique. Perhaps the best known of these hybrids is the *Tampa Bay Times,* a for-profit newspaper owned by the non-profit Poynter Institute, a journalism education organization. The *Times*'s experience illustrates why Lenfest's solution may be no panacea. The original idea was that profits from the *Times* would subsidize Poynter, and that worked well for many years. As newspaper profits disappeared, though, the *Times* had to cut back just like most newspapers — and Poynter suffered financially as a result.[44] (Other for-profit papers owned by nonprofit organizations, including the *New London Day* of Connecticut and the *New Hampshire Union Leader,* have also been hit by serious cuts in recent years.) By contrast with the Poynter setup, the Philadelphia arrangement is based on the notion that the nonprofit organization would subsidize the for-profit newspaper, at least in a limited way.

Among the first members appointed to the nonprofit institute in Philadelphia was David Boardman, dean of the School of Media and Communication at Temple University and former executive editor of the *Seattle Times*. When we spoke, Boardman stressed that the nonprofit arrangement wasn't about providing operating revenues to PMN, or even about saving the papers. Rather, he saw it as a way to funnel resources into experiments that not only might help the Philadelphia papers find a way to sustainability but could benefit the newspaper business as a whole. "It's intended to help support and be a catalyst for innovation and transformation that will help further the cause of public-interest journalism in the region," he said. "We believe that the newsroom of PMN is an important element in that, but I don't think any of us think that the money that is produced by this endowment should be limited to PMN." The kinds of initiatives Boardman envisioned supporting were digital tools, new ways of engaging with the audience, and networking with other news organizations, as well as specific public-interest reporting projects.[45]

Clearly, then, the nonprofit arrangement in Philadelphia has its limits in terms of securing a viable future for the city's newspapers. The three entities need to break even or turn a profit in order to avoid more downsizing. Not to be too downbeat, though — there would be no more musical chairs in the owner's suite and no pressure to generate revenues that would then be sent to some distant corporate headquarters. The Philadelphia model is a promising response to the challenge of trying to operate big city newspapers in the twenty-first century. But it is not in and of itself a solution.

I visited the offices of the *Inquirer* and the *Daily News* just a few days after Gerry Lenfest announced the nonprofit arrangement, meeting with *Inquirer* editor Bill Marimow and Stan Wischnowski, the man who had once replaced Marimow. Wischnowski had only recently been named executive editor and senior vice president of PMN, with each of the three entities having its own editor and reporting to him.[46] The mood in my interviews with Marimow and Wischnowski and at a news meeting I attended later that morning was, to invoke a cliché, one of cautious optimism.

Marimow was still smarting from an article by the newspaper analyst

Ken Doctor in which he mocked Marimow for telling another interviewer that the nonprofit arrangement would "guarantee the perpetuation of values and traditions of the *Inquirer*, the *Daily News*, and Philly.com for generations to come." Doctor's dyspeptic opening: "Say it ain't so."[47] Marimow said he thought Doctor's tone was "mean-spirited."[48]

"In my opinion," Marimow told me, "creating this dual organization is a visionary idea. With a public-benefit corporation, as I understand it — I'm not an attorney — there's a real balance: there's parity between the mandate to do great journalism and the mandate to have an economically viable business. But the priority is no longer maximizing profits. It's having sufficient profits to keep producing good journalism." One advantage Marimow cited was the opportunity to apply for grant money to undertake, say, "a two-year project on the benefits of charter schools." Under the new ownership model, the grant would be awarded to the nonprofit institute, and thus the donor would be able to take a tax write-off.

Marimow acknowledged, however, that achieving economic sustainability would not necessarily be any easier under nonprofit ownership. Given the realities of declining advertising revenues, Marimow's solution was the same one that was being tried elsewhere: moving away from the free web model and instead charging for digital subscriptions. Philly.com and the two newspaper websites (the three were later combined into one site) were free at the time of my visit. Marimow was convinced that readers would pay if they were asked. He recalled speaking to about 200 people at a synagogue. He asked how many people read the *Inquirer* for free, and about sixty hands went up. He then asked how many would pay for a digital subscription, and about forty or fifty people raised their hands. "To me, that demonstrates that there's a solid group of regular readers who'd be willing to pay a small fee, and I don't believe that they were bullshitting me," Marimow said. "I believe most of them were telling the truth."

Significantly, Marimow — like Jeff Bezos in his first town hall meeting at the *Washington Post* — also spoke up for the primacy of the bundle rather than trying to sell journalism one article at a time. Though it might make sense in the digital age for a regional newspaper to focus entirely on local and regional news, Marimow said it was important to offer respectable national and international coverage as well, even if it was pulled together from wire services. "Our mission is to provide indispensable news for residents of Philadelphia, the Pennsylvania suburbs, and South Jersey," he said, "along with a sufficiently deep report on the national and foreign fronts so that people with an interest in those subjects do not have to read the *New York Times* or the *Wall Street Journal,* along with great sports, entertainment, etcetera focused on this region." The question remains, of course, whether the bundle can survive the transition from print to digital. Older readers might like it. But the idea of relying primarily on one (or two or three) news services that you pay for would seem to cut against the online habits of anyone under the age of, say, forty. Or fifty.

Throughout the short history of newspapers and their relationship with the web, opinions have varied — and changed — as to how tightly their digital operations ought to be integrated with the rest of the newsroom. C. W. Anderson, you may recall, thought it was a good idea when Brian Tierney moved Philly.com out of the *Inquirer*'s and *Daily News*'s headquarters so that it could develop its own ethos. Likewise, Washingtonpost.Newsweek Interactive was at one time located across the Potomac in Arlington, Virginia, and the *Boston Globe*'s Boston.com site operated out of two different downtown locations before the operation was finally moved to the *Globe*'s Dorchester facility.

In recent years, though, newspapers have increasingly embraced the model of an integrated newsroom. In Philadelphia, that integration comprises not just digital but also two print properties with very different sensibilities, as stories in either paper could appear in the other as well as online. It was this integration that Stan Wischnowski was working on during my visit in early 2016. "I'm thinking of it as one newsroom with a content/audience-first approach, as opposed to the three operating independently," he told me, explaining that it was no longer economically feasible to, say, assign separate reporters from the *Inquirer* and the *Daily News* to cover the same event. "We've basically broken into teams," he said, "and we have a news team that does all our metropolitan, suburban, business, health news."[49]

It's an unusual idea made possible by the fact that PMN owns both a traditional regional broadsheet and an urban tabloid — the only such arrangement in the country, though it's not unheard of in the United Kingdom and Canada. (Rupert Murdoch's media empire owns both the New York–based *Wall Street Journal* and the *New York Post,* but there is no integration between the two, and the *Journal* does not cover local news.) Wischnowski said the goal was to offer a different sensibility for different audiences in terms of packaging, headlines, and having unique columnists at each paper. But Will Bunch, a columnist at the *Daily News*, told me he was concerned that the tabloid would be marginalized under the arrangement and that long-standing tensions between the two newsrooms might arise anew. "Instead of having two reporters covering that trial," Bunch said, "now you have got one reporter, and the second reporter is free to find the story that nobody was doing. I think most people think that's a great idea. It's the execution. We'll see."[50]

DESPITE (or, perhaps, because of) the shrinkage of Philadelphia's daily newspapers, the city in 2016 remained a vibrant home for all manner of media projects. Although the alt-weekly *Philadelphia City Paper* shut down in the fall of 2015, there were signs of life on a variety of other fronts. Joel Mathis told me that *Philadelphia* magazine had expanded its local news coverage, especially online, because of what he called "the decline of the *Inquirer*." (Cuts later hit the magazine as well. Mathis left a few months after I interviewed him, and in early 2017, a major downsizing of *Philadelphia*'s digital operations was announced.)[51] The city's much-admired public radio station, WHYY, covered local and regional news. Veterans of Philadelphia's media scene had started online projects such as the lifestyle-oriented *Philly Voice* and the civic-minded *Philadelphia Citizen*. None, though, drew as much attention as *Billy Penn*, a for-profit, mobile-first site aimed at millennials that was launched in 2014 by Jim Brady, a pioneer in digital journalism stretching back to the 1990s.[52] *Billy Penn* stands as a paradigmatic example of the kinds of journalistic experiments that can thrive when the local daily newspaper falters. It also stands as an example of the limits of those experiments.

Billy Penn, originally dubbed *Brother.ly*, was hatched at Temple University's Center for Public Interest Journalism.[53] By the time I visited the city, in January 2016, the project had moved to Pipeline, a co-working space for start-ups on the fifteenth floor of a tower that commanded a stunning view of Philadelphia's city hall. Dozens of people were working in an enormous space, but only a few of them worked for *Billy Penn*. Two of what Brady calls "reporter/curators" were sitting on a bench, pecking at their laptops. In a relatively quiet corner I sat down with Brady and *Billy P*[illegible]r, Chris Krewson, a former executive editor of the *Inquirer*'s onlin[illegible]ons who was lured back from the West Coast to help Brady desig[illegible] a new form of local journalism.

I asked Brady to explain *Billy Penn* to me. "I can't pick an exact age, but roughly, the way people thirty-five and under consume news and information is so wildly different from the way people older than that consume news and information," he replied, explaining that the idea was to target that audience by taking advantage of those changing habits. *Billy Penn,* he said, "goes after them on the phone, it goes after them in a way that's heavy on social, heavy on curation — which is, like, 'Come to us and you can find out everything going on in your city without having to bounce all over the web,' which is a pain in the ass on a phone. It has a lot of attitude, it has a lot of voice."[54]

Added Krewson: "We're a very small group, but we don't act our size. We act bigger. We comport ourselves as though we were a much larger news organization."

Brady and Krewson are both older than the audience they seek to serve; Brady was forty-eight when we met, Krewson thirty-nine. Nevertheless, their pursuit of millennials seemed to be going well. Monthly traffic at that point was about 500,000 page views and 300,000 unique visitors. According to a market study they had conducted, more than half the audience was under thirty-five, and 75 percent was under forty — an enormous difference, Krewson pointed out, from the demographics of people who read newspapers or watch television news.

What was most intriguing, though, was the business model. *Billy Penn* is a free site with just a few ads here and there. Its online traffic, though respectable, badly trailed the 8 million monthly unique visitors that Philly.com was receiving in early 2016.[55] So where was the revenue coming from? Brady and Krewson responded that they got fully 85 percent of their income by sponsoring events, ranging from a beer-tasting at a South Philly bar called POPE during a visit by Pope Francis in September 2015, to monthly "Who's Next" get-togethers, to recognizing up-and-comers in fields ranging from entrepreneurs to artists. News organizations have long sponsored events, both free and paid, to extend their brand and to bring in a little extra revenue. The *Billy Penn* model, though, was unusually dependent on them.

Very few people have worked in the trenches of digital journalism for as long as Jim Brady. In 1995, he was hired as sports editor of Digital Ink, the *Washington Post*'s first attempt at online journalism. He was involved in the launch of washingtonpost.com in 1996 and served as executive editor during a time when the site was widely praised as a model for newspapers generally.[56] It was at washingtonpost.com that he clashed with the future *Orange County Register* editor Rob Curley.

Later Brady became general manager of a site called TBD.com (for "to be determined," the joke being that they never came up with a proper name), owned by the Allbritton family — the ancient rivals of the *Washington Post*'s Graham family and the owners of *Politico*. Heavy on aggregation and short bites of information, TBD never properly got off the ground. Brady left within three months, complaining that Robert Allbritton had not fulfilled a pledge to give the site three to five years to find its footing. In part because of Brady's status as a digital news innovator, the experiment had been closely followed, and its passing was lamented by many observers. "It was the James Dean of local websites," Brady once quipped. "Died too young but seems to be remembered fondly."[57]

The mediascape is filled with digital journalism ventures that either failed or, like TBD, were abandoned before they got a chance to prove their worth. Brady's career, though, has been unusually star-crossed. His next move was to become editor-in-chief of the newspaper chain that eventually was named Digital First Media, reporting to John Paton, the brash chief executive whose profane outbursts about the need to transition to digital as quickly as possible were regarded as exactly the sort of truth-telling that was lacking in more traditional circles. Brady ran Project Thunderdome, an ambitious project to centralize content and production functions so that Digital First's newspapers and websites could devote all of their resources to covering local news and selling local advertising. But Paton's reign was relatively brief, as the managers of the hedge fund that was ultimately in charge — Alden Global Capital — began dismantling what Paton had built. Project Thunderdome was shut down in the spring of 2014 after just three years.[58]

"I really like John, and John treated me well," Brady told me when I asked him about Paton. "He treated the Thunderdome staff well. He's a personable guy." But, he added, he knew that his time at Digital First might be short. "If you work for a company owned by a hedge fund, it's like walking through a minefield," Brady said. "Any step can be the one where you hit the mine."

For his next venture, Brady decided to strike out on his own, forming a company he called Spirited Media to launch *Billy Penn.* Brady remained in the Washington suburbs, working in Philadelphia two days a week. He chose Philly, he told me, because he'd gotten to know the city from visiting Digital First papers in the area and, later, as a consultant for the *Inquirer;* because the city had a large number of millennials concentrated in the downtown; and because the turmoil at the daily papers provided him with an opening he thought he could take advantage of.

As a journalistic platform, *Billy Penn* has strengths and weaknesses. The mobile-first design is striking, and in fact looks and feels better on a phone than it does on a computer screen. But much of the content consists of aggregation from social media as well as the dailies — so much so that there could be a shortage of content if and when the paywall Bill Marimow envisioned is fully implemented. Headlines tend to be cheeky and share-friendly; one, which accompanied a tweet about a public official's putting off his swearing-in until his parents could attend, simply read "D'awww-www."[59] The site also makes extensive use of email, Twitter, Instagram, and especially Facebook.

There is some original reporting. Krewson told me he was especially proud of the site's coverage of the pope's visit and of a serious Amtrak crash that took place in April 2015. During the summer of 2016, *Billy Penn* also covered the corruption trial of the state attorney general at the time, Kathleen Kane, who was convicted in federal court of perjury after she lied about leaking grand jury testimony to the *Philadelphia Daily News* in order to harm a political opponent.[60] But Brady and Krewson pick their spots. "It's not that we don't want to be comprehensive," Krewson said. "I know I can't be. It's a city of 1.6 million and a region of four million. I've got eight people, including the ad side. So what are we going to do?"

Billy Penn is a newsy guide to city life, not a substitute for a comprehensive newspaper — and that's not Brady's intention. Starting with $500,000 in personal funds ("We've put in a little bit more since," he told me), Brady may be on his way to a rare business success in online hyperlocal news, with a target of breaking even sometime in 2017. In March 2016, Gannett bought a minority stake in Spirited Media for $2.6 million, which gave Brady the resources he needed to expand hiring and to make plans to start a second site based in Pittsburgh called the *Incline*.[61]

If you believe, as I do, that community news sites serve their audiences best when they are owned at the local level, the Gannett news and the addition of a second site — and possibly more — are both good and bad. The failure of the original Patch.com formula (the sites, formerly owned by AOL, at one time employed hundreds of journalists; by 2016, they continued to limp along with little in the way of original journalism)[62] demonstrated the limits of a cookie-cutter approach to hyperlocal. Meanwhile, vibrant independent for-profit and nonprofit sites have popped up in communities large and small over the past decade, even if none of them is particularly lucrative.

The future depends on experiments like *Billy Penn* and on smart, committed entrepreneurial journalists like Jim Brady. Whether his latest venture succeeds or not, it will be studied for years to come. Still, it is no substitute for a great daily newspaper. The ownership mess at Philadelphia's papers may have provided Brady with the opening he needed to try something new. But the journalism he publishes is a supplement to those papers, not a substitute.

THERE ARE NO billionaire newspaper owners in Vermont. But the state's most populous city, Burlington, has long been an outpost of Gannett Company, the largest American newspaper chain. The publisher of *USA Today* as well as more than a hundred other daily newspapers in thirty-four states, Gannett is the prototype of the sort of publicly traded corporation whose insatiable demand for profits led to drastic downsizing years before the current crisis took hold. As recently as 2008, many Gannett newspapers reported margins of 20, 30, and even 40 percent. But that was a long time ago. In 2015, the company earned just $149 million on revenues of $2.9 billion, or 5 percent. Both those figures were lower than they were in 2014. Gannett may be a behemoth, but like all newspaper companies, it is a wounded behemoth.[63]

Vermont's largest daily newspaper, the *Burlington Free Press*, which traces its roots to 1827, has been part of Gannett since 1971. Burlington is a small place. Although it is the largest city in the state, its population of about 42,000 would be the size of a middling suburb in most parts of the country. Thus the *Free Press* is not a major metro on the order of the *Philadelphia*

Inquirer, the *Boston Globe*, or the *Orange County Register*. And it has been shrinking—in the most literal sense. In 2012, it was reduced from a broadsheet-sized paper to a tabloid, which led to grumbling from more than a few traditionalists. Far worse, paid weekday print circulation dropped from nearly 50,000 around the turn of the century to about 16,000 in 2016 (Sunday circulation was 21,000). Despite Gannett's heavy emphasis on digital, online traffic was just short of 650,000 unique visitors per month, and mobile traffic was minimal. The *Free Press*'s journalistic reach had gotten smaller as well: a newsroom of nearly sixty full-time journalists had been reduced to about twenty-five by late 2015.[64]

Yet something had happened in Burlington and the surrounding area that mirrored what I've observed in other places. In Connecticut, online-only projects such as the *New Haven Independent*, *CT News Junkie*, and the *Connecticut Mirror* were launched and rose to prominence as established newspapers such as the *New Haven Register* and the *Hartford Courant* cut back. The same was true in rural Western New York, where the *Batavian*, a for-profit online-only news service, took its place alongside the *Batavia Daily News*, and in Southern California, where *Voice of San Diego* emerged as one of the most closely watched nonprofit news projects in the country even as the *San Diego Union-Tribune* suffered deep cuts.[65] Likewise, as the *Free Press* withered, other news organizations helped fill the gap—specifically *Seven Days*, a thick, healthy alternative weekly with a strong news sense; *VT Digger*, a nonprofit site that covers politics and public policy at the state level and that was beginning to offer local coverage; and Vermont Public Radio, an NPR affiliate with a decent mix of local and regional reporting.

I don't want to make too much of this. Media diversity is not unique to areas whose dominant daily newspapers have been laid low. Even in Boston, where the *Globe*'s local and regional coverage continues to be strong, a variety of other news organizations thrive, including a second daily paper, neighborhood and community weeklies, multiple television stations, two large public radio stations, and several magazines and websites. My point is that the role of alternative media is especially crucial in places like Vermont, where the *Free Press*'s watchdog journalism can no longer be as comprehensive as it once was.

Traci Griffith, a former Associated Press journalist who is chairwoman of the Media Studies, Journalism, and Digital Arts Department at St. Michael's College in Colchester, Vermont, a short drive from Burlington, has been watching the local media scene since 2001. When I asked her what changes she had seen during that time, she replied, "Well, it was so heavily dominated by the *Free Press* fourteen years ago, right? There was no *VT Digger. Seven Days* was in its infancy. So yeah, the new independents have grown so substantially over the last few years."[66]

Perhaps the most lively of these independents is *Seven Days.* Across the country, alternative weeklies have downsized and even gone out of business. The *Boston Phoenix,* where I worked for fourteen years in the 1990s and 2000s, shut its doors in 2013, the victim of a shriveled-up advertising market.[67] By contrast, *Seven Days* was thick with advertising. Paula Routly, the publisher, coeditor, and co-owner along with her business partner, Pamela Polston, told me something I found astonishing when I visited the paper's deliberately but charmingly funky offices in November 2015: *Seven Days* — founded in 1995 — had never lost money and in fact expanded its staff during the Great Recession.[68]

"When the recession hit, we invested. That's when we ramped up in news," she said. "And that is when the *Free Press* visibly diminished. They just made different business decisions. 'Let's make it smaller, let's lay people off.' That's where I think they made their mistake." One of *Seven Days*'s relatively new reporters, Molly Walsh, had come over from the *Free Press* several months earlier. "The tumult at the *Free Press* was tough on all the employees," she said. "It left people, including me, with some concerns about our job security at the very least."[69]

Comparing the size of *Seven Days,* a free weekly, with that of the paid daily *Free Press* is something of an exercise in apples and oranges. Routly said her paper's print circulation was about 36,000, and web traffic was around 90,000 unique visitors per month. The staff comprised about thirty journalists, some part-time, some in nonjournalistic areas such as proofreading and specialty publications.[70] Overall, it appeared that *Seven Days* was smaller than the *Free Press,* but not overwhelmingly so.

Political editor Paul Heintz joined *Seven Days* in early 2012 after stints in journalism, politics, and thru-hiking the Appalachian Trail. Heintz was covering Senator Bernie Sanders's presidential campaign and had just returned from a trip to Iowa. "Certainly I think that all three of us" — *Seven Days, VT Digger,* and Vermont Public Radio — "have become real competitors to the *Free Press*, and that's healthy," he said. "But we're responding to fill a void to a certain extent."[71]

When I talked with folks at Vermont Public Radio and *VT Digger*, the message was similar. For instance, Taylor Dobbs, a former student of mine, was hired to cover Burlington and the surrounding county for VPR, both online and on the air. "There's news in Burlington to be covered and news in Chittenden County to be covered that the *Free Press* either was missing when the position was created or somebody saw that there would be a hole there," he said. Dobbs, who had broken several important environmental stories, said the *Free Press* still excelled at covering breaking news, but enterprise stories that took some time to develop were more likely to be reported by one of the alternative news outlets.[72]

Likewise, Anne Galloway, who founded the online-only nonprofit *VT Digger* in 2009 after she was laid off by the *Rutland Herald*, said she saw her job as holding state government to account at a time when the *Free Press* and other newspapers were cutting back. "There are thirteen reporters in the statehouse. We have five of them," she told me when I interviewed her at the site's headquarters — a converted old house in Montpelier that was a short walk from the state capitol. At the time that we met, the site had thirteen full-time employees, seven of whom were reporters, and was expanding to offer local coverage in both Chittenden County and Windham County, in the southern part of the state. *Digger* was attracting about 150,000 unique visitors a month. Its annual budget was approaching $1 million, which it raised by tapping small donors, corporate underwriters, and grants from foundations.[73]

There is, of course, another, less bleak perspective regarding the ongoing role of the *Burlington Free Press* in Vermont's media ecosystem. Even after all the cutbacks, the daily remained the largest news organization in the state — larger, certainly, than Vermont Public Radio, *VT Digger*, or even *Seven Days*. Cutbacks have hit daily newspapers everywhere, but I could find little evidence that the pain Gannett had inflicted on the *Free Press* was uniquely awful. Given Gannett's aggressive attempt to buy tronc and its investment in innovative projects such as *Billy Penn*, it seemed clear that its leaders were committed to the newspaper business for the long haul and were not just trying to squeeze out the last remaining profits before shutting down.

Michael Donoghue was a legendary investigative reporter for the *Free Press* before retiring in 2015 after forty-seven years at the paper. I interviewed him at St. Michael's College, where he was a part-time journalism instructor, in a suite of offices named after his father, John D. Donoghue, who had been the college's director of public relations and sports information. Mike Donoghue blamed the decline of the news business on a number of factors — especially on "the dumbing-down of America," as he put it, saying, "There's just not the civic engagement, probably, when you and I went to school and we took pride in knowing who the local officers were in our town and our state and understood what was important in our community."[74]

Given that Donoghue had just left the *Free Press* and was able to speak his mind, I was struck that he had nothing but good things to say about Gannett, praising the company for, among other things, investing in newsroom technology. "Everybody got an iPhone five years ago, and we all learned how to shoot video and take pictures. There's been more changes in the last 10 years in the media than the previous 200 years," he said. "Do I agree with 100 percent of their decisions? No. Do I agree with my wife 100 percent of the time? No. But I understand they make certain decisions for certain reasons, and they've been very supportive of me." As for the effect of the cuts, he said, "Obviously it's a little tougher and you do have to pick your spots. We were always thought of as the newspaper of record because everything would be in there. I'm not sure there's a newspaper of record technically in Vermont anymore."

The next day I visited the *Free Press*'s seventh-floor headquarters, whose windows afforded a 360-degree perspective, including a spectacular view of Lake Champlain extending all the way to the Adirondacks. "We've actually broken stories looking out the window," said Al Getler, the publisher. His favorite: a guy breaking into a car on the roof of a parking garage, which an ad department employee captured on video.[75]

Getler gave me a tour and showed off the *Free Press*'s video equipment, a podcast studio, and other technology. But there was no doubt that the paper was shorthanded. The executive editor, Michael Townsend, had just retired (along with Mike Donoghue and three others), and Getler was filling in until a replacement could be found. I asked him how the paper went about covering the area with fewer resources. "I think the big difference for us today is that we don't spend a lot of time necessarily sitting at long meetings, but we have to choose what meetings we attend," Getler replied. "Would I like to have more feet on the street doing more things? Anybody would. But you have choices that you have to make." The goal, he said, was to cover stories that readers were interested in while maintaining the *Free Press*'s role in holding government accountable.

"You have to understand what's important to the reader," Getler said. "We use metrics a lot. So we really try to be mindful of what people are reading and what people find important. Look, it's a business. And for some reason the public doesn't always equate a newspaper as a business. They look at it as kind of a utility. But it's a business."

What I observed in Vermont — as well as Connecticut and elsewhere — showed that public-interest journalism can survive even when the position of the dominant daily newspaper has eroded. Yes, members of the public have to work harder if they want to be well informed. Twenty years ago, someone living in Burlington might have been able to get away with reading just the *Free Press*; today, anyone who wants to know more about what's going on locally and at the statehouse will also have to listen to Vermont Public Radio and take a look at *Seven Days* and *VT Digger*.

Thus it seemed likely that if major regional papers continued to shrink, then some of the accountability journalism they offer would migrate elsewhere. It's not an ideal solution, since none of these alternatives would command the audience and the attention that large dailies once held. But it is far better than what would happen if important stories went uncovered.

CHAPTER NINE

ALL IN

Jeff Bezos Takes His Place as an "Enemy of the People"

DAVID FAHRENTHOLD'S PHONE RANG. The caller told him that he had some information about Donald Trump. Fahrenthold, a *Washington Post* reporter, had built a reputation for his relentlessness in covering Trump, reporting that many of the wealthy businessman's claims of charitable giving were unsupported by the evidence and that the nonprofit Trump Foundation had engaged in such dubious practices as spending $20,000 to buy a six-foot-tall painting of — well, of Trump.[1]

As Fahrenthold later recalled, he spoke with this particular tipster on Friday, October 7, 2016, around 11 a.m. Within five hours, Trump was dealt a blow that sent his campaign into a tailspin. At about 4 p.m., the *Post* published a story under Fahrenthold's byline reporting that the paper had obtained an eleven-year-old video of Trump in which he could be heard talking with the entertainer Billy Bush, who was then with *Access Hollywood.* In crude language, Trump spoke about having tried to make the moves on a married woman. Far worse, he boasted of having engaged in behavior that could only be described as sexual assault.

"You know I'm automatically attracted to beautiful — I just start kissing them. It's like a magnet. Just kiss. I don't even wait," Trump said. "And when you're a star, they let you do it. You can do anything."

"Whatever you want," Bush responded.

"Grab them by the pussy," Trump said. "You can do anything."

Trump tried to dismiss the tape as irrelevant, telling the *Post* in a statement that what he'd said was merely "locker-room banter, a private conversation that took place many years ago."[2] Nevertheless, his campaign appeared to unravel. At the second presidential debate, CNN's Anderson Cooper pressed Trump on whether he had actually engaged in such behavior. Trump angrily replied that he had not.[3] By Wednesday, though, the *New York Times* was reporting that two women had charged that Trump behaved with them in exactly the manner he described on the tape. "He was like an octopus. His hands were everywhere," said one of the women, Jessica Leeds, about an incident she claimed had taken place three decades earlier.[4] Within weeks, about a dozen women had come forward with similar claims.[5]

Trump's stunning and unexpected victory over Hillary Clinton did nothing to diminish the *Post*'s reporting. For the *Post*, and especially for Fahrenthold, the story about the *Access Hollywood* tape was the culmination of a remarkable run. Fahrenthold was praised for harnessing the power of the crowd in his reporting; among other things, he posted a copy of his handwritten notes on Twitter in an attempt to identify possible charities Trump may have given to. One of his Twitter followers even tracked down another painting of Trump, purchased by his foundation for $10,000, in a sports bar at a Trump golf course in Florida.[6]

In a postelection interview with Duke University professor Philip Bennett (himself a former *Washington Post* managing editor and *Boston Globe* foreign editor), Fahrenthold said he did not regard his work as lacking the desired impact merely because Trump won. "There's this idea that nothing matters with Trump," Fahrenthold said. "I think a lot of journalists get depressed and think, well you know, 'he's shrugged off so many things that would have killed off Mitt Romney or would have killed off Hillary Clinton, and nothing matters.' That's not true. Things matter to him. He cares about his perception. And it matters to voters and readers. They care about this sort of stuff."[7] The following April, Fahrenthold's coverage of Trump was awarded the Pulitzer Prize for National Reporting.[8]

The campaign proved that the *Post* was just as capable of driving the conversation in presidential politics as its ancient rival, the *New York Times*, or upstarts like *Politico*. That was largely symbolic: the *Post* had never stopped being a force in coverage of national politics. But the 2016 race was an opportunity for the new, revitalized *Post* to make a statement — and for Jeff Bezos to show what he was made of. From the beginning, the *Post*'s coverage of Trump was tough and fearless. After Bob Woodward revealed in May 2016 that the *Post* had assembled a team of more than twenty reporters to write a book about Trump, the candidate popped up on Fox News to tell his favorite interlocutor, Sean Hannity, that there was going to be hell to pay once he was safely ensconced in the White House. Amazon,

Trump claimed, had "a huge antitrust problem" and was "getting away with murder, tax-wise." He added that Bezos was "using the *Washington Post* for power so that the politicians in Washington don't tax Amazon like they should be taxed." Trump later banned *Post* reporters from his public events, along with journalists from *Politico*, the *Huffington Post*, *BuzzFeed*, and others, a ban he eventually rescinded.[9]

Right around that time Bezos, speaking at a public event moderated by Marty Baron, alluded to John Mitchell's infamous Watergate-era threat to Katharine Graham's anatomy and said he was up to the challenge. "I have a lot of very sensitive and vulnerable body parts," he said, echoing the message that he wrote to *Post* employees shortly after he purchased the paper. "If need be, they can all go through the wringer rather than do the wrong thing."[10] Bezos proved as good as his word. The *Post* biography, *Trump Revealed: An American Journey of Ambition, Ego, Money, and Power*, was released by Scribner in August. Bezos later said he believed so strongly in the independence of the *Post*'s newsroom that he wasn't even involved in the decision to publish it. "That's Marty Baron's decision," Bezos told the journalist Walter Isaacson at a public event in San Francisco a few weeks before the election. "I do not introduce myself in any way into the daily activities of the newsroom."[11]

Trump's first attack on Bezos was launched on Twitter in December 2015. Presaging what he would tell Sean Hannity several months later, Trump tweeted: "If @amazon ever had to pay fair taxes, its stock would crash and it would crumble like a paper bag. The @washingtonpost scam is saving it!"[12] Bezos, whose business interests include a company developing spacecraft technology, responded: "Finally trashed by @realDonaldTrump. Will still reserve him a seat on the Blue Origin rocket. #sendDonaldtospace."[13] As Bezos quipped to Isaacson, "I have a rocket company so, you know, the capability is there." But Bezos added in his conversation with Isaacson that, in retrospect, he wished he had taken a more serious approach in his initial response to Trump. "I should not have taken it lightly, because we live in an amazing country," he told Isaacson. "One of the things that makes this country so amazing is that we are allowed to criticize and scrutinize our elected leaders. There are other countries where if you criticize the elected leader you might go to jail. Or worse, you may just disappear. The appropriate thing for a presidential candidate to do is to say, 'I am running for the highest office in the most important country in the world. Please scrutinize me. Please scrutinize me.' And that would, by the way, signal great confidence. It would be a leader thing to do. And that's not what we've seen."

Bezos also demonstrated a sophisticated understanding of the difference between free speech in theory and what it takes to guarantee free speech in practice. "We have freedom of speech in this country. It's written into the Constitution," he said. "But the Constitution — except for our norms and our behaviors, the stories we tell ourselves as a nation about who we are — it's just a piece of paper. There are a bunch of nations that have written constitutions that they don't pay any attention to. People still disappear."

At the time that Bezos made those forceful remarks, the Trump campaign seemed to be all but finished. Bezos had not been tested the way Katharine Graham had when the Nixon administration threatened to bring the full weight of the federal government down upon her, her newspaper, and her television stations. Still, Bezos had spoken eloquently about the role of the press — and thus his responsibility as a steward of the First Amendment. It was a good omen for the more difficult tests to come with Trump in the White House.

FOR ANYONE WHO SPENDS MUCH TIME reporting on the shrinking newspaper business, walking around the headquarters of the *Washington Post* feels like a trip to Disney World — a magical place where everyone is optimistic and where all things seem possible. It's an illusion, of course. Jeff Bezos's resources may seem unlimited, but that doesn't mean his approach to spending at the *Post* is unlimited. Remember, he bought a paper with about 560 journalists and boosted that number to 700 — not as many as the more than 1,000 who had worked at the *Post* some years earlier or the 1,300 he would have needed to match the *Times*. Bezos was going about rebuilding the *Post* in a restrained, disciplined manner.

"There's obviously stuff I can't share, but I can tell you that Jeff is a businessman, and there's a reason why he's gotten where he's gotten," said Beth Diaz, the *Post*'s vice president of audience development and analytics. "It's not about spending endless sums of money. Jeff has said that he's given us runway, but he's also made clear that runway doesn't go on forever. And so there is a path that we're on, and I actually feel quite confident that we're getting there."[14] Ken Doctor, the analyst of the media business, said in early 2016 that he understood Bezos had "subsidized a small operating loss" and that the *Post* was working toward narrowing or eliminating that loss in the near future.[15] Marty Baron has described Bezos's approach this way: "We have to have a sustainable economic model. So for him it's certainly not a plaything, and it's not even a charity. It's an effort to create a real business that will last for the long run."[16]

Because the *Post* under Bezos is a privately owned company, most of its numbers are a closely held secret. The *Post* does not report revenues, profits, losses, or even how many customers it has signed up as paid digital subscribers. When I asked Diaz in the spring of 2016 when I might be able to get subscriber totals, she replied, "I wouldn't hold my breath." By the end of 2016, though, the *Post* began reporting numbers that suggested the paper's business strategy was on track.

First Lucia Moses of *Digiday* obtained a memo written by Jed Hartman, the *Post*'s chief revenue officer, claiming that the *Post*'s digital ad revenue had hit "a solid nine-figure total."[17] Then publisher Fred Ryan wrote a memo in which he said that the *Post* would end 2016 "as a profitable and growing company" on the strength of "a 75 percent increase in new subscribers since January" and a 40 percent increase in digital ad revenues. In 2017, Ryan said, the *Post* would bolster its newsroom with new hires in investigative reporting, breaking news, and video.[18] Ken Doctor put the number of likely new hires at about sixty, bringing the size of the newsroom to more than 750.[19]

The word "profitable" in Ryan's memo was especially eye-catching. Earlier in 2016, Shailesh Prakash, the *Post*'s chief technologist, had told me that "nobody, as far as I can tell, has a prescriptive plan for how to get to a sustainable business in media" and that "the combination of monetization capabilities that we will ultimately end up with to give us a sustainable and a highly profitable model is yet to be discovered."[20] That reality hadn't changed in just eight months. No doubt the *Post*'s aggressive, high-profile coverage of the 2016 presidential campaign helped drive subscription growth and bolster the bottom line, but it remained to be seen whether that could be sustained. Then, too, the overall digital advertising picture continued to worsen for news organizations, with an ever-increasing share of revenues being scooped up by Facebook and Google.[21] Without publicly available numbers, it was hard to know exactly what Ryan meant by "profitable" or whether that could be sustained. Still, there was no question that the *Post* under Bezos was in a far better position than nearly every other newspaper.

If the *Post* is to continue growing, it must rely on three ingredients: outstanding journalism, especially of national and international issues; a large and growing digital audience; and a strategy to convert that audience into enough revenue, through advertising and digital subscriptions, to cover the *Post*'s costs. The first two ingredients were already in place. The *Post* was aggressively pursuing the third through a variety of measures. Advertising remained an important part of the revenue mix. But perhaps the more promising strategy was to persuade visitors to become paid digital subscribers.

The idea, not unique to the *Post* or even to the newspaper business, is to pull visitors down through a "customer-engagement funnel," described in a talk to newspaper executives by the former Washington Post Company president Stephen Hills. At the top of the funnel is what might be called drive-by traffic — casual visitors who saw a link on Facebook or Twitter, or in a friend's email, and decided to click. A visitor who sticks around for a few minutes and reads the story will see related stories and perhaps click on a few of those, thus being pulled into the funnel. Farther down are people who begin to visit the *Post* more regularly. And at the very bottom of the funnel are visitors who have become loyal enough *Post* readers that they decide to pay for a subscription to the digital bundle that Bezos himself has identified as a key to the paper's future. The goal is to widen the top of the funnel as much as possible by maximizing total digital traffic and to convert some small percentage of that traffic into loyal, subscription-buying customers.[22]

For the *Post*, this was a new strategy. Don Graham was late to the notion of persuading readers to pay for digital journalism. As recently as 2012, he said the *Post*'s anomalous circulation pattern as a regional newspaper whose online audience was overwhelmingly outside the Washington area because of its coverage of national politics made it unlikely that he'd erect a paywall similar to that of the *New York Times* or the *Wall Street Journal*. "Circumstance has made it so we're the one great news company that's free at this point," he said in July 2012.[23] Later, though, he reversed course. Barely weeks before Graham sold his family's newspaper to Bezos, the *Post* unveiled a metered model of the sort used by the *Times*, the *Boston Globe*, and many other papers, offering a limited amount of free content every month and then asking visitors to pay.[24]

Compared with the paywall put in place in 2011 by the *New York Times*, the *Post*'s was both leaky and inexpensive. Both papers periodically adjust various aspects of their subscription plans, including the overall price as well as the number of free articles that readers can access each month before they have to pay; as of March 2016, the *Post* offered five (down from twenty at launch) while the *Times* offered ten. Social sharing did not count against the monthly limit with either paper, which meant that there were many visitors who never encountered the paywall.[25] Perhaps the most substantial difference in comparison with the *Times* was that a free digital subscription to the *Post* was available to anyone with an email address ending in .edu (education), .gov (government), or .mil (military).[26] That's a lot of people.

In a particularly innovative move, the *Post* also offered free online access to people who subscribed to one of more than 300 local newspapers around the country.[27] Among those papers: Maine's *Portland Press Herald*, *Kennebec Journal*, and *Waterville Morning Sentinel*. Stefanie Manning, vice president of circulation and marketing for the papers' owner, MaineToday Media, said that nearly 5,000 subscribers had registered for access to the *Washington Post*. "It benefits our newspapers in that we can offer an added value benefit to our paid subscribers at no additional cost to them or us," Manning told me. "It increases the perceived value of their subscription."[28]

A digital subscription to the *Post* was also cheaper than a *Times* digital subscription. The *Times* in October 2016 offered a basic digital subscription to all of its platforms for $195 a year. The *Post*, by contrast, offered two different bundles. All digital subscribers received full access to washingtonpost.com. Those who opted for the national digital apps, which were available for smartphones and tablets, paid $99 a year (with frequent discount offers), and those who wanted apps that included all of the *Post*'s journalism, including regional news from Washington, paid $149 a year. Free trial periods and discounts were available for Amazon Prime members (of whom there were more than 60 million in the United States) and customers who purchased the Kindle Fire, on which the national digital edition was preinstalled.[29] It was all rather convoluted, but the bottom line was that there were a lot of *Post* subscribers who were paying less than the full rate.

Perhaps most intriguing, Bezos had leveraged the *Post* in ways that enhanced the value of being an Amazon Prime member. Among the other benefits that Prime members enjoyed, Amazon offered a high-quality national newspaper at such a low price that there was little reason to go to the trouble of canceling it. It was all part of Bezos's long-term strategy of creating an ecosystem around Amazon that took care of an increasingly wide range of his customers' shopping, entertainment, and informational needs. With the *Post,* Amazon could stream news right alongside music, movies, and what we used to think of as television shows.

The Amazon tie-in could also change the calculation for what defines a financially sustainable *Post.* The Amazon Echo is an obvious platform for *Post* journalism, and in fact the *Post* and several other news organizations were early adopters.[30] It is not difficult to imagine the technology behind the Echo and its cloud-based voice recognition system, Alexa, migrating into motor vehicles and mobile devices, enabling users to order up, say, a five-, ten-, or thirty-minute newscast from the *Post.* The *Post*'s new headquarters also have several television studios that were quickly put to use for various live events, including political debates. Why not an Amazon on-demand newscast available to *Post* subscribers and Amazon Prime members?

As I've noted, for quite some time the *Post* did not report how many paid digital subscribers it had attracted, leaving it to outsiders to guess at the numbers.[31] In 2016 and 2017, the *Post* was rushing to catch up with the *New York Times,* whose five-year-old paywall had yielded more than 2 million digital subscribers by early 2017.[32] Occasionally I would check in with Ken Doctor, who would offer his own estimates of how the Post was doing—between 100,000 and 200,000 in March 2016,[33] followed by 300,000 a year later.[34] By summer, he said he had revised that estimate upward to somewhere between 500,000 and 600,000.[35] Finally, in September 2017, the *Post* broke its silence and announced a truly eye-popping figure. Since January, publisher Fred Ryan said, the number of paid digital-only subscriptions had more than doubled and had reached in excess of 1 million.[36] The *Times* was still ahead, but the *Post* was growing rapidly.

DURING MY VISIT to the *Post*, I was exposed to a dizzying array of technology and experimentation. A virtual reality tour of Mars was so immersive that it took me several minutes to get my legs back under me. "This will be the next generation of storytelling," said Micah Gelman, the *Post*'s director of video. When I asked him how such storytelling might contribute to the bottom line, he replied that some companies had already expressed interest in sponsorships.[37] I talked with members of Shailesh Prakash's team about projects they're working on, such as Coral, an open-source collaboration with the Mozilla Foundation, the Knight Foundation, and the *New York Times* to harness technology in order to boost the prominence of high-quality online comments and crack down on trolls.[38] I learned about tools that have been developed to allow a journalist to drop a reader poll or an infographic into a blog post without having to create it from scratch and to help *Post* editors connect with freelance journalists on a moment's notice. I saw the *Post*'s extensive video facilities, which were used for projects such as short documentaries as well as live coverage.

Like Baron, Prakash was a holdover from the Graham era. In 2013, Don Graham called Prakash "a peer of Marty Baron" and said, "He and Baron will create the *Post* digital content in the future jointly"[39]— a judgment with which Bezos apparently agreed. Prakash had been at the *Post* since 2011 following stints at the retail company Sears as well as Microsoft and Netscape. I asked Prakash what he had learned from Sears that he hadn't learned from working at technology companies. "Sears seasoned me to a non-tech company and helped me to do a better job and find a better balance at a place like the *Washington Post*," he replied.[40]

Prakash talked about the top, middle, and bottom of the customer-engagement funnel and threw in a barbell reference as well. Despite his roots in the world of engineering and technology, he explains his work in a way that a layperson can understand.

Perhaps the most technologically important step the *Post* had taken followed a mandate from Bezos himself. After a reader complained to Bezos that it took too long for one of the mobile apps to load, Bezos told Prakash that he needed to do better. "We looked at the problem and I told Jeff I thought we could improve the load time to maybe two seconds. He wrote back and said, 'It needs to be milliseconds,'" Prakash told the *Wall Street Journal*. "He has become our ultimate beta tester."[41] Throughout 2016, in fact, the *Post* became even speedier, as the paper incorporated code from the Google AMP (for "accelerated mobile pages") standard into its own digital products.[42]

Bezos also had a hands-on role in designing a product that serves the bottom of the funnel — the apps for the national digital edition, the development of which was known at one time as Project Rainbow. Although the tablet and smartphone versions look similar, offering a bright-colored, magazine-style layout, there are important differences. The smartphone app is updated throughout the day, and you scroll through it as you would with any news app.[43]

The tablet app is different. For one thing, it's updated just twice a day, publishing 5 a.m. and 5 p.m. editions on the assumption that users are sitting down and reading rather than quickly catching up on the news as they would with mobile. For another, the national app literally has no home page — a design decision that Prakash told *Digiday* was Bezos's idea. Bezos originally wanted the user to see just one article upon launching the app; he and Prakash compromised at two, with the idea being to balance a serious news story with something lighter.[44] Compared with the look of almost any other website or app, this was radical. For instance, the *Post*'s "classic" mobile and tablet app, which is more expensive and includes more content — including local stories — features a traditional home page with multiple stories.

"You have to understand what the problem is that you're trying to solve," Prakash said in explaining the philosophy behind the national apps. "The one issue that Bezos highlighted was it's so easy to enjoy reading a newspaper. Why is it so hard to do digital browsing? What have you lost when you've gone from print to digital? And so the philosophy of the product, the gap you are trying to solve, and we are still trying to solve, is to reduce the cognitive overhead of consuming news digitally."[45]

Not all of Bezos's ideas are similarly inspired. One notorious example was his proposal that readers be given an opportunity to pay to remove the vowels from articles they didn't like. Marty Baron was less than enthusiastic, Prakash told *Fortune* magazine, and the "disemvoweling" initiative was abandoned. "Working together with other smart people in front of a whiteboard," Prakash quipped, "we can come up with a lot of very bad ideas."[46]

To be persuaded to sign on as paid digital subscribers, people first need to be exposed to the *Post*'s journalism and to be enticed into clicking and reading. In other words, the top of the funnel has to be as wide as possible. Prakash and his team have developed several tools in-house to accomplish that. One, called Bandito, automates the process of A/B testing — that is, comparing different digital treatments — that allows the newsroom to write up to five headlines and blurbs for a story, choose several images, and publish all of them to see which combination will most resonate with readers. The treatment that prompts the highest level of engagement in terms of clicks, time spent, and sharing will gradually become the version that all users see. (The A/B testing is done mainly on the *Post*'s home page and on social platforms. Everyone who clicks through to the underlying story sees the same headline and layout.)[47] Prakash told me that the next version of Bandito would include more sophisticated tools that determine which treatment works best with international readers, which with the national audience, which on Facebook, and the like.

Another tool, which Prakash and Marty Baron showed off at the South by Southwest conference in Austin, Texas, in early 2016, is called Loxodo, a suite of metrics displayed prominently on a video screen suspended between the seventh and eighth floors of the *Post*'s headquarters. As Prakash explained it to me, ordinary metrics such as the number of unique visitors and page views are what Bezos refers to as "lag measures" — they're important, but they reflect the results of decisions that have already been made. Bezos, he said, had pushed for the *Post* to embrace "lead measures." For example, Loxodo scoops up journalism from a variety of news organizations such as the *New York Times*, *Business Insider*, and the *Huffington Post* and strips it of branding. About 500 readers are then asked which story treatments they prefer, a process that helps the *Post* refine its own approach with regard to headlines and layout. Loxodo was also being used to measure how quickly the *Post* was pushing out text alerts and whether it was sending too many or too few.

The most valuable customer is someone who visits the *Post*'s website and is gradually enticed into becoming a paying subscriber. But Prakash and other executives understood that there was another huge audience out there that might be interested in the *Post*'s journalism but that might rarely if ever stop by washingtonpost.com. Although the *Post* was making heavy use of a variety of distributed platforms such as Twitter, Apple News,

Google AMP, and Snapchat, Facebook was by far the most important. Like many news organizations, the *Post* shared its journalism on Facebook, driving traffic back to washingtonpost.com. The *Post* and a few others had also gone a step further, publishing all of their content on Facebook as Instant Articles, part of Facebook's mobile platform. With Instant Articles, the content resides on Facebook's servers, meaning that it loads much more quickly than it does when you have to click through to the originating website. When you visit the *Post*'s Facebook page or click on a *Post* story shared by a friend, the Instant Articles version will load automatically if you're reading on your phone. Apple News works the same way; Google AMP depends on publishers rewriting their code to new specifications.

Facebook Instant has advantages and disadvantages for publishers, as Prakash acknowledged. Advertising revenue is shared with Facebook under terms that could be changed in the future — most likely to Facebook's advantage. Publishers do not receive the sort of extensive data they get when users visit their own sites, and the *Post* is nothing if not a data-driven enterprise. On the other hand, with ad-blocking technology proliferating across the web, Facebook offers an environment in which most ad blockers don't work. And then there is the matter of all those Facebook users. As of April 2016, more than a billion and a half unique visitors were dropping in every day, and a billion of them were spending at least twenty minutes on the network.[48] "That's a huge number," Prakash said. "And for us to not piggyback on that platform, especially with our national and international aspirations, I think would not be the right strategy." Indeed, compared with Facebook's traffic, the *Post*'s 80 million or so unique visitors a month was minuscule, as was the one to three minutes per visit people spend at news sites in general.[49]

Which is where the "barbell strategy" comes in. Prakash said that he and Bezos, in talking about how to deal with distributed platforms, have decided that they need to think of their traffic in terms of a barbell, with their website and their customer-engagement funnel on one side and with Facebook, Apple News, and the rest on the other. "It dilutes the bundle a bit," he conceded. "We've discussed this, we've grappled with it. Unfortunately we need to do both. It's not an option."

So how does the *Post* move people to the paid-subscription side of the barbell? Among other things, Facebook users who click on *Washington Post* stories are encouraged to provide their email addresses, which the *Post* uses to try to figure out — algorithmically — which of the *Post*'s sixty newsletters might appeal to them. These newsletters cover a range of topics such as the day's headlines, politics, opinion, science, and entertainment. Arriving by email, with advertising, the newsletters link to various *Post* stories related to the topic. Of course, emailed newsletters are hardly an innovation; they are a standard part of any news organization's repertoire, from the *New York Times* to the *New Haven Independent*, from CNN to local public radio stations. But the *Post*'s efforts are unusually comprehensive, and they are driven by a proprietary platform called Paloma, which is, in turn, based on Amazon technology.[50]

By using Facebook as one of its vehicles to drive newsletter sign-ups, the *Post* is insuring itself against a sudden change in the way Facebook puts content in front of users that harms the distribution of the *Post*'s journalism. That's exactly what happened in 2012. Facebook had encouraged news organizations to build apps based on its Social Reader that would exist within the Facebook environment. The *Post*'s version attracted some 17 million users, who then fled after Facebook redesigned its site and changed the algorithms that determine what users see.[51] David Beard, a veteran journalist who was one of the *Post*'s top digital editors at the time, told me that he gravitated toward newsletters after the Social Reader fiasco because he wanted to develop an outlet that would be totally under the *Post*'s control. "For a while, we had tons of readers in India and the Philippines and some other places. And then Facebook changed the algorithm and we suddenly had none," Beard said. "So my learning from that episode was, is there something we can do without an intermediary, where we own the machinery?"[52]

The *Post* has also developed a content-management system, or CMS, known as Arc. As is the case with a number of tech projects at the *Post*, Arc was begun under Don Graham and then was encouraged and supported once Jeff Bezos took over. "I often like to say that we were working on all this stuff under Don's guidance, but when Jeff bought the company he basically poured gasoline on that effort," said Shailesh Prakash. "It's just really taken off."

Talk with journalists at any news organization and they are likely to tell you how much they hate their unwieldy CMS, which handles tasks such as web publishing, blogging, video, and mobile (and print, a function that has been omitted from Arc). A typical CMS, Prakash explained, falls short in one of two ways: it either handles one task well with mediocre support for other components, or the news organization uses various tools that do a good job with all tasks but that don't communicate with each other. The tools in Arc, by contrast, are discrete but interconnected. Loxodo and Paloma are part of Arc. So, too, is a module called WebSked, which handles group scheduling and tracks the progress of stories. In a whimsical touch, WebSked includes a feature called the "MartyBot" — an image of Marty Baron that pops up on a journalist's screen as a reminder that a deadline is approaching. Arc may not mean much to readers, but they benefit both directly and indirectly when journalists are able to work more efficiently.

Not only is the *Post* using Arc internally, but it's licensing it to other news organizations. Among them is *Willamette Week*, an alternative paper based in Willamette, Oregon. Mark Zusman, the editor and publisher, told me that he got interested in Arc after learning about it while searching for a new CMS. "They flew a team out here and within three months we were up and running," he said. "I was pleasantly surprised with how quickly it happened. Arc creates enormous functionality under the hood. I have a happy news team (talk about unusual) and the *Post* is rolling out improvements on a regular basis." Readers, he added, benefit from "a far cleaner design and better flexibility with art."[53] According to one estimate, Arc could eventually bring in as much as $100 million a year.[54] And in early 2017, the *Post* cut a deal with its largest licensee for Arc yet: the unfortunately named tronc, publisher of the *Los Angeles Times*, the *Chicago Tribune*, and other newspapers.[55]

"I would love it if the platform we built for the *Post* was powering a lot of other media organizations," Prakash said, conjuring up the possibility of a network of Arc-powered news organizations with the *Post* at the center. "That would definitely break down the silos for content sharing, a lot of the silos for analytics, for personalization. The larger the scale the better you can do in some of those scenarios. But those are still aspirational at this point."

One aspect of the *Post*'s business model I haven't discussed much is advertising, which may seem like an oversight given that ads traditionally provided about 80 percent of a newspaper's revenue.[56] It is sometimes said that the news was free, since the 20 percent paid by readers was used mainly to cover the cost of printing and distribution. Even today, daily newspapers, including the *Post,* make most of their money from advertising in their print editions. As I noted earlier, the state of digital advertising is dismal, as its very ubiquity — served up on a programmatic basis by Google and a few smaller competitors — has driven down its value.

Given the realities of the moment, the *Post*'s pursuit of a large digital audience is not necessarily built on the notion that it will lead to advertising riches. A more important goal is turning some percentage of that audience into paying subscribers. But that hardly means that online advertising is being ignored. As Jed Hartman said in his memo about the *Post* being a "growing business," digital advertising was on the rise. Beth Diaz told me that getting big not only had increased the revenues the *Post* received from programmatic ads of the type that Google serves up, but had also improved the sales force's ability to sell digital ads directly. "We did need to achieve a certain level of scale just to be in the game," she said. "Suddenly nobody is laughing at us when we come to present ourselves as the place to reach a broad audience, a leadership audience, etcetera."[57]

The *Post,* like the *New York Times,* the *Boston Globe,* and many other newspapers, had also embraced a controversial form of online advertising known as native advertising, or sponsored content. There is, in fact, nothing new about sponsored content. Decades ago, *Time* and *Newsweek* would publish multipage sections extolling the virtues of various repressive foreign regimes, and you had to look closely to discover that the sections had been bought and paid for by those regimes. So it is with online native content, whose critics argue is inherently aimed at fooling readers into thinking it's not really advertising.

That sort of criticism, though, leaves no room for native advertising that *is* properly labeled. Flip through the *Post*'s apps and peruse its website and you'll come across occasional features from the "WP BrandStudio." At the top of the screen it says (for example), "Content from Siemens." In place of a byline, we see "Content created by WP BrandStudio." At the bottom it says, "This content is developed and paid for by Siemens. The Washington Post Newsroom is not involved in the creation of this content." That strikes me as more than sufficient.

Given how difficult it is to persuade readers to pay for online subscriptions and the plummeting value of programmatic digital advertising, it appears that sponsored content is here to stay. According to one report, native advertising accounted for 11 percent of revenues at news media companies in 2016 and was projected to rise to 25 percent in 2018.[58] Moreover, native advertising can be an effective way to fight back against the proliferation of ad-blocking software, which got a huge boost in the fall of 2015 when Apple allowed ad blockers into its app store for iPhones and iPads. Ad blockers deprive publishers of revenue, of course, and the *Post* has experimented with blocking the blockers; Prakash told me those experiments would continue. But they also are a response to a real problem: the spread of abusive ads at many sites that pop up on your screen, chew up the data you paid for, slow down access, invade your privacy, and in some cases carry spyware or malware.[59] (The *Post*, like most subscription-based sites, is relatively free of such abominations.) By contrast, native ads can't be blocked because they reside on a news organization's own server. And, properly designed, they can be attractive and even provide information that users might be interested in. "I think there's a future for branded content or sponsored content as long as we keep it clearly demarcated as such," Prakash said.

IN LATE OCTOBER 2015, Bob Woodward, the legendary *Washington Post* reporter who was one-half of the duo that brought down a president, spoke at the First Parish Church in Cambridge, Massachusetts, to promote a new book. *The Last of the President's Men* was about Alexander Butterfield, the aide who revealed the existence of the taping system in Richard Nixon's White House, thus proving that he really was a crook. Toward the end of the evening, a member of the audience asked Woodward how the media business had changed over the years. Woodward responded by praising Jeff Bezos.

"I think he's helping us as a business," Woodward said. "It's a better website. I find things much more authoritative, quite frankly, than the *New York Times*." He continued: "Bezos is good news for the newspaper, the *Washington Post*. I think he has a long-range view, staying in for fifteen or twenty years and making sure the *Washington Post* is one of the surviving news sources in the country." And when the moderator, the veteran presidential counselor and CNN commentator David Gergen, asked, "Are newspapers as strongly committed to investigative journalism as they were?," Woodward responded: "I know the *Washington Post* is, because I asked Jeff Bezos.

He has the money. We talked about this, and he said I could quote him on this, and I will. And he said, 'Rest assured, Marty' — Baron, the editor — 'will have the resources he needs.'"[60]

Bezos's *Post* probably doesn't offer much in the way of concrete lessons for the rest of the struggling newspaper business. His success has been built on three strategies that are not available to most newspaper owners. First, he was able to transform the *Post* almost overnight into a national digital publication by virtue of its being in Washington. Second, he has leveraged the *Post* in ways that enhance the value of Amazon, a strategy that he is likely to build on. Third, his immense wealth allows him the luxury of experimenting with various initiatives, some of which may work and some of which may not.

But if specific "do this" lessons are few, there are nevertheless matters of tone and approach Bezos has brought to the *Post* that every newspaper executive ought to ponder. I've identified five, some obvious, some counterintuitive:

There are significant benefits to private ownership. Even though the Graham family held a majority of the voting stock before they sold the Washington Post Company to Bezos, they were still constrained by demands from Wall Street to produce quarterly profits. Bezos, like John Henry at the *Boston Globe,* is free to do what he likes in charting a future for the *Post.*

There is value in getting big. At a time when some are warning that the decline of online advertising prices means it no longer makes sense to build as large a digital audience as possible, Bezos has pursued size and scale. This has given him an opportunity to convert some percentage of that audience into paying customers and to be in a position to benefit from revenue opportunities that may not currently exist.

Do not pursue change for change's sake. Perhaps the most important statement Bezos made about his management style was to leave Marty Baron and Shailesh Prakash in place. Both enjoy reputations as among the best in the business, but no one would have begrudged a new owner for wanting to bring in his own people. Bezos realized he already had the right people.

Technology is central to the mission. Very few organizations have the resources to develop their own technology to the extent that the *Post* has. Still, every newspaper executive who wants to succeed online needs first-rate tools and products, whether they are built in-house or licensed from outside developers.

Embrace change even when you can't control it. The *Post* decided early on to publish its content as Facebook Instant Articles, on Apple News, and as part of Google AMP. Though using such distributed platforms runs counter to the goal of selling more digital subscriptions and deprives the paper of customer data, *Post* executives believe they have to be where their audience is.

As a technologist himself, Shailesh Prakash has a unique perspective on what Bezos has meant to the *Post.* "The money has helped us, of course. I wouldn't deny it," he told me. "But I don't think that's the main thing Jeff has brought. And I don't just say that because he's my boss. I truly believe that. Of course he's helped with money. He's helped me hire people, he's helped Marty hire people, and so on. But it's not like it's open-check season where we can do anything we want. So what has he really done? I personally think that the biggest thing Jeff has done is to set the right tone for our culture — which is one of experimentation, which is one of encouragement, which is one of 'find the positive surprises and double down.' We believe we have an owner who respects the past but at the same time wants us to be innovative."

As you walk through the *Post*'s newsroom, you encounter inspirational quotes from a number of the paper's legendary figures, past and present. One is from Jeff Bezos. It reads: "I strongly believe that missionaries make better products. They care more. For a missionary, it's not just about the business. There has to be a business, and the business has to make sense, but that's not why you do it. You do it because you have something meaningful that motivates you."[61]

Bezos is smart and tough. In considering his stewardship of the *Washington Post,* it's important to maintain a sense of realism. No doubt he wants the *Post* to succeed, but that success has to come on his terms. Ultimately, that means it has to succeed as a profitable business. Still, we should take him at his word that saving a great newspaper is more important to him than turning around the fortunes of "a snack-food company," as he has put it. Bezos is someone who cares about his reputation and who has spoken with fervor about the role of journalism. As he said at the dedication of the new headquarters, "This needs to be a sustainable business because that's healthy for the mission."

No newspaper executive has figured out a way to prosper during the twenty-year era of the commercial internet. As is the case with the *Post*, news organizations need to be willing to experiment, to abandon experiments that aren't working, and to keep embracing new ideas in the hope that some of them will prove to be not only journalistically sound but an enhancement of the bottom line as well.

In his public interview with Walter Isaacson, Bezos spoke passionately about the history and traditions of the *Washington Post*. "What makes the *Post* great is not our business model. What makes the *Post* great is the tradition of investigative journalism and all the things that they have in the newsroom," he said. "I started to get a very powerful sense of it when I went to Ben Bradlee's funeral. There's a long tradition at the *Post* of just putting a lot of shoe leather into things and finding stories that nobody else can find."[62] More than anything, Bradlee's death in 2014 underscored the *Post*'s ongoing importance in American life and of Bezos's role not just as its owner but as the curator of its culture and the guarantor of its continued relevance.

In the early months of the Trump presidency, journalism faced an unprecedented challenge. The president, besieged by evidence that his campaign had colluded with the Russian government, lashed out at the press, declaring it to be "an enemy of the people."[63] And just as during the Nixon era, the two news organizations that took the lead in holding the White House to account were the *New York Times* and the *Washington Post*.

Jeff Bezos is a brilliant businessman and a visionary. The times call for an idealist as well. Bezos appears to understand what it means to own the newspaper where Ben Bradlee made his mark — and where Woodward and Bernstein brought down a president, and where Katharine Graham demonstrated the crucial importance of a publisher who was willing to stand up to power.

By late 2017, it was as yet unclear what challenges Bezos would face. What mattered was that he appeared willing to face them.

EPILOGUE

THE FALL AND RISE OF JOURNALISM IN THE AGE OF TRUMP

THE IMMEDIATE AFTERSHOCKS of Donald Trump's stunning election in 2016 carried with them a wave of unexpected good news for some media organizations. Trump had won his Electoral College victory in part by attacking members of the media as "scum," "slime," "dishonest," and "disgusting."[1] Such rhetoric played well with his most devoted supporters. But Americans who were appalled by Trump's rise responded by offering financial support for journalism aimed at holding him to account.

The comedian John Oliver urged his viewers to donate to the nonprofit investigative reporting project ProPublica and to subscribe to the *New York Times* and the *Washington Post.* The response was heartening. Contributions to ProPublica shot up by a factor of ten, according to the organization's president, Richard Tofel. From Election Day through the end of November, the *Times* reported a net increase of about 132,000 paid print and digital subscriptions. The *Post,* characteristically cryptic, said in a statement that there had been a "steady increase in subscriptions across the course of this year." Liberal-leaning magazines such as the *Atlantic* and *Mother Jones* reported a postelection boost as well. Indeed, anti-Trump sentiment was proving to be so good for business that when the president-elect went after *Vanity Fair* for trashing one of his restaurants, it responded with a marketing campaign calling itself the "magazine Trump doesn't want you to read" — and new subscribers flocked in. At the regional level, the *Boston Globe* also reported a sharp increase in digital subscribers.[2]

Of course, anger over Trump's election could not itself serve as the basis of a sustainable business model. At the dawn of 2017, it appeared that the economic problems that had long plagued journalistic enterprises were about to become much, much worse. The continued domination of Facebook and Google was strangling the news business, even though journalists supplied much of the content on which the two internet behemoths relied. Advertising in 2017 was expected to reach $547 billion, with 77 percent of it going to digital. The trouble was that about 85 percent of all new online ad spending was going to Facebook and Google. Facebook's status as a "frenemy" of the news business was becoming increasingly fraught, especially following reports that it had been overstating the amount of time its users spent watching videos — touted as a revenue opportunity for media organizations — by 60 to 80 percent. Facebook was also found to be overreporting traffic to Instant Articles by 10 percent or more.[3]

Within the newspaper business, disappointment over the failure of digital to provide revenue growth led to a backlash. The *Columbia Journalism Review* published a special report arguing that newspaper owners had made a monumental mistake by heading down the digital path and letting their print publications wither. Incongruously, the article was written by Michael Rosenwald, a reporter for the *Washington Post*, one of the few newspapers to experience some financial success in the digital realm. Two decades after the first newspaper websites flickered into view, Rosenwald wrote, nothing "has come close to matching the success of print in revenue or readership."[4]

Rosenwald was not wrong. As I have shown throughout, print continues to provide the majority of revenues to most papers, even the *Post*. It was the animating theory behind Aaron Kushner's ownership of the *Orange County Register*, and it might have worked if Kushner's emphasis on print hadn't been accompanied by an unaffordable hiring spree. But a strategy disproportionately geared to print was not realistic given the precipitous decline of print advertising revenues. No doubt print will persist for quite some time as a high-priced "artisanal product," as Kathleen Kingsbury, the *Boston Globe*'s former managing editor for digital, has put it.[5] But if newspapers are to survive and thrive, they will ultimately have to do so through some combination of print, digital, and perhaps other sources yet to be discovered.

In addition to economic woes, newspapers in early 2017 faced a crisis of legitimacy. The term "fake news" — originally applied to for-profit hoax stories designed for viral shareability — began to be applied indiscriminately. When the *Washington Post* erroneously reported that Russian hackers had gained access to the electrical grid in Vermont, in some circles it was not labeled a mistake but "fake news." And when CNN reported — accurately — that intelligence officers had briefed President-elect Trump and President Obama about unverified personal and financial information regarding Trump that Russian sources had compiled into a dossier, Trump labeled CNN a purveyor of "fake news."[6]

Since 1970, when Vice President Spiro Agnew denounced the media as "nattering nabobs of negativism," Republicans have been working to undermine trust in mainstream journalism by claiming that it is hopelessly suffused with liberal bias.[7] That campaign reached its apotheosis under Trump, as traditional news organizations such as the *Times*, the *Post*, and others were equated with right-wing media organizations and personalities that did little or no reporting and often spread ideologically motivated falsehoods, such as Breitbart News, the Fox News Channel, and the conspiracy-minded radio host Alex Jones. A major study by scholars at Harvard and MIT found that media usage during the 2016 campaign was characterized by "asymmetric polarization," which they described as a tendency among Hillary Clinton supporters to consume a wide array of mainstream and left-leaning media and among Trump supporters to stick with a small number of right-wing outlets.[8]

Still, we shouldn't lose hope. As the journalist James Fallows observed, the very same people who voted for Trump as an expression of their fear and anger over the state of the nation nevertheless retained their ability to function as cooperative members of their local communities. Fallows wrote in the *Atlantic* that "at the level of politics where people's judgments are based on direct observation rather than media-fueled fear, Americans still trust democratic processes and observe long-respected norms." He added:

> The American public has just made a decision of the gravest consequence, largely based on distorted, frightening, and bigoted caricatures of reality that we all would recognize as caricature if applied to our own communities. Given the atrophy of old-line media with their quaint regard for truth, the addictive strength of social media and their unprecedented capacity to spread lies, and the cynicism of modern politics, will we ever be able to accurately match image with reality?[9]

Fallows underscored a crucial truth: that constructive engagement still takes place at the regional and local levels. At a time of national divisive-ness, any hope we have of coming together must be rooted in our communities and in our ability to find a common understanding with the friends, neighbors, and strangers among us.

Although this book is largely about three newspapers, one is not the same as the other two. Jeff Bezos's great accomplishment was to restore the *Washington Post* to its status as a leading national news organization. The *Boston Globe* and the *Orange County Register* are in a very different situation. Along with other large regional newspapers, from the *Los Angeles Times* to the *Philadelphia Inquirer,* from the *Chicago Tribune* to the *Dallas Morning News,* it is their role to serve as the glue that binds together their communities.

They are engaged in a difficult balancing act. Many of us care about what's going on nationally and in our immediate neighborhoods. Metropolitan newspapers, though, tend to be too small to do a good job with the former and too large to cover the latter. And yet they are uniquely suited to build the bridges we need in order to identify problems and come up with solutions that cut across lines of neighborhood, race, and class. I live in a medium-sized city outside of Boston. But when I travel, I tell people that I live in Boston. It's an idea as much as it is a geographic entity, and the local media — led by the *Globe* — help to define that idea.

Journalism will endure regardless of how it is distributed. But newspapers, whether in print or online, are still the most elegant vehicles for delivering that journalism. The way forward for newspapers will not be easy. It's not even clear that there *is* a way forward. But our democracy will be much the poorer if they lose their struggle for survival.

ACKNOWLEDGMENTS

THIS BOOK GREW out of a series of conversations I had with Stephen Hull of ForeEdge at University Press of New England. I had only recently completed *The Wired City: Reimagining Journalism and Civic Life in the Post-Newspaper Age* (University of Massachusetts Press, 2013), and I wasn't sure how eager I was to dive into another book so soon. But Steve was persistent. We kicked around several ideas before external events intervened. On the Friday of the first weekend in August 2013, John Henry announced he would buy the *Boston Globe*. The following Monday, Jeff Bezos said he would purchase the *Washington Post*. Aaron Kushner was garnering praise for his efforts to remake the *Orange County Register*. After years of gloom in the newspaper business, public-spirited people of means were taking an interest in revitalizing the economics of journalism. Steve and I knew we had our project. As with any book, there were bumps and delays along the way. Steve's patience, understanding, and support were crucial in bringing this project home.

I'm not sure I would have been able to complete this book were it not for my good fortune in being named a Joan Shorenstein Fellow at the Shorenstein Center for Media, Politics and Public Policy, part of the Harvard Kennedy School, during the Spring 2016 semester. I have spent the better part of my career attending events at Shorenstein. Coming inside as a fellow proved every bit as intellectually stimulating and collegial as I had hoped. I greatly enjoyed working alongside the other fellows, Johanna Dunaway, Joanna Jolly, and Marilyn Thompson, brilliant women whose presence pushed me to do my best. They were also wonderful lunch companions. We all enjoyed our time with Bob Schieffer of CBS News, who was the Walter Shorenstein Media and Democracy Fellow. Bob took an interest in my project and was kind enough to feature me on a podcast he hosts with

H. Andrew Schwartz, *About the News,* through the Center for Strategic and International Studies.

I also owe a debt of gratitude to Thomas Patterson, Shorenstein's Bradlee Professor of Government and the Press, who was interim director during my fellowship. Tom offered valuable advice and counsel in helping me carve out part of my project so that I could write a proper Shorenstein paper. That paper, "The Bezos Effect," served as the template for my chapters on the *Washington Post.* Shorenstein faculty members Matthew Baum, Michael Ignatieff, Marion Just, Richard Parker, and Robert Picard provided useful suggestions and support as well. Executive director Nancy Palmer, fellows program manager Katie Miles, and events manager Tim Bailey were always available to assist with logistics and to answer questions. Nilagia McCoy provided expert copy-editing. My research assistant, Stephanie Desanges, did a terrific job of tracking down books, articles, facts, and figures. I know she has a great career ahead of her.

My research would have benefited greatly from the guidance of Stephen Burgard, the director of the School of Journalism at Northeastern University, who died after a brief illness in the fall of 2014. Steve was a friend and mentor. It was my honor to serve as interim director after his death until our current director, Jonathan Kaufman, joined us the following summer. Earlier in his career Steve had worked as the editorial page editor of the *Los Angeles Times*'s Orange County edition. He had expressed great enthusiasm for my project, and I was looking forward to the assistance he had promised with the Orange County chapters — as well as to attending a few more Red Sox games with him.

My former *Boston Phoenix* colleague Susan Ryan-Vollmar, a communications specialist and the principal of Influence Consulting, edited the entire manuscript, making a number of excellent suggestions for improving it. Susan's mother, Patricia Ryan, provided me with the use of her cottage in Jay, Vermont, for a crucial final week of writing in March 2017. Two other former *Phoenix* colleagues also weighed in with valuable suggestions: Catherine Tumber, the research manager for the University of Massachusetts Donahue Institute and the author of *Small, Gritty, and Green: The Promise of America's Smaller Industrial Cities in a Low-Carbon World* (MIT Press, 2012), and Jon Keller, political analyst for WBZ-TV in Boston and the author of *The Bluest State: How Democrats Created the Massachusetts Blueprint for American Political Disaster* (St. Martin's Griffin, 2008).

In addition to Steve Hull, a team of people at University Press of New England worked diligently on this book, including Lauren Seidman, the production editor; and her successor, Amanda Dupuis; Mindy Basinger Hill, the designer; Mary Becker, my exceedingly skilled and patient copy editor; Barbara Briggs, the publicist; and Andrew Lohse, Sherri Strickland, Katy Grabill, and Susan Sylvia, who are handling marketing and sales.

Brian Halley, the senior editor at University of Massachusetts Press, helped bring to life *The Wired City*, without which *The Return of the Moguls* would not be possible. My wonderful colleagues at Northeastern are ever supportive and understanding. Natasha Chang, a recent graduate of Northeastern's journalism program, gave the page proofs one final read. There are many others whom I could and should acknowledge, if not for their specific contributions to this book, then for their friendship and guidance. We write alone, yet we can't do it well without a community.

During the years that I was working on this book, our children, Tim, a professional photographer, and Becky, an aspiring writer, embarked on their early years of adulthood. They are a joy, and we are blessed to have them in our lives.

My wife, Barbara Kennedy, is my source of love, support, and friendship, as well as my favorite editor. I admire her and try to live up to the example that she sets in her daily life.

NOTES

INTRODUCTION
The Rise and Fall of Newspapers in a Time of Turmoil

1. Paul Farhi, "The *Washington Post*'s New Slogan Turns Out to Be an Old Saying," *Washington Post*, February 24, 2017; William Cummings, "Trump Declares 'Fake News' Media 'the Enemy of the American People,'" *USA Today*, February 17, 2017.

2. "Our Mission: Why We Do What We Do," *Boston Globe*, accessed on April 3, 2017, www.bostonglobe.com.

3. It should be noted that Aaron Kushner is not related to Donald Trump's son-in-law, Jared Kushner, who has also invested in media properties. Aaron Kushner, email message to the author, February 17, 2017.

4. Dan Kennedy, "The War on 'Fake News' Is Over. So What's Next in Restoring Media Credibility?," WGBH News, December 27, 2016, news.wgbh.org.

5. Eric Bradner, "Conway: Trump White House Offered 'Alternative Facts' on Crowd Size," CNN.com, January 23, 2017, www.cnn.com.

6. Pete Vernon, "Subscription Surges and Record Audiences Follow Trump's Election," *Columbia Journalism Review*, December 6, 2016, www.cjr.org.

7. Alex S. Jones, *Losing the News: The Future of the News That Feeds Democracy* (New York: Oxford University Press, 2009), 2–4.

8. Philip Meyer, *The Vanishing Newspaper: Saving Journalism in the Information Age* (Columbia: University of Missouri Press, 2004), 5.

9. "Boston Daily Newspapers 20th Century," Boston Public Library, accessed on June 8, 2017, www.bpl.org.

10. The *Washington Post*'s rivalry with other Washington newspapers is covered in depth in Katharine Graham, *Personal History* (New York: Alfred A. Knopf, 1997), and in David Halberstam, *The Powers That Be* (Urbana: University of Illinois Press, 2000).

11. "Sun Myung Moon Paper Appears in Washington," *New York Times*, May 18, 1982.

12. Katerina Eva Matsa, "Network News Fact Sheet," *State of the News Media, 2015* (Washington, DC: Pew Research Center, April 29, 2015), 36.

13. Alliance for Audited Media, www.auditedmedia.com; the circulation is a Monday-through-Friday average for the twelve-month period ending September 30, 2015, and includes print (614,781) and digital (1,511,426).

14. A. J. Liebling, *The Press* (New York: Ballantine Books, 1964), 4.

15. The Pulitzer Prizes, accessed on June 8, 2017, www.pulitzer.org.

16. Leonard Downie Jr. and Michael Schudson, "The Reconstruction of American Journalism," *Columbia Journalism Review*, November/December 2009, www.cjr.org.

17. "Stopping the Presses," *On the Media*, National Public Radio, February 20, 2009, www.onthemedia.org.

18. Meyer, *The Vanishing Newspaper*, 38.

19. John B. Horrigan and Maeve Duggan, *Home Broadband, 2015* (Washington, DC: Pew Research Center, December 21, 2015), www.pewinternet.org.

20. John Markoff, "Apple Introduces Innovative Cellphone," *New York Times*, January 10, 2007.

21. Clay Shirky, "Newspapers and Thinking the Unthinkable," *Clay Shirky* (blog), March 13, 2009, www.shirky.com.

22. *Newspaper Circulation Volume* (Arlington, VA: Newspaper Association of America, March 30, 2015). By September 2016, the organization had changed its name to the News Media Alliance and had moved much of its data to a members-only section of its website, located at www.newsmediaalliance.org. Estimates for 2016 are from "Newspapers Fact Sheet," *State of the News Media, 2017* (Washington, DC: Pew Research Center, June 1, 2017), www.journalism.org.

23. Ibid.; Barthel, "Newspapers Fact Sheet," *State of the News Media, 2015*, 27.

24. Suzanne Vranica and Jack Marshall, "Plummeting Newspaper Ad Revenue Sparks New Wave of Changes," *Wall Street Journal*, October 20, 2016.

25. Barthel, "Newspapers Fact Sheet," *State of the News Media, 2015*, 27.

26. Mark J. Perry, "Free-Fall: Adjusted for Inflation, Print Newspaper Advertising Will Be Lower This Year than in 1950," *Carpe Diem* (blog), April 8, 2014, mjperry.blogspot.com.

27. Barthel, "Newspapers Fact Sheet," *State of the News Media, 2015*, 28; Rick Edmonds, "Newspaper Industry Lost 3,800 Full-Time Editorial Professionals in 2014," Poynter.org, July 28, 2015, www.poynter.org.

28. Richard Pérez-Peña, "*Rocky Mountain News* Fails to Find Buyer and Will Close," *New York Times*, February 26, 2009; William Yardley and Richard Pérez-Peña, "Seattle Paper Shifts Entirely to the Web," *New York Times*, March 16, 2009.

29. Curt Nickisch, "N.Y. Times Co. Threatens to Close *Boston Globe*," NPR.org, April 9, 2009, www.npr.org.

30. Michael Hirschorn, "End Times," *Atlantic*, January/February 2009, www.theatlantic.com.

31. Michael J. de la Merced, "Freedom Communications Files for Bankruptcy Protection," *New York Times*, September 1, 2009.

32. *Citizen Kane*, directed by Orson Welles, screenplay by Herman J. Mankiewicz and Orson Welles, RKO Radio Pictures and Mercury Productions, 1941. The scene depicts Welles as the newspaper magnate Charles Foster Kane and George Coulouris as his former guardian, Walter Parks Thatcher. Additional information from the *Citizen Kane* entry at the Internet Movie Database, www.imdb.com.

33. Jack Shafer, "The New Vanity Press Moguls," *Slate*, June 22, 2006, www.slate.com.

34. Jack Shafer, "Pierre Omidyar and the Bottomless Optimism of Billionaire Publishers," Reuters, October 17, 2013, blogs.reuters.com/jackshafer.

35. Maria Bustillos, "News Isn't for the Billionaire Few," *Nieman Journalism Lab*, December 2015, www.niemanlab.org.

CHAPTER ONE

The Swashbuckler: Jeff Bezos Puts His Stamp on a Legendary Newspaper

1. Justin Jouvenal and Michael Laris, "As Region Returns to Life, Some Still Snowbound Feel Abandoned," *Washington Post*, January 27, 2016.

2. Remarks at the dedication ceremony are from video at "Jeff Bezos, John Kerry Attend the *Washington Post* Grand Opening," *Washington Post*, January 28, 2016.

3. Paul Fahri, "*Washington Post* Closes Sale to Amazon founder Jeff Bezos," *Washington Post*, October 1, 2013.

4. Nikki Usher, "The *Washington Post* Celebrates Its New Building with DC Elite and High-End Catering," *Columbia Journalism Review*, January 29, 2016, www.cjr.org.

5. Andrew Roth, "*Post* Owner Jeff Bezos Flies Reporter Jason Rezaian to U.S. after Iran Release," *Washington Post*, January 22, 2016.

6. Laura Hazard Owen, "Jeff Bezos Says the *Washington Post*'s Goal Is to Become the 'New Paper of Record,'" *Nieman Journalism Lab*, November 15, 2015, www.niemanlab.org.

7. Matthew Hindman, *Stickier News: What Newspapers Don't Know about Web Traffic Has Hurt Them Badly — But There Is a Better Way* (Cambridge, MA: Shorenstein Center on Media, Politics and Public Policy, Harvard Kennedy School, Fall 2014).

8. Nick Wingfield, "Move Over, Bill Gates. Jeff Bezos Gets a Turn as World's Richest Person," *New York Times*, July 27, 2017.

9. Jordan Valinsky, "*Washington Post* Tops *New York Times* Online for First Time Ever," *Digiday,* November 13, 2015, www.digiday.com. A unique visitor is a person — or, more precisely, a specific location on the internet known as an Internet Protocol, or IP, address. Web traffic is most commonly measured as unique visitors per month.

10. "The *Washington Post* Surpasses 890 Million Page Views, 73 Million Users in February," *WashPost PR Blog, Washington Post,* March 17, 2016, www.washington post.com.

11. "The *Washington Post* Records Nearly 100 Million Visitors in October, Greatly Exceeding Previous Traffic Records," *WashPost PR Blog, Washington Post,* November 14, 2016, www.washingtonpost.com.

12. "The *Washington Post* Records More than 78 Million Users in April, up 22% Year over Year," *WashPost PR Blog, Washington Post,* May 15, 2017, www.washington post.com.

13. September 2015 circulation figures are from the Alliance for Audited Media, www.auditedmedia.com; the 1993 figure is from Steven Mufson, "As Jeff Bezos Prepares to Take Over, a Look at Forces That Shaped the *Washington Post* sale," *Washington Post,* September 27, 2013; the 2008 figure is from Frank Ahrens, "Post Co. Reports First Operating Loss in 37 Years," *Washington Post,* August 2, 2008.

14. "*Washington Post* Executive Editor Martin Baron on Journalism's Transition from Print to Digital," *WashPost PR Blog, Washington Post,* April 8, 2015, www.wash ingtonpost.com; email messages to the author from Molly Gannon Conway, lead publicist for the *Washington Post,* March 10 and 30, July 1 and 7, 2016; Ravi Somaiya, "*New York Times* Plans to Eliminate 100 Jobs in the Newsroom," *New York Times,* October 1, 2014; Ken Doctor, "'Profitable' *Washington Post* Adding More than Five Dozen Journalists," *Politico Media,* December 27, 2016, www.politico.com/media.

15. Baxter Holmes, "Is Martin Baron the Best Editor of All Time?," *Esquire,* November 24, 2015, www.esquire.com.

16. Brian Stelter, "*Spotlight* Wins Best Picture, and the Real-Life Journalists Are Overjoyed," CNN.com, February 29, 2016, money.cnn.com.

17. The Pulitzer Prizes, accessed on October 13, 2016, www.pulitzer.org.

18. David Beard, interview by the author, October 16, 2015.

19. Robert C. Kennedy, "On This Day" for August 1, 1863, *New York Times,* no publication date provided, accessed on October 13, 2016, www.nytimes.com.

20. Chalmers Roberts, *The Washington Post: The First 100 Years* (Boston: Houghton Mifflin, 1977), 1.

21. Ibid., 12–27, quote on 16.

22. Ibid., 78.

23. Ibid., 64.

24. Ibid., 57–69, quote on 57.

25. Ibid., 85–120, quote on 87.

26. Ibid., 134–56, quote on 136.

27. Ibid., 170–93.

28. David Halberstam, *The Powers That Be* (Urbana: University of Illinois Press, 2000), 180–81; Roberts, *The Washington Post: The First 100 Years*, 194–95.

29. Halberstam, *The Powers That Be*, 177–83; Katharine Graham, *Personal History* (New York: Alfred A. Knopf, 1997), 170.

30. John Huey, Martin Nisenholtz, Paul Sagan, and John Geddes, *Riptide: An Oral History of the Epic Collision between Journalism and Digital Technology, from 1980 to the Present* (Cambridge, MA: Shorenstein Center on Media, Politics and Public Policy, April 4, 2013), www.digitalriptide.org.

31. Martin Baron, interview by the author, March 16, 2016.

32. Huey et al., *Riptide.*

33. Halberstam, *The Powers That Be*, 305.

34. Graham, *Personal History*, 131.

35. Ibid., 187–221.

36. Halberstam, *The Powers That Be*, 301–4.

37. Huey et al., *Riptide.*

38. Halberstam, *The Powers That Be*, 582–83.

39. James Fallows, *Breaking the News: How the Media Undermine American Democracy* (New York: Vintage Books, 1997), 70–71.

40. Brooke A. Masters, "*N.Y. Times* Control Challenged," *Washington Post*, April 19, 2006; Graham, *Personal History*, 441–42.

41. Graham, *Personal History*, 511–12.

42. Halberstam, *The Powers That Be*, 714–16; Graham, *Personal History*, 537–65.

43. Ben H. Bagdikian, "Maximizing Profits at the *Washington Post*," *Washington Monthly*, January 1976, 31.

44. Graham, *Personal History*, 570.

45. Ibid., 537–97.

46. Jeff Bercovici, "Nice Guy, Finishing Last: How Don Graham Fumbled the Washington Post Co.," *Forbes*, February 27, 2012, www.forbes.com.

47. Megan Garber, "Encyclo: TBD," *Nieman Journalism Lab*, August 22, 2012, www.niemanlab.org.

48. Craig Timberg, Chico Harlan, and Peter Whoriskey, "*Post* Names Frederick J. Ryan Jr. as New Publisher," *Washington Post*, September 2, 2014.

49. Halberstam, *The Powers That Be*, 522–36; Graham, *Personal History*, 379–83.

50. Halberstam, *The Powers That Be*, 571–78; Graham, *Personal History*, 446–51.

51. Graham, *Personal History*, 455–56, 479.

52. Harvey Silverglate, "The Gray Lady in Shadow," *Boston Phoenix*, January 6, 2006.

53. Graham, *Personal History*, 465.

54. Jeff Bezos, "Jeff Bezos on *Post* Purchase," *Washington Post*, August 5, 2013.

55. Halberstam, *The Powers That Be*, 536; Graham, *Personal History*, 415–16.

56. Alicia C. Shepard, *Woodward and Bernstein: Life in the Shadow of Watergate* (Hoboken, NJ: John Wiley and Sons, 2007), 161–84, 192–245; Douglas Brinkley, "A Force of Nature," *Boston Globe*, June 17, 2007.

57. Dan Kennedy, "Print Is Dying, Digital Is No Savior: The Long, Ugly Decline of the Newspaper Business Continues Apace," WGBH News, January 26, 2016, news.wgbh.org.

58. David Carr, "Digital Ink Reboots," *Washington City Paper*, February 16, 1996.

59. "WPNI Press Materials" and "Make the WPNI Advantage Your Own," washingtonpost.com, outdated materials accessed on April 5, 2016, www.washingtonpost.com.

60. Graham Holdings Company, accessed on June 8, 2017, www.ghco.com.

61. "QuickFacts," U.S. Census Bureau, accessed on June 8, 2017, www.census.gov.

62. Russell Adams, "Big Daily's 'Hyperlocal' Flop," *Wall Street Journal*, June 4, 2008; Rob Curley, "After the 'Flop' Flap: Lessons Learned from Loudoun," *Rob Curley* (blog), June 8, 2008, www.robcurley.com.

63. Jim Brady, interview by the author, January 26, 2016.

64. Eric Convey, "*Boston Globe* Lays Off Hyper-Local Your Town Correspondents," *Boston Business Journal*, March 6, 2014.

65. John Hazard, "Authentically Local Declares: Local Doesn't Scale," *Street Fight*, May 12, 2011, www.streetfightmag.com.

66. David Kirkpatrick, *The Facebook Effect: The Inside Story of the Company That Is Connecting the World* (New York: Simon & Schuster Paperbacks, 2011), 123.

67. Ibid., 107–14, quote on 107–8.

68. Ibid., 121–23.

69. Ibid., 123–25, quotes on 123.

70. Brady, interview by the author.

71. Bercovici, "Nice Guy, Finishing Last."

72. Yahoo! Finance, accessed on April 2, 2017, finance.yahoo.com.

73. Huey et al., *Riptide*.

74. Dan Kennedy, "Truth, Lies and the *Washington Post*," *Comment Is Free* (blog), *Guardian*, October 20, 2009, www.theguardian.com.

75. Mufson, "Could Don Graham Have Saved the *Washington Post*?"

76. "Martin 'Marty' Baron Named Executive Editor of the *Washington Post*," *Washington Post*, November 13, 2012.

77. David Remnick, "Donald Graham's Choice," *New Yorker*, August 5, 2013, www.newyorker.com.

78. Frank Ahrens, "Post Co. Reports First Operating Loss in 37 Years," *Washington Post*, August 2, 2008.

79. Bercovici, "Nice Guy, Finishing Last."

80. *2012 Annual Report*, Washington Post Company, 91; "Don Graham's Remarks to *Washington Post* Employees August 5, 2013," *2013 Annual Report*, Graham Holdings Company, 10–11.

81. Huey et al., *Riptide*.

CHAPTER TWO

The *Crux* of the Matter: John Henry's Culture of Experimentation

1. Account of the Boston College event is from Dan Kennedy, "The Catholic Church, the *Boston Globe* and a Jolt of Cognitive Dissonance," WGBH News, September 12, 2014, news.wgbh.org.

2. Steve Marantz, "Law Raps Ex-Priest Coverage," *Boston Globe*, May 24, 1992.

3. David France, *Our Fathers: The Secret Life of the Catholic Church in an Age of Scandal* (New York: Harmony, 2004), 537.

4. David Boeri, "Cardinal O'Malley Praises *Spotlight* Film Following Best Picture Oscar," WBUR.org, March 1, 2016, www.wbur.org.

5. Dan Kennedy, The *Globe* Will Shutter *Crux* and Reposition *BetaBoston*," *Media Nation* (blog), March 11, 2016, www.dankennedy.net.

6. "*Crux* Will Continue with the Knights of Columbus as Its Partner," *Crux*, March 15, 2016, www.cruxnow.com.

7. Dan Kennedy, "Mobile-First *Stat*: Can the *Boston Globe* Engineer Profits through the Life Sciences?," WGBH News, November 4, 2015, news.wgbh.org.

8. Dan Kennedy, "The *Boston Globe* Is Headed for Another Round of Buyouts," *Media Nation* (blog), May 3, 2016, www.dankennedy.net; Dan Adams, "*Globe* Reaches Agreement to Sell Dorchester Headquarters," *Boston Globe*, July 16, 2016; "*Globe* Editor McGrory: It's Time to Rethink Everything We Do," April 7, 2016, *Media Nation* (blog), www.dankennedy.net.

9. Shaun Sutner, "Halifax Media of Florida to Buy *Telegram & Gazette*," *Worcester Telegram & Gazette*, May 22, 2014.

10. Catherine Carlock, "Sources: New York Developer to Pay up to $80M for *Boston Globe* HQ," *Boston Business Journal*, July 19, 2016; Jon Chesto, "*Boston Globe* Says Buyer of Its Dorchester Site Backs Out," *Boston Globe*, May 17, 2017.

11. Mark Arsenault, "It's Been One Problem after Another for *Globe* Presses," *Boston Globe*, September 16, 2017.

12. Louis M. Lyons, *Newspaper Story: One Hundred Years of the "Boston Globe"* (Cambridge, MA: Belknap Press, 1971), 3.

13. Ibid., 5–16.

14. Ibid., 26–27.

15. Ibid., 107.

16. "John Irving Taylor," RedSox.com, accessed on December 1, 2016, boston.redsox.mlb.com.

17. "MLB World Series Winners," ESPN.com, accessed on December 1, 2016, www.espn.com.

18. Dan Shaughnessy, *The Curse of the Bambino* (New York: Penguin Books, 2004).

19. Dan Duquette Jr., "Report: New York Times Company Sells Minority Stake in Red Sox for $63 Million," NESN.com, May 11, 2012, www.nesn.com.

20. Casey Ross, "Despite Objections, Red Sox Win Rights to Street Use," *Boston Globe*, September 27, 2013.

21. Bob Hohler, "Inside the Collapse," *Boston Globe*, October 12, 2011.

22. Jason Schwartz, "Will John Henry Save the *Globe*?," *Boston*, March 2014, www.bostonmagazine.com.

23. Dan Shaughnessy, interview by the author, November 17, 2016.

24. Dan Kennedy, "Dan Shaughnessy Defends *Boston Globe* over Deleted Sentence in Don Orsillo Column," WGBH News, September 1, 2015.

25. Shaughnessy, interview by the author.

26. Ibid.

27. Lyons, *Newspaper Story*, 13.

28. Ibid., 14.

29. Ibid., 71.

30. Ibid., 3–4.

31. Ibid., 27–60; on "the maid's paper," see Fox Butterfield, "The *Globe*'s Own Family Is a Story unto Itself," *New York Times*, June 13, 1993.

32. Herbert A. Kenny, *Newspaper Row: Journalism in the Pre-Television Era* (Chester, CT: Globe Pequot Press, 1987), 2–3.

33. Erin Ailworth, "*Boston Herald* Moving to Seaport," *Boston Globe*, September 6, 2011.

34. Kenny, *Newspaper Row*, 121–25.

35. Lyons, *Newspaper Story*, 75–76; J. Anthony Lukas, *Common Ground: A Turbulent Decade in the Lives of Three American Families* (New York: Vintage Books, 1986), 479–80.

36. Lyons, *Newspaper Story*, 161–62; Lukas, *Common Ground*, 480, 492; Kenny, *Newspaper Row*, 36–37.

37. Kenny, *Newspaper Row*, 1–2, 22–25, 35, 185–204, 218; The Pulitzer Prizes, accessed on June 8, 2017, www.pulitzer.org.

38. Kenny, *Newspaper Row*, 218.

39. Oswald Garrison Villard, *The Disappearing Daily: Chapters in American Newspaper Evolution* (New York: Alfred A. Knopf, 1944), 175–84. Accessed through the Internet Archive, www.archive.org.

40. Kenny, *Newspaper Row*, 218–23.

41. Ibid., 223–27; "John Fox, Boston Publisher," Associated Press, as published in the *New York Times*, January 25, 1985.

42. Lukas, *Common Ground*, 483–84.

43. Ibid.

44. Ibid., 484–85.

45. Peter Braestrup, "What the Press Has Done to Boston and Vice Versa," *Harper's*, October 1960, 85, 90.

46. Lukas, *Common Ground*, 485–86, 495; Lyons, *Newspaper Story*, 274, 332–33.

47. Dan Kennedy, "How Tip Saved the *Globe*," *Boston Phoenix*, February 9, 2001.

48. Lukas, *Common Ground*, 486; Kennedy, "How Tip Saved the *Globe*."

49. John Aloysius Farrell, *Tip O'Neill and the Democratic Century* (Boston: Back Bay Books, 2001), 154, 161.

50. Margery Eagan, "Forst a Force in Mentoring Journalists," *Boston Herald*, January 6, 2014.

51. Dudley Clendinen, "Murdoch Gets Union Deal; Will Buy Boston Paper," *New York Times*, December 4, 1982.

52. George Garneau, "Purcell to Buy *Boston Herald*," *Editor & Publisher*, February 26, 1994, 10.

53. Adam Clymer, *Edward M. Kennedy: A Biography* (New York: William Morrow, 2015), Kindle edition, "The Apprentice"; Lukas, *Common Ground*, 489; Kennedy, "How Tip Saved the *Globe*."

54. Kennedy, "How Tip Saved the *Globe*."

55. Ibid.

56. Lukas, *Common Ground*, 474.

57. The Pulitzer Prizes, accessed on June 8, 2017, www.pulitzer.org.

58. Doug Bailey and Charles Stein, "*N.Y. Times* to Acquire the *Globe*," *Boston Globe*, June 11, 1993.

59. Allen R. Myerson, "Times Co. to Buy Its Shares, Spending up to $100 Million," *New York Times*, June 22, 1993.

60. Mitchell Zuckoff, "Newspaper Giants Trod Rocky Path to the Altar," *Boston Globe*, June 13, 1993.

61. Ibid.; Bailey and Stein, "*N.Y. Times* to Acquire the *Globe*."

62. Dan Kennedy, "Don't Mess with Matt," *Boston Phoenix*, August 9, 1996.

63. Charles Fountain, *Another Man's Poison: The Life and Writing of Columnist George Frazier* (Chester, CT: Globe Pequot Press, 1984), 308.

64. Dan Kennedy, "Barnicle's Game," *Boston Phoenix*, August 13, 1998; Dan

Kennedy, "Striking Similarities," *Boston Phoenix*, August 20, 1998; Howard Kurtz and Pamela Ferdin, "Mike Barnicle Forced Out at *Boston Globe*," *Washington Post*, August 20, 1998.

65. Howell Raines, "Editorial Observer; The High Price of Reprieving Mike Barnicle," *New York Times*, August 13, 1998; Jacques Steinberg, "Executive Editor of the *Times* and Top Deputy Step Down," *New York Times*, June 5, 2003.

66. Matthew Storin, interview by the author, December 9, 2015.

67. "New Publisher at *Boston Globe*," *New York Times*, December 6, 1996.

68. Dan Kennedy, "Taylor Unmade," *Boston Globe*, July 15, 1999.

69. Dan Kennedy, "Disappearing Ink," *CommonWealth*, April 26, 2007, www.commonwealthmagazine.org.

70. Dan Kennedy, "Goodbye to All That," *Boston Phoenix*, July 20, 2001.

71. Sarah Larson, "*Spotlight* and Its Revelations," *New Yorker*, December 8, 2015, www.newyorker.com.

72. The first of these articles was Kristen Lombardi, "Cardinal Sin," *Boston Phoenix*, March 23, 2001.

73. Larson, "*Spotlight* and Its Revelations."

74. Clay Shirky, *Here Comes Everybody: The Power of Organizing without Organizations* (New York: Penguin Books, 2009), Kindle edition, "Collective Action and Institutional Challenges."

75. Dan Kennedy, "Baron Rushes to Injured Reporter's Bedside," *Boston Phoenix*, April 4, 2002.

76. Rick Gladstone, "At Work in Syria, *Times* Correspondent Dies," *New York Times*, February 16, 2012.

77. Kennedy, "Goodbye to All That"; Mark Jurkowitz, "*Globe*-al Anxiety," *Boston Phoenix*, January 13, 2006.

78. Gabriel Sherman, "Good News at the *Washington Post*," *New York*, June 28, 2016, www.nymag.com.

79. Richard Pérez-Peña, "*Boston Globe* Surprised by Size of Demand for Cuts," *New York Times*, April 8, 2009.

80. "Employees Hold Rally to Save *Boston Globe*," Associated Press, April 24, 2009, www.masslive.com.

81. Beth Healy, "Times Co. Isn't Selling *Globe*, Taylor Discusses Failed Bid," *Business Updates* (blog), *Boston Globe*, October 14, 2009, no longer online as of December 20, 2016.

82. Adam Reilly, "Brave New *Globe*?," *Boston Phoenix*, January 29, 2010.

83. Casey Ross, "Brian McGrory Named *Globe*'s New Editor," *Boston Globe*, December 21, 2012.

84. Roger Yu, "New York Times Co. Selling *Boston Globe*," *USA Today*, February 20, 2013.

85. Lauren Fox, "*Crux* Columnist Margery Eagan Wins Religion Association Excellence Award," *Boston Globe*, September 1, 2015.

86. John Henry, interview by the author, February 11, 2016.

87. Brian McGrory, interview by the author, January 9, 2017.

88. Kathleen Kingsbury, interview by the author, November 29, 2016.

89. "Kathleen Kingsbury Named Deputy Editorial Page Editor, the *New York Times*," New York Times Company, June 20, 2017, investors.nytco.com.

90. John Allen, interview by the author, November 28, 2016.

91. Alexander Russo, "*Boston Globe* Launches Expanded Education Effort," *Washington Monthly*, September 18, 2015, www.washingtonmonthly.com; Michael Cooper, "Nonprofits to Help *Boston Globe* Pay Classical Music Critic," *New York Times*, October 31, 2016.

92. John Henry, email message to the author, June 9, 2016.

93. Henry, interview by the author.

CHAPTER THREE

Unrequited Love: Spurned in Boston and Maine, Aaron Kushner Looks West

1. I've written about Kushner for the *Huffington Post*, for WGBH News, and for my blog, *Media Nation*. An index can be found at www.dankennedy.net/tag/aaron-kushner.

2. As a privately held newspaper during the Kushner era, the *Register* did not report exact staffing levels, and its financial numbers were obscure. The estimates I've offered are from Ryan Chittum, "A Reply to Clay Shirky," *Columbia Journalism Review*, June 19, 2014, www.cjr.org.

3. Christine Haughney, "For Aaron Kushner, a Difficult Foray into Newspapers," *New York Times*, August 19, 2014.

4. Aaron Kushner, interviews with the author, September 14 and 19, 2016. Unless otherwise indicated, all quotes from Kushner are from one of these two interviews.

5. Jessica Heslam, "Mass. Group Wants to Buy *Globe*," *Boston Herald*, October 21, 2010.

6. Katherine Ozment, "Can Aaron Kushner Save the *Globe*?," *Boston*, February 2011, www.bostonmagazine.com; Gustavo Arellano, "Is Aaron Kushner the Pied Piper of Print?," *OC Weekly*, December 13, 2012; MyMove.com, accessed on March 23, 2017, www.mymove.com.

7. Ozment, "Can Aaron Kushner Save the *Globe*?"

8. Ibid.

9. Ibid.

10. Beth Healy, "Times Co. Isn't Selling *Globe*, Taylor Discusses Failed Bid,"

Business Updates (blog), Boston.com, October 19, 2009, accessed through the Internet Archive, web.archive.org; Beth Healy and Casey Ross, "Potential *Globe* Suitors May Include Local Investors," *Boston Globe*, February 22, 2013.

11. Healy and Ross, "Potential *Globe* Suitors May Include Local Investors." The estimate that Kushner's offer for the *Globe* was $200 million is from Beth Healy, "Kushner Group to Acquire *Portland Press Herald*," *Boston Globe*, January 7, 2012.

12. Benjamin Taylor, email message to the author, December 7, 2015.

13. Casey Ross, "Taylors Back Local Bid to Buy *Globe*," *Boston Globe*, January 21, 2011.

14. Ben Bradlee Jr., interview by the author, November 10, 2015.

15. Alex Jones, interview by the author, October 13, 2015.

16. Ozment, "Can Aaron Kushner Save the *Globe*?"

17. Arellano, "Is Aaron Kushner the Pied Piper of Print?"

18. *The 2100 Trust Business Summary*, September 20, 2010, 2.

19. Ibid., 12–13.

20. Martin Baron, email message to the author, June 9, 2016.

21. Christopher Mayer, email message to the author, June 9, 2016.

22. *The 2100 Trust Business Summary*, 2–3, quote on 2.

23. Dan Kennedy, "Publisher Chris Mayer on the *Globe*'s New Pay Model," *Media Nation* (blog), October 1, 2010, www.dankennedy.net.

24. *The 2100 Trust Business Summary*, 5.

25. Ibid., 6–7, 18, quote on 18.

26. Michael Barthel, "Newspapers Fact Sheet," *State of the News Media, 2015* (Washington, DC: Pew Research Center, April 29, 2015), 27.

27. *The 2100 Trust Business Summary*, 22.

28. Ibid., 22–23.

29. Ibid., 23–24.

30. Gustavo Arellano, "Aaron Kushner's Wrecking Ball," *OC Weekly*, June 26, 2014.

31. "*Globe* Readers and Non-Profits Together," accessed on June 15, 2016, manage.bostonglobe.com/grant.

32. Tom Bell and Greg Kesich, interview by the author, December 9, 2015. Unless otherwise indicated, all quotes from Bell and Kesich are from this interview.

33. "History of the *Portland Press Herald* and *Maine Sunday Telegram*," *Portland Press Herald*, accessed through the Internet Archive on June 16, 2016, web.archive.org; pronunciation is based on the personal knowledge of the author.

34. "History of the *Portland Press Herald* and *Maine Sunday Telegram*."

35. Steve Wilmsen, "Seattle Times Co. Buys Maine Newspapers from Guy Gannett," *Boston Globe*, September 2, 1998.

36. Ibid.

37. Lynda V. Mapes, "Times Co. Completes Long-Stalled Sale of Maine News-

papers," *Seattle Times*, June 16, 2009; Tania deLuzuriaga, "Portland Shaken by Warning That Its Daily Could Fold," *Boston Globe*, August 15, 2008.

38. "New Owner: Maine Papers Poised to Be Profitable," *Seattle Times*, June 16, 2009.

39. Matt Wickenheiser, "*Press Herald* Gets 'Significant New' Investment," *Bangor Daily News*, January 2, 2012; Jason Singer, "Investors Plan to Buy Big Stake in MaineToday Media," *Portland Press Herald*, January 6, 2012; Healy, "Kushner Group to Acquire *Portland Press Herald*"; Colin Woodard, "Black and White and Red All Over," *DownEast*, March 2012, www.downeast.com.

40. Singer, "Investors Plan to Buy Big Stake in MaineToday Media"; Woodard, "Black and White and Red All Over"; Wickenheiser, "*Press Herald* Gets 'Significant New' Investment."

41. Bell and Kesich, interview by the author; Janelle Hartman, "'Longest of Long Shots' Pays Off in Portland," *Guild Reporter*, March 1, 2012, www.newsguild.org.

42. Michael Socolow, interview by the author, December 18, 2015.

43. Lisa DeSisto, interview by the author, December 9, 2015; the $13 million figure is from Tux Turkel, "Purchase of Maine's Largest Media Company Completed," *Portland Press Herald*, June 1, 2015.

44. Turkel, "Purchase of Maine's Largest Media Company Completed"; Emily Heil, "Rep. Chellie Pingree and Donald Sussman Divorcing," *Washington Post*, September 9, 2015.

45. Socolow, interview by the author.

46. Paul Heintz, "Media Note: Mitchells to Sell *Rutland Herald, Times Argus*," *Off Message* (blog), *Seven Days*, August 11, 2016, www.sevendaysvt.com.

47. Greg Kesich, email message to the author, October 10, 2016.

48. Eric Platt, "Warren Buffett Makes Another Major Newspaper Investment," *Business Insider*, May 17, 2012, www.businessinsider.com.

49. Horace Greeley, letter to R. L. Sanderson, November 15, 1871, Gilder Lehrman Institute of American History, accessed on October 3, 2016, www.gilderlehrman.org.

50. Ian Wheeler, "A Timeline of Freedom Communications and the *Orange County Register*," *Orange County Register*, March 19, 2016.

CHAPTER FOUR

This Is Your Brain on the Internet: Can News Break Free of the Distraction Machine?

1. Kristine Lu and Jesse Holcomb, "Digital News Audience: Fact Sheet," and Michael Barthel, "Newspapers: Fact Sheet," *State of the News Media, 2016* (Washington, DC: Pew Research Center, June 15, 2016), www.journalism.org.

2. Marshall McLuhan, *Understanding Media: The Extensions of Man* (Cambridge, MA: MIT Press, 1994), 7–21.

3. Virginia Heffernan, *Magic and Loss: The Internet as Art* (New York: Simon & Schuster, 2016), Kindle edition, preface.

4. Ibid.

5. Nicholas Carr's website is www.nicholascarr.com; his blog, *Rough Type,* is at www.roughtype.com.

6. Nicholas Carr, *The Shallows: What the Internet Is Doing to Our Brains* (New York: W. W. Norton, 2010), 3.

7. Ibid., 32.

8. Ibid., 64–65.

9. Ibid., 137.

10. Heffernan, *Magic and Loss,* chap. 2.

11. Nicholas Carr, "News in the Age of Now," *Nieman Reports,* June 29, 2010, www.niemanreports.org.

12. Ibid.

13. Heffernan, *Magic and Loss,* chap. 2.

14. Sarah Marshall, "Why *Quartz* Does Not Publish 500 to 800 Word Articles," Journalism.co.uk, October 15, 2013, www.journalism.co.uk.

15. Julia Beizer, interview by the author, March 17, 2016.

16. Carr, *The Shallows,* 56.

17. "1981 Primitive Internet Report on KRON," accessed on October 12, 2016, www.youtube.com.

18. John Huey, Martin Nisenholtz, Paul Sagan, and John Geddes, *Riptide: An Oral History of the Epic Collision between Journalism and Digital Technology, from 1980 to the Present* (Cambridge, MA: Shorenstein Center on Media, Politics and Public Policy, April 4, 2013), www.digitalriptide.org.

19. Michael S. Rosenwald, "For Tablet Computer Visionary Roger Fidler, a Lot of What-Ifs," *Washington Post,* March 10, 2012.

20. "The Tablet Newspaper: A Vision for the Future," Knight Ridder, 1994, accessed on October 12, 2016, www.youtube.com. (Knight Ridder dropped the hyphen in its name in the final years of its existence, and, for the sake of consistency, so have I.)

21. Dan Kennedy, "Gatekeepers," *Boston Phoenix,* May 12, 1995.

22. Peter H. Lewis, "The *New York Times* Introduces a Web Site," *New York Times,* January 22, 1996.

23. Clay Shirky, "Newspapers and Thinking the Unthinkable," *Clay Shirky* (blog), March 13, 2009, www.shirky.com.

24. Dave Kellogg, "Half Your Advertising Budget Is Wasted," *Kellblog* (blog), April 18, 2006, www.kellblog.com.

25. Nicco Mele spoke at the Shorenstein Center on February 18, 2016.

26. For instance, the *Batavian*, in Genesee County, New York, often cited as a successful example of a for-profit community news site, charges its advertisers a flat rate. Dan Kennedy, *The Wired City* (Amherst: University of Massachusetts Press, 2013), 72–73.

27. Tony Haile spoke at a session titled "A Data State of the Union: Can We Make Quality Pay Online?," Online News Association, September 26, 2014.

28. Shailesh Prakash, interview by the author, April 8, 2016.

29. Brad Esposito, "This Cat Stuck in a Grate Is All of Us," *BuzzFeed*, July 19, 2016, www.buzzfeed.com.

30. Tony Haile, "What You Think You Know about the Web Is Wrong," *Time*, March 9, 2014, www.time.com.

31. Max Willens, "What's Really Killing Digital Media: The Tyranny of the Impression," *International Business Times*, April 27, 2016, www.ibtimes.com.

32. Howard Rheingold, *The Virtual Community: Homesteading on the Electronic Frontier* (Cambridge, MA: MIT Press, 1993).

33. "The Top 20 Valuable Facebook Statistics — Updated July 2016," Zephoria Digital Marketing, www.zephoria.com.

34. Emily Bell, "Facebook Is Eating the World," *Columbia Journalism Review*, March 7, 2016, www.cjr.org.

35. Emily Bell, "Who Owns the News Consumer: Social Media Platforms or Publishers?," *Columbia Journalism Review*, June 21, 2016, www.cjr.org.

36. Carmel DeAmicis, "Facebook Shifts Its Algorithm to Fight Clickbait. Will It Kill Off *Upworthy* and *BuzzFeed*?," *Gigaom*, August 25, 2014, www.gigaom.com.

37. Mathew Ingram, "Facebook Tweaks the News Feed Algorithm and Media Companies Tremble," *Fortune*, June 30, 2016, www.fortune.com.

38. Michael Nunez, "Former Facebook Workers: We Routinely Suppressed Conservative News," *Gizmodo*, May 9, 2016, www.gizmodo.com; Mike Isaac, "Facebook 'Trending' List Skewed by Individual Judgment, Not Institutional Bias," *New York Times*, May 20, 2016; Kurt Wagner, "Facebook Is Tweaking Trending Topics to Counter Charges of Bias," *Recode*, May 23, 2016, www.recode.net.

39. "News and Facebook," *Charlie Rose*, July 5, 2016, www.charlierose.com.

40. Carr, *The Shallows*, 6.

CHAPTER FIVE

Getting Big Fast: How the *Washington Post* Is Becoming the Amazon of News

1. Paul Farhi, "*Washington Post* to Be Sold to Jeff Bezos, the Founder of Amazon," *Washington Post*, August 5, 2013.

2. Sheryl Gay Stolberg, "The Next Edition: Katharine Weymouth Takes Charge at the *Washington Post*," *New York Times*, August 4, 2013.

3. David Remnick, "Donald Graham's Choice," *New Yorker*, August 5, 2013, www.newyorker.com.

4. Farhi, "*Washington Post* to Be Sold to Jeff Bezos."

5. Craig Timberg and Paul Farhi, "Jeffrey P. Bezos Visits the *Post* to Meet with Editors and Others," *Washington Post*, September 3, 2013; Paul Farhi and Craig Timberg, "Jeff Bezos to His Future *Washington Post* Journalists: Put the Readers First," *Washington Post*, September 4, 2013; Steven Mufson, "Bezos Courts *Washington Post* Editors, Reporters," *Washington Post*, September 4, 2013.

6. Craig Timberg, Chico Harlan, and Peter Whoriskey, "*Post* Names Frederick J. Ryan Jr. as New Publisher," *Washington Post*, September 2, 2014.

7. Farhi and Timberg, "Jeff Bezos to His Future *Washington Post* Journalists: Put the Readers First"; Mufson, "Bezos Courts *Washington Post* Editors, Reporters"; Max Fisher, "9 Questions about Syria You Were Too Embarrassed to Ask," *Washington Post*, August 29, 2013.

8. Mufson, "Bezos Courts *Washington Post* Editors, Reporters"; David Carr, "Let's Invent an iTunes for News," *New York Times*, January 11, 2009.

9. Jeff Bezos was interviewed by Walter Isaacson on October 20, 2016, at the Vanity Fair New Establishment Summit 2016. Video online at "Watch Full Panels from the Vanity Fair New Establishment Summit 2016," *Vanity Fair*, October 19, 2016, www.vanityfair.com. The date discrepancy is the result of the web page's having been set up before the Bezos video was published.

10. Timothy B. Lee, "Sorry, Jeff Bezos, the News Bundle Isn't Coming Back," *Washington Post*, September 5, 2013.

11. "In March, the *Washington Post* Had More than 988 Million Page Views and 73 Million Users," *WashPost PR Blog, Washington Post*, April 14, 2016, www.washingtonpost.com; Adam Lella, "Why Are Millennials So Mobile?," comScore Public Relations Blog, February 7, 2014, www.comscore.com.

12. Stephanie Desanges, my research assistant during my fellowship at the Shorenstein Center on Media, Politics and Public Policy, part of the Harvard Kennedy School, interviewed David T. Z. Mindich in April 2016.

13. Amanda Hess, "How to Escape Your Political Bubble for a Clearer View," *New York Times*, March 3, 2017.

14. Jeffrey Gottfried and Michael Barthel, "Among Millennials Engaged in Primaries, Dems More Likely to Learn about the Election from Social Media," *Fact-Tank: News in the Numbers* (blog), Pew Research Center, February 9, 2016, www.pewresearch.org.

15. Julia Beizer, interview by the author, March 17, 2016.

16. Mufson, "Bezos Courts *Washington Post* Editors, Reporters."

17. Mike Isaac, "Amazon's Jeff Bezos Explains Why He Bought the *Washington Post*," *Bits* (blog), *New York Times*, December 2, 2014, bits.blogs.nytimes.com.

18. Brad Stone, *The Everything Store: Jeff Bezos and the Age of Amazon* (New York: Back Bay Books, 2014), 21–27.

19. Ibid., 18–19.

20. Farhad Manjoo, "The Echo from Amazon Brims with Groundbreaking Promise," *New York Times*, March 9, 2016.

21. David Streitfeld, "Amazon Sales Soared 22% in Holiday Quarter, but Profit Fell Short," *New York Times*, January 28, 2016; Adam Levy, "Is Amazon's AWS Too Profitable?," *Motley Fool*, April 7, 2016, www.fool.com.

22. William Alden, "Bezos Buys a Landmark in Washington," *Dealbook* (blog), *New York Times*, August 6, 2013, dealbook.nytimes.com.

23. Brad Stone, interview by the author, March 7, 2016.

24. Jeff Sommer, "The Mind-Boggling Ascent of Amazon and Jeff Bezos," *New York Times*, July 28, 2017.

25. Stone, *The Everything Store*, 13; the review by MacKenzie Bezos was published on November 4, 2013, beneath the entry for Stone's book at www.amazon.com; Jodi Kantor and David Streitfeld, "Inside Amazon: Wrestling Big Ideas in a Bruising Workplace," *New York Times*, August 15, 2015.

26. Stone, *The Everything Store*, 265–66.

27. Shailesh Prakash, interview by the author, April 8, 2016. Unless otherwise indicated, all quotes from Prakash are from this interview.

28. Martin Baron, interview by author, March 16, 2016. Unless otherwise indicated, all quotes from Baron are from this interview.

29. Stone, *The Everything Store*, 4–5.

30. Ibid., 28.

31. Ibid., 32–33, 51, 325–26.

32. Ibid., 32–33; Martin Baron spoke at the Harvard Kennedy School on April 4, 2016.

33. Clayton M. Christensen, *The Innovator's Dilemma: When New Technologies Cause Great Firms to Fail* (Boston: Harvard Business Review Press, 2000), Kindle edition, introduction.

34. Stone, *The Everything Store*, 48–49, 234.

35. Clayton M. Christensen, David Skok, and James Allworth, "Breaking News: Mastering the Art of Disruptive Innovation in Journalism," *Nieman Reports*, Fall 2012, www.niemanreports.org.

36. Subscription rates for the *New York Times* and the *Washington Post* were accessed from their respective websites on October 26, 2016.

37. Ken Doctor, interview by the author, March 10, 2016; also, see Ken Doctor, *Newsonomics: Twelve New Trends That Will Shape the News You Get* (New York: St. Martin's Press, 2010), and his blog *Newsonomics*, www.newsonomics.com.

38. Jeff Bezos was interviewed by the technology journalist Walt Mossberg on May 31, 2016. A video of their conversation is available at "Amazon CEO Jeff Bezos at Code 2016," *Recode*, June 1, 2016, www.recode.com.

39. Stone, *The Everything Store*, 336.

40. Andy Alexander, "*Post*'s National Weekly Edition to Close," *Omblog* (blog), *Washington Post*, August 10, 2009, voices.washingtonpost.com.

41. "The *Washington Post* Launches a National Weekly Print Edition," *WashPost PR Blog, Washington Post*, October 17, 2014, www.washingtonpost.com.

42. Michele Norris and Wesley Lowery spoke at Harvard University's Nieman Foundation on February 19, 2016.

43. Rick Edmonds, "Ranking of Newspapers' Market Penetration Indicates the Market Matters as Well as the Content," Poynter.org, March 31, 2011, www.poynter .org.

44. David Kindred, *Morning Miracle: Inside the Washington Post — A Great Newspaper Fights for Its Life* (New York: Doubleday, 2010), Kindle edition, chap. 10.

45. Isabell Hülsen, "News Lab: Jeff Bezos Takes *Washington Post* into Digital Future," *Spiegel Online*, February 20, 2015, www.spiegel.de.

46. Scott Sherman, "The Long Good-Bye," *Vanity Fair*, November 30, 2012, www.vanityfair.com; Christine Haughney and Eric Pfanner, "At 125 Years, a Rechristening for the *Herald Tribune*," *New York Times*, February 25, 2013.

47. Steve Coll, interview by the author, May 29, 2014.

48. Mathew Ingram, "Is the *Guardian*'s Former Editor to Blame for Its Financial Woes?," *Fortune*, May 13, 2016, www.fortune.com.

49. Joe Pompeo, "Bezos on 'The Thing We're Changing' at the *Washington Post*," *Politico Media*, December 2, 2014, www.politico.com/media.

50. Brian Stelter, "Jeff Bezos Just Shut Down My Hometown Newspaper," CNN. com, June 12, 2015, money.cnn.com; Tom Grubisich, "*Washington Post*'s *Gazette* Community Sites Were Stuck in a Print Past," *Street Fight*, June 18, 2015, www.street fightmag.com.

51. Martin Baron was interviewed by Bob Schieffer and H. Andrew Schwartz on the podcast *About the News*, Center for Strategic and International Studies, June 13, 2016, www.csis.org.

52. Matthew Hindman, *Stickier News: What Newspapers Don't Know about Web Traffic Has Hurt Them Badly — but There Is a Better Way* (Cambridge, MA: Shorenstein Center on Media, Politics and Public Policy, April 2015), 4.

53. Emily Heil and Kathy Orton, "Jeff Bezos Is the Anonymous Buyer of the Biggest House in Washington," *Washington Post*, January 12, 2017.

54. Stone, *The Everything Store*, 9–10.

55. Beth Diaz, interview by the author, April 13, 2016.

56. Jack Shafer, interview by the author, January 28, 2016.

57. Beizer, interview by the author.

58. Jim Tankersley, "Baby Boomers Are What's Wrong with America's Economy," *Washington Post*, November 5, 2015.

59. Molly Gannon, email message to the author, April 21, 2016. Gannon also told me that she was unable to provide a breakdown of how much of the *Post*'s digital content never finds its way into the print edition, but it is clearly a substantial amount.

60. Dan Kennedy, "The Debates Gave Trump the Nomination, and It's the Media's Fault," *In Theory* (blog), *Washington Post*, July 12, 2016, www.washington post.com.

61. "In March, the *Washington Post* Had More than 988 Million Page Views and 73 Million Users."

62. Erik Wemple, interview by the author, February 9, 2016.

63. Mufson, "Bezos Courts *Washington Post* Editors, Reporters."

64. Peter Whoriskey, "For Bezos, the *Post* Represents New Frontier," *Washington Post*, August 10, 2013.

65. According to Cet Parks, executive director of the Washington-Baltimore Newspaper Guild, the two sides reached an agreement on a new contract in 2015: "We gained decent percentage wage increases and beat back most of management's proposals. Unfortunately, we could not stop management from freezing the defined benefit pension plan. The freezing of the pension plan wasn't necessary as it was overfunded and very beneficial to the members/employees." The union's contract with the *Post* was due to expire in June 2017. Cet Parks, email message to the author, October 27, 2016.

66. Whoriskey, "For Bezos, the *Post* Represents New Frontier."

67. Kimberly Kindy, interview by the author, March 4, 2016.

68. The Pulitzer Prizes, accessed on June 9, 2017, www.pulitzer.org.

69. Kantor and Streitfeld, "Inside Amazon."

70. Mathew Ingram, "Amazon: Dystopian Nightmare, or Just Another Successful Tech Company?," *Fortune*, August 17, 2015, www.fortune.com.

71. Jay Carney, "What the *New York Times* Didn't Tell You," *Medium*, October 19, 2015, www.medium.com.

72. "Amazon Spokesman: *NYT* Story 'Way Off Base,'" CNN.com, August 18, 2015, money.cnn.com.

73. John Cook, "Full Memo: Jeff Bezos Responds to Brutal *NYT* Story, Says It Doesn't Represent the Amazon He Leads," *GeekWire*, August 16, 2015, www.geekwire.com.

74. Taylor Soper, "Jeff Bezos Says Amazon Has the 'Gold Standard Culture for Innovation and Pioneering Work,'" *GeekWire,* May 31, 2016, www.geekwire.com.

75. Shafer, interview by the author.

76. Wemple, interview by the author.

77. Dan Kennedy, "Marty Baron Warns Press against Fear and Timidity," *Media Nation* (blog), February 10, 2012, www.dankennedy.net.

78. "*Washington Post* Executive Editor Martin Baron on Journalism's Transition from Print to Digital," *WashPost PR Blog, Washington Post,* April 8, 2015, www.washingtonpost.com.

79. Martin Baron, "*Washington Post* Editor Marty Baron Has a Message to Journalists in the Trump Era," *Vanity Fair,* November 30, 2016, www.vanityfair.com.

CHAPTER SIX
The End of Free: The *Boston Globe* Tells Readers to Pay Up

1. "John Henry Invades *Felger & Massarotti,*" CBS Boston, October 14, 2011, boston.cbslocal.com.

2. John Henry, address to the Greater Boston Chamber of Commerce, held at the Mandarin Oriental Boston, January 8, 2014.

3. John Henry, interview by the author, February 11, 2016. Unless otherwise indicated, all quotes are from this interview.

4. Ricardo Bilton, "The *Boston Globe* Is Getting Smarter about Digital Subscriptions — and Tightening Up Its Paywall," *Nieman Journalism Lab,* May 31, 2017, www.niemanlab.org; Pete Doucette, email message to the author, June 2, 2017.

5. Alan D. Mutter, "Mission Possible? Charging for Web Content," *Reflections of a Newsosaur* (blog), February 8, 2009, newsosaur.blogspot.com.

6. Dan Adams, "Here's a New List of the Richest People in Mass.," *Boston Globe,* June 10, 2016.

7. Seth Mnookin, *Feeding the Monster: How Money, Smarts, and Nerve Took a Team to the Top* (New York: Simon & Schuster), Kindle edition, chap. 9.

8. Ibid.; HobokenBaseball.com, accessed on March 5, 2017, www.hobokenbaseball.com.

9. Mnookin, *Feeding the Monster,* chap. 9.

10. Ibid.

11. Ibid.

12. Ibid.

13. Martin Baron, email message to the author, January 26, 2017.

14. Dan Shaughnessy, "John Harrington Sold Out Red Sox Fans in Sale," *Boston Globe,* December 21, 2001.

15. Robert McG. Thomas Jr., "Jean R. Yawkey, Red Sox Owner and Philanthropist, Is Dead at 83," *New York Times*, February 27, 1992.

16. Adrian Walker, "It's Time to Banish the Racist Legacy of Tom Yawkey," *Boston Globe*, December 7, 2015.

17. Shaughnessy, "John Harrington Sold Out Red Sox Fans in Sale"; Meg Vaillancourt, "Red Sox Reach Deal to Sell Team for Record $700m," *Boston Globe*, December 21, 2001.

18. Scott Lauber, "David Ortiz's Finest Moment with the Red Sox Wasn't at the Plate," ESPN.com, April 10, 2016, www.espn.com.

19. Steve Bailey, "Local Group May Bid for *Globe*," *Boston Globe*, October 24, 2006.

20. Dan Kennedy, "Disappearing Ink," *CommonWealth*, April 26, 2007, www.commonwealthmagazine.org.

21. Beth Healy, "A Familiar Name, an Interrupted Record," *Boston Globe*, October 8, 2009; Casey Ross and Beth Healy, "An Iron Fist, a Golden Touch," *Boston Globe*, October 7, 2009.

22. Brian McGrory, interview by the author, January 9, 2017. Unless otherwise indicated, all quotes are from this interview.

23. Christine Haughney, "New York Times Company Sells *Boston Globe*," *New York Times*, August 3, 2013; David Carr, "Newspaper as Business Pulpit," *New York Times*, June 10, 2012; Jason Schwartz, "Will John Henry Save the *Globe*?," *Boston*, March 2014, www.bostonmagazine.com.

24. Schwartz, "Will John Henry Save the *Globe*?"

25. Brian McGrory fleshed out some of the details in an email message to the author, January 26, 2017.

26. Linda Pizzuti Henry, email message to the author, March 3, 2017.

27. Ibid.

28. Simon van Zuylen-Wood, "Can Linda Henry Save the *Boston Globe*?," *Boston*, June 2017, www.bostonmagazine.com.

29. Peter Gammons, "Source: John Henry Selected as New *Boston Globe* Owner," *Gammons Daily* (blog), August 2, 2013, www.gammonsdaily.com.

30. Haughney, "New York Times Company Sells *Boston Globe*"; Edmund Lee, "*New York Times* Sells *Boston Globe* to John Henry for $70M," *Bloomberg Technology*, August 4, 2013, www.bloomberg.com.

31. Schwartz, "Will John Henry Save the *Globe*?"

32. Haughney, "New York Times Company Sells *Boston Globe*."

33. William Glaberson, "Times Co. Acquiring *Boston Globe* for $1.1 Billion," *New York Times*, June 11, 1993.

34. Alliance for Audited Media, publisher's statement for the six-month period ending September 29, 2013, www.auditedmedia.com.

35. Dan Kennedy, "The Challenge of Counting Digital Subscribers," *Media Nation* (blog), November 14, 2013, www.dankennedy.net.

36. Craig Douglas, "John Henry's Shrinking *Boston Globe*," *Boston Business Journal*, August 30, 2013.

37. The *Globe* employed 274 full-time journalists as of November 2013. Because the *Globe*'s and Boston.com's operations were intertwined at that time, the actual number was slightly higher than that. A precise count could not be determined, but 285 represents an informed estimate.

38. John Henry, "Why I Bought the *Globe*," *Boston Globe*, October 27, 2013.

39. Ibid.

40. Schwartz, "Will John Henry Save the *Globe*?"

41. Beth Healy, "*Boston Globe* Publisher Christopher Mayer to Step Down," *Boston Globe*, January 8, 2014; Beth Healy, "John Henry Assumes Role of *Globe* Publisher, Names CEO," *Boston Globe*, January 30, 2014.

42. Christopher Mayer, interview by the author, February 12, 2016.

43. Sacha Pfeiffer, "How the One Fund Became Reality in 7 Hours," WBUR.org, October 22, 2013, www.wbur.org.

44. Michael Sheehan, interview by the author, January 23, 2017.

45. Lisa Eckelbecker, "John Henry Seeks 'Right' Buyer for *Telegram & Gazette*," *Worcester Telegram & Gazette*, November 26, 2013.

46. Dan Kennedy, "John Henry Sells *Worcester T&G* to Florida Chain," WGBH News, May 21, 2014, news.wgbh.org.

47. Skyler Swisher, "GateHouse Acquires *News-Journal*, Halifax Media," *Daytona Beach News-Journal*, January 9, 2015.

48. Mayer, interview by the author.

49. Bruce Mohl, "The Man Who Lied to Worcester," *CommonWealth*, November 15, 2014, www.commonwealthmagazine.org.

50. Dan Kennedy, "With New Political Section, the *Boston Globe* Seeks to Spend Its Way Out of the Newspaper Doldrums," WGBH News, June 6, 2014, news.wgbh.org.

51. Joe Sullivan, email message to the author, March 17, 2017.

52. Jed Gottlieb, "Curtains Fall on Arts Critics at Newspapers," *Columbia Journalism Review*, January 6, 2017, www.cjr.org.

53. The Pulitzer Prizes, accessed on June 9, 2017, www.pulitzer.org.

54. Hadas Gold, "Peter Canellos to Take on Investigative Role, Paul Volpe to Join Politico as Executive Editor," *Politico*, November 3, 2016, www.politico.com.

55. Ellen Clegg, email message to the author, April 15, 2017.

56. Benjamin Mullin, "Layoffs Hit the *Boston Globe*," Poynter.org, October 15, 2015, www.poynter.org.

57. Dan Kennedy, "The *Globe* Shrinks Its Saturday Edition as It Straddles the Print-Digital Divide," WGBH News, October 6, 2015, news.wgbh.org.

58. Henry, email message to the author, February 8, 2017.

59. Jon Chesto, "*Boston Globe* Publisher Chris Mayer Plans Changes Even as Paper Is Up for Sale," *Boston Business Journal*, March 29, 2013.

60. Prices were checked at "Today's Front Pages," Newseum, accessed on March 7, 2017, www.newseum.org.

61. Kathleen Kingsbury, "Print as a Premium Offering," *Nieman Journalism Lab*, December 2017, www.niemanlab.org.

62. Mark Arsenault and Dan Adams, "*Globe*, Distributor Trade Blame as Delivery Woes Persist," *Boston Globe*, January 4, 2016.

63. Dan Kennedy, "How the *Globe*'s Home-Delivery Woes Morphed from an Annoyance into a Crisis," WGBH News, January 4, 2016, news.wgbh.org.

64. John W. Henry, "We Apologize to Our Loyal Readers," *Boston Globe*, January 5, 2016.

65. Paid print circulation figures were included in the "Statement of Ownership, Management, and Circulation," published in the *Boston Globe* on October 4 and 6, 2015, and October 2 and 3, 2016. The author has used a measure of the number of copies of a single issue published nearest to the filing date.

66. Pete Doucette, email message to the author, March 17, 2017.

67. Pete Doucette, interview by the author, January 19, 2017.

68. Sheehan, interview by the author.

69. Michelle Johnson, interview by the author, November 2, 2015.

70. Baron made his quip about the "Red Sox diaspora" in a conversation with the author in 2007 or 2008.

71. Dan Kennedy, "Will BostonGlobe.com Give Papers a Blueprint to Avoid Apple's 30% Cut?," *Nieman Journalism Lab*, September 12, 2011, www.niemanlab.org.

72. Jeremy C. Fox, "Boston.com Editor Suspended over T-Shirt Mocking Story Subject," *Boston Globe*, December 13, 2014.

73. Nestor Ramos, "Boston.com Story Mocking Boehner Threat Draws Ire," *Boston Globe*, January 14, 2015.

74. Pizzuti Henry, email message to the author.

75. Kathleen Kingsbury, email message to the author, November 23, 2016.

76. Bilton, "The *Boston Globe* Is Getting Smarter about Digital Subscriptions — and Tightening Up Its Paywall"; Pete Doucette, email message to the author, June 2, 2017.

77. Dan Kennedy, "The Daily Trump: Katie Kingsbury on the *Globe*'s Interactive Transition Graphic," *Media Nation* (blog), January 19, 2017, www.dankennedy.net.

78. "Our Mission: Why We Do What We Do," *Boston Globe,* accessed on March 8, 2017, www.bostonglobe.com.

79. Subscription information accessed on March 10, 2017, subscribe.bostonglobe .com.

80. Doucette, interview by the author.

81. Mayer, interview by the author.

82. Henry, email message to the author, February 8, 2017.

83. Sheehan, interview by the author.

84. Kathleen Kingsbury, interview by the author, November 23, 2016.

85. Henry, email message to the author, February 27, 2017.

86. Ike Swetlitz, "One-on-One with Trump's Doctor: Hecklers, House Calls, and Why Obamacare Must Be Shut Down," *Stat,* December 21, 2016, www.statnews .com.

87. Charles Ornstein, "Help Us Fact-Check What Members of Congress Say about the Health Care Law," *Stat,* March 10, 2017, www.statnews.com.

88. Dan Kennedy, "Mobile-First *Stat*: Can the *Boston Globe* Engineer Profits Through the Life Sciences?," WGBH News, November 4, 2015, news.wgbh.org.

89. Dan Kennedy, "At the *Globe,* a Downsizing That Was Preordained," *Media Nation* (blog), October 16, 2015, www.dankennedy.net.

90. Rick Berke, email message to the author, March 3, 2017.

91. Dan Kennedy, "*Boston Globe*'s *Stat* Marks First Anniversary by Unveiling Paid 'Plus' Service," WGBH News, December 6, 2016, news.wgbh.org.

92. Information about *Politico*'s paid services is from a confidential source.

93. Berke, email message to the author.

94. Joseph Lichterman, "*Stat* Is Publishing a Print Section in Sunday's *Boston Globe* — and It Might Be Coming to a Paper Near You," *Nieman Journalism Lab,* April 21, 2017, www.niemanlab.org.

95. Dan Kennedy, "Doug Franklin to Succeed Mike Sheehan as *Globe* CEO," WGBH News, December 8, 2016, news.wgbh.org.

96. Sheehan, interview by the author.

97. Doug Franklin, email message to the *Boston Globe* staff, a copy of which was obtained by the author, March 16, 2017.

98. Dan Kennedy, "Doug Franklin Is Out as CEO of Boston Globe Media; Vinay Mehra Is Named President," WGBH News, July 18, 2017, news.wgbh.org.

99. Mark Arsenault, "*Globe* Chief Executive Doug Franklin Steps Down," *Boston Globe,* July 18, 2017.

100. Information based on customer-service emails the author has received as well as internal communications obtained confidentially by the author; Mark Arsenault, "It's Been One Problem after Another for *Globe* Presses," *Boston Globe,* September 16, 2017.

101. John Henry, email message to the author, July 18, 2017.

102. Confidential email message to the author, July 18, 2017.

103. Walter Robinson, interview by the author, October 8, 2015; Mayer, interview by the author.

104. Dan Kennedy, "*Globe* Editor McGrory: It's Time to Rethink Everything We Do," *Media Nation* (blog), April 7, 2016, www.dankennedy.net.

105. Dan Kennedy, "No More 'Paper of Record': McGrory Offers More Details on the *Globe*'s Reinvention," WGBH News, January 5, 2017, news.wgbh.org.

106. Adrian Walker, interview by the author, February 20, 2017.

107. Frank Phillips, interview by the author, February 27, 2017.

108. Clegg, email message to the author.

109. Robinson, interview by the author.

CHAPTER SEVEN

Orange Crush: From California Dreaming to an Epic Nightmare

1. Al Franken, *I'm Good Enough, I'm Smart Enough, and Doggone It, People Like Me! Daily Affirmations by Stuart Smalley* (New York: Dell, 1992).

2. Gustavo Arellano, interview by the author, March 12, 2015.

3. Aaron Kushner, interview by the author, September 14, 2016; Eric Spitz, interview by the author, September 23, 2016. Unless otherwise indicated, all quotes from Kushner and Spitz are from these interviews or from a second interview with Kushner that the author conducted on September 19, 2016; Marilyn Kalfus, "Gustavo Arellano, Editor in Chief of *OC Weekly*, Says He Quit Instead of Laying Off Staffers," *Orange Country Register*, October 14, 2017.

4. "Quick Facts: Orange County, California," United States Census Bureau, accessed on June 22, 2016, www.census.gov.

5. Gustavo Arellano, *Orange County: A Personal History* (New York: Scribner, 2008), Kindle edition, "My Mexican Awakening."

6. Ibid.

7. Ibid., "Becoming 'The Mexican.'"

8. Gustavo Arellano, speech at a conference of the Puenta Project in Claremont, CA, March 12, 2015.

9. Arellano, interview by the author; Gustavo Arellano, "Is Aaron Kushner the Pied Piper of Print?," *OC Weekly*, December 13, 2012.

10. Jim Sleeper, *Turn the Rascals Out! The Life and Times of Orange County's Fighting Editor Dan M. Baker* (Traduce Canyon: California Classics, 1973), 98–119, 341.

11. Jim Sleeper, "How Orange County Got Its Name," accessed on October 9, 2016, www.oc.ca.gov. An address delivered on March 11, 1974, on the occasion of the

county's eighty-fifth anniversary, reprinted from *Jim Sleeper's 2nd Orange County Almanac of Historical Oddities* (New York: Ocusa Press, 1974).

12. Sleeper, *Turn the Rascals Out!*, 2–8, 24–25, 98.

13. Ruth Ellen Taylor, ed., *Legacy: The Orange County Story* (Santa Ana, CA: The Register, 1980), 181.

14. Sleeper, *Turn the Rascals Out!*, 98–119.

15. Ibid., 98.

16. Ibid., 280, 386n1.

17. Taylor, ed., *Legacy*, 181.

18. Ibid.

19. Arellano, *Orange County: A Personal History*, "Where All the Good Idiot Republicans Go to Die."

20. "Making Money by Making Enemies," *Time*, April 19, 1963, 108.

21. Marty Smith, interview by the author, March 11, 2015; Marty Smith, email message to the author, June 24, 2016.

22. Jim Seale, "Nipping Otis in the Orange," *Los Angeles*, February 1984, 102–3, quote on 103.

23. "*Times* O.C. Edition Names Martin Baron, 38, as Its New Editor," *Los Angeles Times*, March 17, 1993.

24. Martin Baron, LinkedIn profile, accessed on October 3, 2016, www.linkedin .com.

25. Ian Wheeler, "A Timeline of Freedom Communications and the *Orange County Register*," *Orange County Register*, March 19, 2016; The Pulitzer Prizes, accessed on June 9, 2017, www.pulitzer.org.

26. Kimberly Kindy, interview by the author, March 4, 2016.

27. M. L. Stein, "Harry Hoiles, Libertarian, Former Freedom Exec," *Editor & Publisher*, May 2, 1998, 21.

28. Peter Lattman and Russell Adams, "Paper Owner Freedom Plans to File for Chapter 11," *Wall Street Journal*, August 31, 2009; Michael J. de la Merced, "Freedom Communications Files for Bankruptcy," *DealBook* (blog), *New York Times*, September 1, 2009, dealbook.nytimes.com.

29. Christopher Smith, "The Curious Quest of Aaron Quixote," *Orange Coast Magazine*, February 11, 2013, www.orangecoast.com.

30. Arellano, "Is Aaron Kushner the Pied Piper of Print?"; Jason Schwartz, "Will John Henry Save the *Globe*?," *Boston*, March 2014, www.bostonmagazine.com.

31. Smith, "The Curious Quest of Aaron Quixote."

32. William D'Urso and Walter Hamilton, "Sale of *Orange County Register*'s Owner Is Completed," *Los Angeles Times*, July 26, 2012.

33. Arellano, "Is Aaron Kushner the Pied Piper of Print?"

34. Ibid.

35. Smith, "The Curious Quest of Aaron Quixote"; Ken Doctor, "The Newso-

nomics of Aaron Kushner's Virtuous Circles," *Nieman Journalism Lab*, January 31, 2013, www.niemanlab.org.

36. Smith, "The Curious Quest of Aaron Quixote."

37. Ibid.

38. Ryan Chittum, "An Ink-Stained Stretch," *Columbia Journalism Review*, May/June 2013, www.cjr.org.

39. Doctor, "The Newsonomics of Aaron Kushner's Virtuous Circles."

40. Ibid.

41. Chittum, "An Ink-Stained Stretch."

42. Mary Ann Milbourn, "*Register* to Launch Long Beach Newspaper," *Orange County Register*, August 21, 2013; Mary Ann Milbourn, "*Riverside Press-Enterprise* Deal Completed," *Orange County Register*, November 22, 2013; Wheeler, "A Timeline of Freedom Communications and the *Orange County Register*."

43. Adam Elmahrek, "*OC Register* Alters Ad Policy after Politicians Complain," *Voice of OC*, February 27, 2013, www.voiceofoc.org.

44. Ken Bensinger, "Dozens Laid Off at Freedom Papers," *Los Angeles Times*, January 18, 2014; Wendy Lee, "*OC Register* Says More than 30 Employees and Its Editor Are Leaving the Paper," Southern California Public Radio, January 16, 2014, www.scpr.org; Jim Romenesko, "Reports: *Orange County Register* Lays Off Dozens of Staffers," JimRomenesko.com (blog), January 16, 2014, www.jimromenesko.com; Michael Hiltzik, "The *O.C. Register*'s Supremely Ghoulish Financial Strategy," *Los Angeles Times*, January 28, 2014; Michael Hiltzik, "*O.C. Register* Boss Resents Being Labeled a 'Ghoul,'" *Los Angeles Times*, January 29, 2014.

45. Mary Ann Milbourn, "*Register* Owner to Launch L.A. Paper Wednesday," *Orange County Register*, April 14, 2014.

46. Ken Doctor, "Six Things to Consider about the New *Los Angeles Register*," *Nieman Journalism Lab*, April 16, 2014, www.niemanlab.org.

47. Ibid.

48. "*OC Register* Owner Aaron Kushner Talks Future of Newspaper Empire," Southern California Public Radio, June 4, 2014, www.scpr.org.

49. Gustavo Arellano, "Exclusive: Read Aaron Kushner's Secret PowerPoint Pitch to Investors to Save the *OC Register*," *OC Weekly*, June 5, 2014.

50. Ryan Chittum, "Why the *Orange County Register*'s Bold Experiment Hit the Skids," *Columbia Journalism Review*, June 11, 2014, www.cjr.org.

51. Ibid.; Alliance for Audited Media, www.auditedmedia.com.

52. Ken Doctor, "The Newsonomics of the *Orange County Register*'s Swerves All over the Freeway," *Nieman Journalism Lab*, June 4, 2014, www.niemanlab.org.

53. Gustavo Arellano, "Aaron Kushner's Wrecking Ball," *OC Weekly*, June 26, 2014.

54. Ibid.

55. Christine Haughney, "For Aaron Kushner, a Difficult Foray into Newspapers," *New York Times*, October 19, 2014; Christine Haughney, "California Paper

Asks Its Employees to Produce, Then Deliver, the News," *New York Times*, November 18, 2014.

56. Michael Hiltzik, interview by the author, March 10, 2015; Haughney, "For Aaron Kushner, a Difficult Foray into Newspapers."

57. Chuck Salter, "Hyper-Local Hero," *Fast Company*, November 1, 2006, www.fastcompany.com.

58. Rob Curley, "After Abandoning the Web, the *Orange County Register* Is Focused on a Digital Do-Over," *Rob Curley* (blog), February 22, 2016, www.robcurley.com.

59. Gustavo Arellano, "Aaron Kushner and Eric Spitz Resign from *Orange County Register* Effective Immediately," *OC Weekly*, March 10, 2015.

60. Kindy, interview by the author.

61. Richard Mirman was a guest on KCRW Radio's program *To the Point* on March 12, 2015. He was interviewed by the host, Warren Olney.

62. Lukas I. Alpert, "Tribune Publishing to Buy *San Diego Union-Tribune*," *Wall Street Journal*, May 7, 2015; Jason Felch, "*O.C. Register* Owner Aaron Kushner Bets Heavily on Print," *Los Angeles Times*, August 20, 2013.

63. Eric Spitz, "Start the Presses! It's How You Sell Newspapers," *Wall Street Journal*, August 18, 2013.

64. "OC Business Summit 2014 with Eric Spitz," Saddleback Church, July 18, 2014, www.youtube.com. The event was actually held on March 8, 2014. See Marni Usheroff, "Entrepreneurs Get Expert Advice at Saddleback Church Event," *Orange County Register*, March 8, 2014.

65. Aaron Kushner, email message to the author, September 23, 2016.

66. Haughney, "For Aaron Kushner, a Difficult Foray into Newspapers."

67. Dave Chafey, "Display Advertising Clickthrough Rates," *Smart Insights*, April 26, 2016, www.smartinsights.com.

68. Gabriel Kahn, interview by the author, March 10, 2015.

69. Ibid.; Gabriel Kahn, email message to the author, September 22, 2016.

70. *The 2100 Trust Business Summary*, September 20, 2010, 2.

71. Jonathan Lansner, "With Bankruptcy Filing, Local Group Bids for Ownership of Freedom Communications," *Orange County Register*, November 2, 2015; Jim Romenesko, "*Orange County Register* Parent Files for Bankruptcy Protection," JimRomenesko.com (blog), November 1, 2015, www.jimromenesko.com.

72. Nina Culver, "Rob Curley Named Editor of the *Spokesman-Review*," *Spokane Spokesman Review*, July 21, 2016.

73. Deirdre Newman, "*Register* to Move to Anaheim," *Orange County Business Journal*, September 21, 2016.

CHAPTER EIGHT

Money Isn't Everything: Why Wealthy Ownership Doesn't Guarantee Success

1. Michael J. de la Merced, "Berkshire Bets Again on Newspapers with Media General Deal," *DealBook* (blog), *New York Times*, May 17, 2012, dealbook.nytimes.com; Anupreeta Das, "Buffett's Media General Deal Makes a Lot More Financial Sense Now," *Wall Street Journal*, January 4, 2014; Aaron Kushner, interview by the author, September 19, 2016; quote from Tanzina Vega, "Buffett to Buy Omaha Newspaper Company," *Media Decoder* (blog), *New York Times*, November 30, 2011, mediadecoder.blogs.nytimes.com.

2. Anupreeta Das, "At Papers, Berkshire Rewrites Its Script," *Wall Street Journal*, January 2, 2014.

3. Katharine Graham, *Personal History* (New York: Alfred A. Knopf, 1997), 530.

4. Scott Patterson, "Buffett Sees 'Unending Losses' for Many Newspapers," *Wall Street Journal*, May 2, 2009.

5. Rem Rieder, "Rieder: Newspapers Haven't 'Cracked Code,' Buffett Says," *USA Today*, May 28, 2016.

6. Fred Imbert, "Warren Buffett Names the Only 2 Newspapers That Have an 'Assured Future,'" CNBC.com, February 27, 2017, www.cnbc.com.

7. Steve Jordan, "BH Media Cuts 289 Jobs; None Are at *World-Herald*," *Omaha World-Herald*, April 4, 2017.

8. Melissa Matczak's memo was published on the media reporter Jim Romenesko's Facebook page, May 11, 2017, www.facebook.com/jimromenesko.

9. "The World's Billionaires," *Forbes*, accessed on July 26, 2016, www.forbes.com.

10. The story of how Otis Chandler built the *Los Angeles Times* into a great newspaper is told in David Halberstam, *The Powers That Be* (Urbana: University of Illinois Press, 2000); "The Oldest US Newspaper in Continuous Publication," ConnecticutHistory.org, accessed on August 2, 2016, www.connecticuthistory.org.

11. Jay Rosen, "Journalists as 'Hit Squad': Connecting the Dots on Sheldon Adelson, the *Review-Journal* of Las Vegas and Edward Clarkin in Connecticut," *Press Think* (blog), January 27, 2016, www.pressthink.org.

12. Ryan Tate, "Exclusive: Sam Zell Says 'Fuck You' to His Journalist," *Gawker*, February 4, 2008, www.gawker.com.

13. Ibid.

14. David Carr, "At Flagging Tribune, Tales of a Bankrupt Culture," *New York Times*, October 5, 2010.

15. Christine Haughney and David Carr, "To Cut Taxes, Tribune Is to Split into Broadcasting and Publishing Units," *New York Times*, July 10, 2013.

16. Christopher Goffard and Stuart Pfeifer, "Publisher Austin Beutner Is Fired after a Yearlong Drive to Reshape the *Times*," *Los Angeles Times*, September 8, 2015; Beutner spoke at the Shorenstein Center for Media, Politics and Public Policy, part of the Harvard Kennedy School, on February 24, 2016.

17. Leslie Picker and Sydney Ember, "A Tech Mogul's Fight to Keep Control of a Newspaper Empire," *New York Times*, August 15, 2016; Lukas A. Alpert, "Tribune Publishing Shareholder Files Lawsuit against Board," *Wall Street Journal*, June 2, 2016.

18. "Tribune Publishing Announces Corporate Rebranding, Changes Name to tronc," tronc.com, June 2, 2016, investor.tronc.com.

19. "Newspaper Deal Falls Apart as Gannett Gives Up on Tronc," Associated Press, November 1, 2016, bigstory.ap.org; James Rufus Koren, "Tronc to Billionaire Soon-Shiong: 'L.A. Times Is Not for Sale," *Los Angeles Times*, April 6, 2017.

20. Consolidated Media Reports for the quarter ending December 31, 2015, submitted to the Alliance for Audited Media, www.auditedmedia.com.

21. "Annual Estimates of the Population of Metropolitan and Micropolitan Statistical Areas: April 1, 2010 to July 1, 2015," *American FactFinder*, United States Census Bureau, accessed on August 8, 2016, factfinder.census.gov.

22. The Pulitzer Prizes, accessed on August 8, 2016, www.pulitzer.org.

23. Douglas Martin, "Thomas Winship, Ex-Editor of *Boston Globe*, Dies at 81," *New York Times*, March 15, 2002; Alex S. Jones, "Media Business; Editor Leaving *Philadelphia Inquirer*," *New York Times*, August 1, 1990.

24. Joel Mathis, interview by the author, January 25, 2016.

25. Michael Massing, "Now They Tell Us," *New York Review of Books*, February 26, 2004, www.nybooks.com.

26. Felicity Barringer, "Publisher Who Resigned Urges Editors to Put Readers First," *New York Times*, April 7, 2001.

27. Dan Kennedy, "The Baron of Morrissey Boulevard," *Boston Phoenix*, December 6, 2001.

28. Katharine Q. Seelye, "Knight Ridder Chief Expresses His Regrets over Deal to Sell Newspapers," *New York Times*, March 15, 2006.

29. Julia M. Klein, "Brian Tierney's Grand Experiment," *Columbia Journalism Review*, July/August 2007, www.cjr.org; Michael J. de la Merced, "Tensions Flare in Philadelphia Newspaper Bankruptcy," *Dealbook* (blog), *New York Times*, March 4, 2009, dealbook.nytimes.com.

30. Klein, "Brian Tierney's Grand Experiment"; Roy J. Harris Jr., *Pulitzer's Gold: A Century of Public Service Journalism* (New York: Columbia University Press, 2016), Kindle edition, chap. 9; quote in Klein, "Grand Experiment."

31. Michael Schaffer, interview by the author, February 2, 2016.

32. C. W. Anderson, interview by the author, January 15, 2016.

33. David Carr, "Defending the Papers He Fought," *New York Times*, April 11, 2010.

34. Harris, *Pulitzer's Gold*, chap. 9.

35. Andrew Beaujon and Julie Moos, "New Owners Bring Bill Marimow Back to the *Philadelphia Inquirer*," Poynter.org, April 4, 2012, www.poynter.org.

36. Steve Volk, "Exclusive: Internal Documents Tell the Tale of *Inquirer* Editor Bill Marimow's Dismissal," *Philadelphia*, October 7, 2013, www.phillymag.com; Erik Wemple, "Marimow Reinstated as Top Editor of *Philadelphia Inquirer*," *Erik Wemple Blog, Washington Post*, November 22, 2013, www.washingtonpost.com.

37. Alfred Lubrano, "Lewis Katz, Co-Owner of the *Inquirer*, Dies in Plane Crash," Philly.com, June 3, 2014, articles.philly.com.

38. Mathis, interview by the author.

39. Chris Krewson, "Could the *Philadelphia Inquirer* Become Part of Temple University?," *Billy Penn*, September 30, 2015, www.billypenn.com.

40. Alison Burdo, "*Inquirer, Daily News*, Philly.com Newsrooms to Merge; Layoffs Coming," *Philadelphia Business Journal*, October 30, 2015.

41. Ken Doctor, "Newsonomics: The Hard Realities of Philly's Hail Mary Nonprofit Reorganization," *Nieman Journalism Lab*, January 21, 2016, www.niemanlab.org.

42. James Warren, "New Nonprofit to Run Philly Newspapers," Poynter.org, January 12 2016, www.poynter.org.

43. Jeff Gammage, "For Journalism Institute, a New Name to Honor Its Founder," Philly.com, February 11, 2017, www.philly.com.

44. T. R. Goldman, "What Will Happen to the *Tampa Bay Times*?," *Columbia Journalism Review*, March/April 2015, www.cjr.org; Andrew Beaujon, "The Poynter Institute Lost $3.5 Million in 2013, Makes Progress toward New Revenue Sources," Poynter.org, November 14, 2014, www.poynter.org.

45. David Boardman, interview by the author, February 8, 2016.

46. Chris Mondics, "One Editor Now to Run *Philadelphia Inquirer, Daily News* and Philly.com," Philly.com, January 8, 2016, www.philly.com.

47. Doctor, "The Hard Realities of Philly's Hail Mary Nonprofit Reorganization."

48. Bill Marimow, interview by the author, January 26, 2016.

49. Stan Wischnowski, interview by the author, January 26, 2016.

50. Will Bunch, interview by the author, January 26, 2016.

51. Jeff Blumenthal, "*Philadelphia* Magazine Continues Newsroom Restructuring," *Philadelphia Business Journal*, March 14, 2016, www.bizjournals.com/philadelphia; Chris Krewson, "More Cuts Hit Philly Mag; Writers Laid Off, *Birds 24/7* Shut Down," *Billy Penn*, January 12, 2017, www.billypenn.com.

52. Benjamin Mullin, "Shuttering of *Philadelphia City Paper* Latest in Series of

Alt-Weekly Closures," Poynter.org, September 30, 2015, www.poynter.org; Mathis, interview by the author; Joel Mathis, "Media Startup Showdown: Ranking Philly's Three New Online News Sites," *Philadelphia*, January 14, 2015, www.phillymag.com.

53. Joseph Lichterman, "How Philly's *Billy Penn* Is Building a Local News Audience from Scratch," *Nieman Journalism Lab*, December 17, 2014, www.niemanlab.org.

54. Jim Brady and Chris Krewson, interviews with the author, January 26, 2016.

55. "Consolidated Media Report," Philadelphia Media Network, March 31, 2016, Alliance for Audited Media, www.auditedmedia.com.

56. "Jim Brady," *Billy Penn*, accessed on August 17, 2016, www.billypenn.com.

57. Simon van Zuylen-Wood, "Jim Brady Profile: The Billy Pulpit," *Philadelphia*, September 24, 2014, www.phillymag.com.

58. Ken Doctor, "The Newsonomics of Digital First Media's Thunderdome Implosion (and Coming Sale)," *Nieman Journalism Lab*, April 2, 2014, www.niemanlab.org.

59. Jan Murphy, Twitter post, August 16, 2016, 3:39 p.m., twitter.com/JanMurphy. The headline that accompanies the tweet was published on *Billy Penn* at billypenn.com/2016/08/16/dawwwwww/.

60. Anna Orso, "Jury Convicts PA Attorney General Kathleen Kane on All Charges," *Billy Penn*, August 15, 2016, www.billypenn.com.

61. Kelsey Sutton, "Spirited Media Prepares to Launch the *Incline* in Pittsburgh," *Politico Media*, May 12, 2016, www.politico.com/media.

62. Jack Marshall, "Patch Rebounds after Split from AOL," *Wall Street Journal*, February 2, 2016.

63. "Who We Are," accessed on August 24, 2016, www.gannett.com; Jim Hopkins, "Documents Reveal Double-Digit Profit Margins at Scores of Papers Now on Verge of Massive Layoffs," *Gannett Blog*, November 28, 2008, gannettblog.blogspot.com; "Gannett Co., Inc. (GCI)," Yahoo! Finance, accessed on August 24, 2016, finance.yahoo.com.

64. David J. Blow, *Historic Guide to Burlington Neighborhoods*, ed. Lilian Baker Carlisle, vol. 2 (Burlington, VT: Chittenden County Historical Society, 1997), 33–34; "Quick Facts," United States Census Bureau, accessed on August 24, 2016, www.census.gov; Christine Haughney, "In Vermont, a Venerable Paper Fights for Readers," *New York Times*, September 30, 2012; Michael Donoghue, interview by the author, November 17, 2015; reports submitted to the Alliance for Audited Media, www.auditedmedia.org.

65. All of these projects are described in detail in Dan Kennedy, *The Wired City: Reimagining Journalism and Civic Life in the Post-Newspaper Age* (Amherst: University of Massachusetts Press, 2013).

66. Traci Griffith, interview by the author, November 17, 2015; "Faculty Profile:

Traci Griffith, JD," St. Michael's College, accessed on August 25, 2016, www.smcvt .edu.

67. Dan Kennedy, "How the *Boston Phoenix* Kept Its Readers but Lost Its Advertisers," *MediaShift*, March 19, 2013, www.mediashift.org.

68. Paula Routly, interview by the author, November 18, 2015.

69. Molly Walsh, interview by the author, November 18, 2015.

70. Information on circulation and staff size from Routly, interview by the author, November 18, 2015, and Routly, email message to the author, November 20, 2015.

71. Paul Heintz, interview by the author, November 18, 2015.

72. Taylor Dobbs, interview by the author, November 17, 2015.

73. Anne Galloway, interview by the author, November 19, 2015; additional information from *VT Digger* publisher Diane Ziegler, interview by the author, November 19, 2015.

74. Donoghue, interview by the author.

75. Al Getler, interview by the author, November 18, 2015.

CHAPTER NINE

All In: Jeff Bezos Takes His Place as an "Enemy of the People"

1. David A. Fahrenthold, "How Donald Trump Retooled His Charity to Spend Other People's Money," *Washington Post*, September 10, 2016.

2. David A. Fahrenthold, "Trump Recorded Having Extremely Lewd Conversation about Women in 2005," *Washington Post*, October 8, 2016. An earlier version of the story, no longer available, had been published online the day before.

3. "Fact Check: Clinton and Trump Debate for the 2nd Time," NPR.org, October 9, 2016, www.npr.org.

4. Megan Twohey and Michael Barbaro, "Two Women Say Donald Trump Touched Them Inappropriately," *New York Times*, October 12, 2016.

5. "An Exhaustive List of the Allegations Women Have Made Against Donald Trump," *The Cut* (blog), *New York*, October 20, 2016, www.nymag.com.

6. Ricardo Bilton, "How One *Washington Post* Reporter Uses Pen and Paper to Make His Tracking of Trump Get Noticed," *Nieman Journalism Lab*, September 9, 2016, www.niemanlab.org; David A. Fahrenthold, "David Fahrenthold Tells the Behind-the-Scenes Story of His Year Covering Trump," *Washington Post Magazine*, December 29, 2016.

7. David Fahrenthold was interviewed by Philip Bennett at the John Fisher Zeidman Colloquium on Politics and the Press at Duke University's Sanford School of Public Policy. The interview was published on YouTube on December 15, 2016, www.youtube.com.

8. Paul Farhi, "*Washington Post*'s David Fahrenthold Wins Pulitzer Prize for Dogged Reporting of Trump's Philanthropy," *Washington Post*, April 10, 2017.

9. Paul Bedard, "*Washington Post* Assigns Army of 20 to Dig into 'Every Phase' of Trump's Life," *Washington Examiner*, May 11, 2016, www.washingtonexaminer.com; David Goldman, "Donald Trump's War on Jeff Bezos, Amazon and the *Washington Post*," CNN.com, May 13, 2016, money.cnn.com; Brian Stelter, "Donald Trump Ending Press 'Blacklist,'" CNN.com, September 7, 2016, money.cnn.com.

10. Katharine Graham, *Personal History* (New York: Alfred A. Knopf, 1997), 465; "Jeff Bezos Wants to See an Entrepreneurial Explosion in Space," *Washington Post*, May 20, 2016.

11. Jeff Bezos was interviewed by Walter Isaacson on October 20, 2016, at the Vanity Fair New Establishment Summit 2016. Video online at "Watch Full Panels from the Vanity Fair New Establishment Summit 2016," *Vanity Fair*, October 19, 2016, www.vanityfair.com. The date discrepancy is the result of the web page's having been set up before the Bezos video was published.

12. Donald J. Trump, Twitter post, December 7, 2015, 10:22 a.m., twitter.com/realDonaldTrump.

13. Jeff Bezos, Twitter post, December 7, 2015, 6:30 p.m., twitter.com/JeffBezos.

14. Beth Diaz, interview by the author, April 13, 2016.

15. Ken Doctor, email message to the author, May 10, 2016.

16. Martin Baron was interviewed by Bob Schieffer and H. Andrew Schwartz on the podcast *About the News*, Center for Strategic and International Studies, June 13, 2016, www.csis.org.

17. Lucia Moses, "The *Washington Post*: We Are a Growing Business," *Digiday*, September 7, 2016, www.digiday.com.

18. Andrew Beaujon, "The *Washington Post* Says It Was Profitable in 2016," *Washingtonian*, December 13, 2016, www.washingtonian.com.

19. Ken Doctor, "'Profitable' *Washington Post* Adding More than Five Dozen Journalists," *Politico Media*, December 27, 2016, www.politico.com/media.

20. Shailesh Prakash, interview by the author, April 8, 2016.

21. Peter Kafka, "Google and Facebook Are Booming. Is the Rest of the Digital Ad Business Sinking?," *Recode*, November 2, 2016, www.recode.net.

22. Former Washington Post Company president Stephen Hills discussed the *Post*'s funnel strategy in an address before the New England Newspaper and Press Association in Boston on February 19, 2016.

23. Jennifer Reingold, "Don Graham: Why a Paywall Won't Work for the *Post*," *Fortune*, July 17, 2012, www.fortune.com.

24. Andrew Beaujon, "*Washington Post* Paywall Will Launch June 12," Poynter.org, June 5, 2013, www.poynter.org.

25. Josh Sternberg, "*Washington Post* Starts Its Paywall," *Digiday*, June 5, 2013, www.digiday.com; "Digital Subscriptions," *New York Times*, accessed on April 25, 2016, www.nytimes.com/subscriptions; *Washington Post* spokeswoman Molly Gannon, email message to the author, April 25, 2016; New York Times Company spokeswoman Eileen Murphy, email message to the author, April 25, 2016.

26. "How Do I Activate My .gov/.mil/.edu Free Subscription?," *Washington Post*, accessed on October 27, 2016, helpcenter.washingtonpost.com.

27. Molly Gannon, email message to the author, April 27, 2016.

28. Stefanie Manning, email message to the author, March 11, 2016.

29. Subscription rates for the *New York Times* and the *Washington Post* were accessed from their respective websites on October 26, 2016; "Amazon Prime Members Enjoy Digital Access to the *Washington Post* for Free," *WashPost PR Blog, Washington Post*, September 16, 2015, www.washingtonpost.com; Audrey Shi, "Amazon Prime Members Now Outnumber Non-Prime Customers," *Fortune*, July 11, 2016, www.fortune.com; "The *Washington Post* Launches New Tablet App, Free for Amazon Fire Customers," *WashPost PR Blog, Washington Post*, November 20, 2014, www.washingtonpost.com; Gannon, email message to the author, April 25, 2016.

30. Joseph Lichterman, "Alexa, Give Me the News: How Outlets Are Tailoring Their Coverage for Amazon's New Platform," *Nieman Journalism Lab*, August 30, 2016, www.niemanlab.org.

31. Diaz, interview by the author.

32. Brian Stelter, "*New York Times* Has Record Subscriber Growth — and Some Bad News Too," CNN.com, May 3, 2017, money.cnn.com.

33. Ken Doctor, interview by the author, March 10, 2016.

34. Ken Doctor, "Trump Bump Grows into Subscription Surge — and Not Just for the *New York Times*," TheStreet.com, March 3, 2017, www.thestreet.com.

35. Ken Doctor, email message to the author, June 7, 2017.

36. Paul Farhi, Twitter post, September 26, 2017, 12:53 p.m., twitter.com/farhip.

37. Micah Gelman, interview by the author, March 16, 2016.

38. Joseph Lichterman, "The Coral Project Unveils Its First Product to Make Comments Better," *Nieman Journalism Lab*, March 15, 2016, www.niemanlab.org.

39. John Huey, Martin Nisenholtz, Paul Sagan, and John Geddes, *Riptide: An Oral History of the Epic Collision between Journalism and Digital Technology, from 1980 to the Present* (Cambridge, MA: Shorenstein Center on Media, Politics and Public Policy, April 4, 2013), www.digitalriptide.org.

40. Shailesh Prakash, interview by the author, April 8, 2016. Unless otherwise indicated, all quotes from Prakash are from this interview.

41. Lukas I. Alpert and Jack Marshall, "Bezos Takes Hands-On Role at *Washington Post*," *Wall Street Journal*, December 20, 2015.

42. "The *Washington Post* Introduces New Progressive Web App Experience," *WashPost PR Blog, Washington Post,* May 19, 2016, www.washingtonpost.com.

43. Joshua Benton, "Cory Haik on How the *Washington Post* Is Rethinking Its Strategy for Mobile," *Press Publish* (podcast), *Nieman Journalism Lab,* August 5, 2015, www.niemanlab.org.

44. Brian Morrissey, "'The Best Product People Come Out of the Newsroom': How the *Washington Post* Adopted a Product Mindset," *Digiday Podcast, Digiday,* September 11, 2015, www.digiday.com.

45. Ibid.

46. Adam Lashinsky, "Bezos Prime," *Fortune,* April 1, 2016, www.fortune.com.

47. Shailesh Prakash, email message to the author, June 16, 2017.

48. "Imperial Ambitions," *Economist,* April 9, 2016, www.economist.com.

49. Kenneth Olmstead and Elisa Shearer, "Digital News — Audience Fact Sheet," *State of the News Media 2015* (Washington, DC: Pew Research Center, April 29, 2015), 10–14.

50. "The *Washington Post* Unveils 'Paloma' Newsletter Delivery Platform," *WashPost PR Blog, Washington Post,* July 20, 2016, www.washingtonpost.com.

51. Matthew Hindman, *Stickier News: What Newspapers Don't Know about Web Traffic Has Hurt Them Badly — but There Is a Better Way* (Cambridge, MA: Shorenstein Center on Media, Politics and Public Policy, April 2015), 21.

52. David Beard, interview by the author, October 16, 2015.

53. Mark Zusman, email message to the author, March 9, 2016.

54. Kyle Pope, "Revolution at the *Washington Post,*" *Columbia Journalism Review,* Fall/Winter 2016, www.cjr.org.

55. Jack Marshall, "*Washington Post* Licenses Publishing Technology to Tronc," *Wall Street Journal,* March 13, 2017.

56. Newspaper Association of America, accessed on April 27, 2016, www.naa.org. The organization subsequently changed its name to the News Media Alliance and moved its data to a members-only section of its website.

57. Diaz, interview by the author.

58. Rick Edmonds, "Native Ads Will Provide 25 Percent of News Media Revenues by 2018, Says Media Association," Poynter.org, October 31, 2016, www.poynter.org.

59. Dan Kennedy, "The Real Battle over Ad-Blocking Is between Big Tech and Independent Media," WGBH News, September 23, 2015, news.wgbh.org.

60. Bob Woodward spoke at the First Parish Church in Cambridge, Massachusetts, on October 20, 2015. Thanks to Boston University journalism student Kylie Ayal, who provided me with an audio file of Woodward's talk after I botched my own recording of it.

61. JP Mangalindan, "Jeff Bezos's Mission: Compelling Small Publishers to Think Big," *Fortune*, June 29, 2010, www.fortune.com.

62. Vanity Fair New Establishment Summit 2016.

63. David Jackson, "Trump Again Calls Media 'Enemy of the People,'" *USA Today*, February 24, 2017.

EPILOGUE

The Fall and Rise of Journalism in the Age of Trump

1. Jeremy Diamond, "Trump Launches All-Out Attack on the Press," CNN.com, June 1, 2016, www.cnn.com.

2. Joseph Lichterman, "After Trump's Win, News Organizations See a Bump in Subscriptions and Donations," *Nieman Journalism Lab*, November 14, 2016, www.niemanlab.org; Matthew J. Belvedere and Michael Newberg, "*New York Times* Subscription Growth Soars Tenfold, Adding 132,000, after Trump's Win," CNBC.com, November 29, 2016, www.cnbc.com; Daniel Politi, "*Vanity Fair* Subscriptions Soar after Trump Blasts Magazine on Twitter," *Slate*, December 17, 2016, www.slate.com; Ken Doctor, "Trump Bump Grows into Subscription Surge — and Not Just for the *New York Times*," *Newsonomics*, March 4, 2017, www.newsonomics.com.

3. Theodore Ross, "The Year Everyone Realized Digital Media Is Doomed," *New Republic*, December 13, 2016, www.newrepublic.com; "This Year, Next Year: 2017 Global Advertising to Reach $547B," GroupM, December 5, 2016, www.groupm.com; Suzanne Vranica and Jack Marshall, "Facebook Overestimated Key Video Metric for Two Years," *Wall Street Journal*, September 22, 2016; Mike Shields, "Facebook Discloses Another Metrics Mishap Affecting Publishers," *Wall Street Journal*, December 16, 2016.

4. Michael Rosenwald, "Print Is Dead. Long Live Print.," *Columbia Journalism Review*, Fall/Winter 2016, www.cjr.org.

5. Kathleen Kingsbury, "Print as a Premium Offering," *Nieman Journalism Lab*, December 2016, www.niemanlab.org.

6. Taylor Dobbs, "Botched *Washington Post* Report Launches Burlington Electric into National Spotlight," Vermont Public Radio, January 3, 2017, www.vpr.org; Warner Todd Huston, "*Washington Post*'s Fake News of Russian Vermont Power Plant Hack," *Breitbart*, December 31, 2016, www.breitbart.com; Evan Perez, Jim Sciutto, Jake Tapper, and Carl Bernstein, "Intel Chiefs Presented Trump with Claims of Russian Efforts to Compromise Him," CNN.com, January 12, 2017, www.cnn.com; Michael M. Grynbaum, "Donald Trump's News Session Stars War with and within Media," *New York Times*, January 11, 2017.

7. David Remnick, "Nattering Nabobs," *New Yorker*, July 10, 2006, www.new yorker.com.

8. Yochai Benkler, Robert Faris, Hal Roberts, and Ethan Zuckerman, "Study: Breitbart-Led Right-Wing Media Ecosystem Altered Broader Media Agenda," *Columbia Journalism Review*, March 3, 2017, www.cjr.org.

9. James Fallows, "Despair and Hope in Trump's America," *Atlantic*, January/ February 2017, www.theatlantic.com.

INDEX